# 100 Years of Women's Suffrage

# 100 Years of Women's Suffrage

A University of Illinois Press Anthology

Compiled by
**DAWN DURANTE**

Introduction by Nancy A. Hewitt

**UNIVERSITY OF ILLINOIS PRESS**
Urbana, Chicago, and Springfield

This anthology was compiled with the assistance of Alison Syring.

Library of Congress Cataloging-in-Publication Data
Names: Durante, Dawn, editor | Hewitt, Nancy A., 1951– author
    of introduction.
Title: 100 years of women's suffrage : a University of Illinois
    Press anthology / edited by Dawn Durante ; introduction by
    Nancy A. Hewitt.
Other titles: One hundred years of women's suffrage
Description: Urbana : University of Illinois Press, 2019. |
    Includes bibliographical references and index.
Identifiers: LCCN 2019021437 (print) | LCCN 2019981530 (ebook)
    | ISBN 9780252042928 (hardcover) | ISBN 9780252084744
    (paperback) | ISBN 9780252051784 (ebook)
Subjects: LCSH: Women—Political activity—United States—
    History. | Women—Suffrage—United States—History. |
    Feminism—United States—History. | Women's rights—United
    States—History.
Classification: LCC HQ1236.5.U6 A17 2019 (print) | LCC HQ1236.5.U6
    (ebook) | DDC 305.420973—dc23
LC record available at https://lccn.loc.gov/2019021437
LC ebook record available at https://lccn.loc.gov/2019981530

# CONTENTS

# PREFACE

Publications by the University of Illinois Press (UIP) over the last several decades have contributed to the project of illuminating key figures and diverse types of work across gender, race, and class that contributed to the suffrage movement and to women's voting issues. In the pages of this anthology, you will find interesting and influential pieces on women's suffrage that have appeared between the covers of previously publishe UIP books. I have approached this project as a curator, assembling previously published pieces that are valuable on their own, but that also work cohesively among the other pieces—or so I hope. As with any curatorial project, there are constraints. Were there no limitation on time, resources, copyright, or length, I know there are many other pieces that could have easily augmented this volume. Luckily, though, those important works are all out in the world, in libraries and on bookshelves and e-readers, and I hope you will seek them out.

This project arose with the simple realization that 2020 and the centennial of the women's vote was nearing, and that the University of Illinois Press has a legacy of publishing works on this history. That simple realization led to the much larger task of this book, which is the model of a collaborative effort across the Press's many departments. Particularly, Alison Syring took on the essential tasks of reviewing permissions, gathering files, and coordinating groundwork for this volume's publication— her support on this project transitioned a work in progress to a reality. The Press and I also owe a debt of gratitude to Nancy Hewitt, whose development advice and introduction are a gift to this volume, UIP, and discussions of women's suffrage. Her involvement in this book has been a great honor.

The chapters in this collection represent scholarship from different disciplines over a range of years. These reproductions of previously published material do not always reflect current conventions and terminology, but do give a sense of how the field of women's studies has developed. There is an obvious inconsistency in how authors refer to the very topic of the anthology itself. For the title and original materials, this volume uses the term "women's suffrage."

As you turn the pages of this book, I think we are right to celebrate the 100th anniversary of the Nineteenth Amendment. I also think we must recognize the great work that is left to do and that is being done to extend all forms of equality and acceptance to marginalized and underrepresented groups throughout the world. As we know well, the equal right to vote, to marry, to immigrate, to religious freedom, does not mean equal or equitable treatment. While many pieces in this volume serve as a celebration of the centennial of an important landmark, other essays serve to remind us there is always more work to be done.

# Introduction

NANCY A. HEWITT

This volume captures the long history of women's suffrage in the United States through intricate snapshots of key developments. The dozen articles gathered here illuminate the views and experiences of diverse groups of women suffragists as well as the wider political and cultural debates that their campaigns inspired. American politicians, journalists, and even some scholars point to the 1920 ratification of the Nineteenth Amendment to the U.S. Constitution as the dawn of female enfranchisement. However, that claim obscures as much as it reveals. In fact, millions of women across the United States voted before 1920, and millions more were denied the right to vote after 1920. In addition, the national stage was only one arena in which women fought for first-class citizenship. In the 1830s and 1840s, women pressured churches, reform societies, and state governments to grant them the ballot. From the 1860s on, battles over local, state, territorial, and federal suffrage transformed the social and cultural as well as political landscape in the United States and reverberated with sister movements in Britain, Australia, New Zealand, Finland, China, and other countries.

As campaigns for women's votes gained strength in the late nineteenth and early twentieth centuries, suffragists faced hostility, ridicule, imprisonment, and forced feeding and were attacked as blue stockings, freaks, and sexual inverts. Rather than being silenced, however, suffragists escalated their efforts by staging mass marches, public protests, hunger strikes, and other spectacles in hopes of gaining publicity and support. The ratification of the Nineteenth Amendment on August 26,

1920, did not end these activist endeavors, but instead reshaped them as African American women in the South, Puerto Rican women on their island home, and Latinas, Asian American, and American Indian women across the country fought to be included in the Amendment's promises.[1] The articles collected here address the significance of these campaigns both before and after ratification of the Nineteenth Amendment as well as women's efforts to turn voting rights into political power. They introduce readers to crucial issues—of ideology and tactics, religion and race, sexuality and culture—that marked the battle for enfranchisement and to additional issues—gender unity and disunity and the gender gap—that arose as women entered the electoral arena en masse.

Although Abigail Adams begged her husband to "remember the ladies" in 1776 when John Adams was helping to forge a new compact of government for the rebellious colonies, it was several decades before groups of American women consistently pressed for the right to vote. Many of these requests—sometimes stated as demands—emerged independently, but by the 1860s, the idea of enfranchising women had gained widespread attention if not support. As Ellen Carol DuBois argues in chapter 1, a path-breaking article from 1975, the radical character of women's suffrage lay in advocates' focus "on the public sphere, and particularly on citizenship" and their demand for "a kind of power and connection with the social order not based on the institution of the family and their [women's] subordination within it." DuBois also claims that the "exclusion of women from participation in political life in the early nineteenth century was so absolute and unchallenged that it did not require explicit proscription."

More recent scholarship shows that growing numbers of women did voice political opinions, publicly and collectively, from the 1820s on and, in the following decades, wielded their right of petition as they fought for voting rights in diverse arenas. Women petitioned Congress against Indian removal and slavery; joined abolitionist organizations and supported antislavery political parties; spoke out in progressive religious meetings, such as the African Methodist Episcopal Church and the Society of Friends; demanded rights as workers; entreated state constitutional conventions to expand their legal and political rights; and demanded full citizenship at woman's rights conventions. These early ventures into political life by black and white women attracted the support of reform-minded men, including William Lloyd Garrison, Frederick Douglass, William C. Nell, and the Reverend Samuel J. May.[2]

By the mid-1860s, amid the upheavals engendered by Civil War, many activists hoped to enfranchise both African Americans and women. However, in 1869, Congress agreed only to remove race as a barrier to voting for black men. That decision, embedded in the Fifteenth Amendment to the U.S. Constitution, led to divisions between advocates of black and women's suffrage as well as among women suffragists. While those divisions fractured the movement, they also inspired tens of thousands of women to organize on behalf of female enfranchisement locally, regionally, and nationally in the late nineteenth century.[3]

Amid these conflicting efforts, women gained an important victory: In 1869, Wyoming's territorial legislature granted them equal suffrage, and in 1890, when that territory gained statehood, it also became the first state to enfranchise women. However, Wyoming's decision to grant its female population the vote had little to do with feminist agitation. Instead, Wyoming legislators hoped to attract more women to the region as a means of stabilizing a rowdy frontier society. Over the next fifty years, between 1869 and 1919, fifteen more states and territories—most of them in the West—followed Wyoming's lead in granting women "full suffrage," that is, the right to vote in elections of all kinds. In a dozen others, local or state legislators passed partial suffrage bills, allowing women to cast ballots in school board and/or municipal elections, in primaries, or in federal presidential elections, but denying them the entire array of voting rights accorded men.[4]

In addition, for a decade following the Fifteenth Amendment's ratification, suffragists sought to win the vote by attempting to register and to vote in towns and cities across the country. Five black suffragists in Charleston, South Carolina, were among the first to execute this plan in 1869, as they sought to extend the enfranchisement of black men— instituted in the 1868 South Carolina Constitution—to women. Likely led by suffragist Louisa Rollin, five women successfully registered and voted, but they were arrested and fined, and the male registrars who accepted their ballots were fined and imprisoned.[5] Other groups of women— black, white, and interracial—joined this effort, some following the lead of the South Carolina activists and many more following a plan known as the New Departure, which was devised by Missouri lawyers Francis and Virginia Minor. They argued that the Fourteenth Amendment made all people born or naturalized in the United States citizens, including women. The Fifteenth Amendment then guaranteed voting as a right of citizenship, even if it did not explicitly mention sex in the same way it did "race, color and previous condition of servitude."[6] The Minors urged suffragists to make coordinated excursions to registrars and to the polls, creating test cases that would force judicial recognition of their position.

Thousands of women across the country participated in these efforts to gain the vote by insisting they were already enfranchised, but their claims were refuted by the U.S. Supreme Court in 1875, when the justices ruled against the New Departure in *Minor v. Happersett*. Still, activists in cities, states, and territories across the country continued to organize. Indeed, as fractious relations escalated between the two national organizations based in the East—the American Woman Suffrage Association and the National Woman Suffrage Association—many women in the Midwest and in the Far West focused on state and territorial campaigns.[7] Utah Territory granted women full voting rights in 1870, a victory rooted in Mormon leaders' desire to maintain control of state government as well as in women's desire to vote. However, in 1887, the U.S. Congress used its power over territorial policies to rescind Utah women's right to vote as punishment for the practice of polygamy among members of the Church of the Latter-day Saints. That decision engendered intense debates among women suffragists, who opposed the federal government's action but did not want to be seen as approving of polygamy. To win suffragists to their side, Mormon activists used the 1893 World's Columbian Exposition in Chicago, a spectacular months-long event, to make the case for their re-enfranchisement. In chapter 2, "Mormon Women, Suffrage, and Citizenship," Andrea Radke-Moss examines the strategies wielded by Utah delegates to the World's Congress of Representative Women, which was held in conjunction with the Exposition. The delegates embraced "a public opportunity to assert their identity as modern women" who were "on the cutting edge of suffrage activism." Mormon activists, such as Emily Richards and Emmeline Wells, who were not part of polygamous marriages, pointed to the Church's 1890 Manifesto ending polygamy to reassure mainstream suffragists of their morality. Non-Mormon Utah women also joined the delegation, and together they emphasized the territory's progressive and patriotic views. By the time Utah claimed statehood in 1896, national suffrage leaders applauded the return of Mormon women to the ballot box.

While Mormon women used a spectacular event to make the case for their respectability, other suffragists, in the United States and in Great Britain, created spectacles and wielded popular culture to promote the cause. As Mary Chapman and Barbara Green show in chapter 3, "In both its vibrant print culture and its innovative spectacular politics, the modern suffrage movement . . . developed new and varied forms of persuasion." Through suffrage newspapers; newly founded women's presses; the publication of politically progressive romance novels, cartoons, newsreels, and advertising; and soapbox oratory, street theater, and sensational stunts, suffragists created a "counter-public sphere" in the early twentieth century that promoted women's rights. In both the United States and Great Britain, younger women and new suffrage organizations, such as those created by college students, wielded popular cultural forms to garner attention. Increasingly successful at gaining media access, they multiplied the audience for mass marches, automobile caravans, and other events by the coverage they received in daily newspapers and monthly magazines, many accompanied by photographs that captured the size and enthusiasm of suffrage events.[8]

However, some militant suffragists offended their more-moderate co-workers as well as the political leaders whose support moderates sought to win. When members of the National Woman's Party picketed the White House on a daily basis in 1917 to protest President Woodrow Wilson's refusal to support women's suffrage, their actions horrified many Americans, including members of the National American Woman Suffrage Association, which had been forged by the merger of the National and American Associations in 1890. Still, when these militants were arrested, organized a prison hunger strike, and were then force fed by prison authorities, they gained widespread publicity—and sympathy—across the country.[9]

Militant suffragists in Britain, who used even more violent tactics, faced even harsher responses from government and prison officials as Lady Constance Lytton reveals in the excerpt offered in chapter 4 from her 1914 memoir *Prisons and Prisoners*. Once again, harsh reprisals by government officials aroused public interest and, eventually, sympathy for female militants. That these protests took place during World War I, when women, like men, were asked to make tremendous sacrifices for their countries, lent them greater power. And autobiographical narratives, like that of Lytton, aided the cause by presenting suffragists' actions in spiritual and communal as well as political terms.

Kimberly Jensen provides a fascinating counterpart to the many studies of the militant wing of the suffrage movement in chapter 5, "Whether We Vote or Not—We are Going to Shoot." In the very same years that suffragists made spectacles of themselves, 1914–1919, tens of thousands of American women insisted on their right to bear arms. Having read stories about the rapid fall of Belgium and northern France to German troops and the horrifying rapes that followed, American women insisted that wives, mothers, and sisters needed to be able to defend themselves and their homes. Stories of men weakened by "shell shock" only increased women's insistence that they needed to protect themselves. For some women, including suffragists and pacifists who hoped to stay out of Europe's war, military preparedness and self-defense training for women were "part of more complete female citizenship." At the same time, popular magazines like the *Delineator,* newspapers like the *New York Times,* and organizations like the National Rifle Association publicized and often supported women's rifle and pistol training, even as the federal government directed its military preparedness programs solely to men and boys.

Jensen shows that even as the debate over the appropriateness of women's military training raged, Women's Defense Clubs, rifle training schools, and the American Women's League for Self-Defense attracted thousands of participants from Maine to Texas and Indiana to Florida. While only a small percentage of American women ended up serving in formal positions in self-defense and military operations during World War I, the debates over women's right to bear arms and to protect themselves and the nation raised issues with significant implications for peacetime.

Wielding banners and bullets, militant suffragists and female advocates of "home protection" shocked many people who still imagined the "fairer" sex as meek, motherly, and subordinate. In chapter 6, "Unsightly Evidence," Laura L. Behling reminds us of the backlash against women who demanded new roles and rights in the early twentieth century. Anti-suffragist women and men, writers for popular magazines, and a rising school of male sexologists disparaged suffragists as "oddities" and "freaks," claiming that they had evolved into "a new sex" that, along with flappers, embodied "the menace of the hour." Behling traces the growing chorus that critiqued suffragists as unwomanly and suggested their activism was a sign, in the worst cases, of sexual inversion. She thus makes clear that even as some nations moved toward enfranchising women, a powerful backlash took hold that identified outspoken women as sexually, psychologically, and socially anathema.

As cultural and political debates swirled around the suffrage movement, growing numbers of women engaged in the practical work of winning and wielding the ballot. These activists emerged in every state and from every racial, ethnic, and socio-economic community. Yet most national, state, and city suffrage associations did not welcome all who sought to enfranchise women. Instead, in chapter 7, an excerpt from "Fighting for Rights in the 1910s and 1920s," Julie A. Gallagher argues, "Fault lines surfaced repeatedly over critical issues like the embrace or rejection of racial equality and over strategies like the targeting of the U.S. Congress or the states." Such conflicts erupted in the late 1860s, during debates over the Fourteenth and Fifteenth Amendments, and they remained powerful in the following decades, even as the suffrage movement gained victories and adherents. When New York State activists sought enfranchisement by referendum in the 1910s, black suffragists, who had been organizing in New York City for half a century, still contended with white women's indifference and antagonism. They also faced hostility from some black men and argued among themselves over ideology and tactics. Despite these hurdles, leaders emerged from New York City's diverse black communities, and their citizenship education programs helped ensure the success of the 1917 referendum granting women the ballot statewide. In the aftermath of that victory, however, black women faced indifference from major political parties. While Republicans and Democrats sought women's votes, they rarely ran black male or white female candidates; and black women remained even more marginal to the vision and plans of party leaders. The Socialist Party did run a black female candidate in New York City, but whatever clout it had was ended by the post-World War I Red Scare that demonized "radicals." Nonetheless, black women continued to engage in politics in New York City and nationwide, fighting not only for political access but also for power.[10]

Three years after New York State women won the vote, the ratification of the Nineteenth Amendment was celebrated as enfranchising women nationwide. Yet its ratification did not eliminate numerous restrictions on voting already in place to disenfranchise African American, Asian American, Latino, and Native American men; these restrictions were soon extended to women in those groups. Congressional restrictions on citizenship—such as those passed in the late nineteenth century to exclude Chinese immigrants, and state efforts in the South and West to disenfranchise people of color via literacy tests, white primaries, poll taxes, and other means—ensured that female disenfranchisement remained a critical issue. It took decades of organizing and litigating for these disenfranchised women and men to gain first-class citizenship. Although they fought these battles side-by-side, women's efforts have received far less attention until recently.[11]

In most cases, only concerted action by the disenfranchised and the support of white allies moved state and federal governments to action. One important step—the repeal of the 1882 Chinese Exclusion Act in 1943, which allowed Chinese in the United States to become citizens and to vote—was driven by the wartime alliance between the United States and China.[12] In far more cases, collective action and litigation expanded the electorate. In 1944, for instance, the U.S. Supreme Court ruled in *Smith v. Allwright* that the white primary, which excluded black voters from participating in the only meaningful elections in the one-party South, was unconstitutional. It was two decades later, in response to the growing power of the civil rights movement, that Congress finally passed the 1965 Voting Rights Act, which removed most remaining barriers to minority voting rights. Still, it was not until the Act's 1975 renewal that bilingual election materials for Spanish-speaking voters were required.[13] And still, the disenfranchisement of felons, gerrymandering, voter ID laws, and other devices continue to be used to suppress the votes of women and men in targeted communities.

It is thus crucial that scholars recognize both the significance of women's enfranchisement and its limits. Carolyn Daniels and I address these issues in this volume. Chapter 8, "New Women," examines the political efforts of Anglo-American, African American, and Cuban and Italian immigrant women in Tampa, Florida, in the years surrounding 1920. Women in all three groups were active in charitable and reform work, but immigrant women were considered by far the most radical. The large number of Cuban and Italian women in the cigar industry and their participation in industry-wide strikes between 1919 and 1921 garnered significant publicity in Tampa and nationwide. Yet few immigrant women, or men, became U.S. citizens in this period, so for Cuban and Italian women, speaking and voting in union meetings proved their most powerful political weapon. In October 1920, "more than twenty-five thousand strikers, 'about 50 percent of them women,'" attended a mass meeting at the Centro Asturiano club to demonstrate their support for strike leaders and their confidence in achieving victory. That same month, white civic leaders sought to change the ward system of city governance to an at-large system via a municipal referendum. When Florida's Supreme Court ruled that fall that all women in the state must be allowed to vote because there was insufficient time to implement normal registration procedures for newly enfranchised voters, black as well as white women mobilized. The efforts of women in Tampa's distinct racial and ethnic communities to cast votes in critical civic matters, the response of white officials and editors, and the victory for at-large elections illuminate the possibilities and limits of the Nineteenth Amendment.[14]

The limits of the Amendment would become even clearer in the years ahead, as southern states forced to allow black women to vote in 1920 quickly extended literacy tests, poll taxes, and other efforts to disenfranchise black men to black women. Nonetheless, the efforts of black suffragists and their experience in casting ballots in 1920 ensured that they would continue to fight, alongside black men and other women of color, for full political rights. In chapter 9, "We Just Kept Going," Carolyn Daniels provides a vivid account of these efforts in Dawson, Georgia, the county seat of Terrell County. Daniels's son Roy was inspired to join the civil rights movement in high school and became friends with a leader of the Student Nonviolent Coordinating Committee, Charles Sherrod, who organized voting rights efforts with his wife Shirley Sherrod across southwest Georgia. When Roy Daniels was beaten by the local sheriff, his mother joined the movement.

A beautician by trade, Mrs. Daniels was not dependent on white clients and was thus freer than many blacks to take political action.[15] Still, this did not make her immune to intimidation and violence or make it easy to find allies. Her local A.M.E. Church refused to allow the building to be used for civil rights meetings for fear it would be burned down, and black teachers and others dependent on white superiors were reluctant to attend such meetings. But Daniels was persistent and, with the support of Sherrod, national black leaders, and other women and men in her community, black voter registration slowly increased. The response, however, was everything that civil rights activists feared. Mrs. Daniels sent Roy to Jacksonville to keep him out of harm's way as white vigilantes targeted churches and families that harbored civil rights workers. Daniels's home and the civil rights workers staying there were attacked by nightriders, and eventually a bomb destroyed her house. Still, Daniels never gave up, but "kept on going."[16]

The stories of black, immigrant, and other disenfranchised women offer powerful tales of the courage entailed in fighting for first-class citizenship both during the battle for and after the ratification of the Nineteenth Amendment.[17] They also suggest the challenges of forging any kind of women's voting bloc, a threat that anti-suffragists popularized in their attempt to derail state and federal efforts to enfranchise women. As Bonnie Thornton Dill argues in chapter 10, her widely reprinted 1983 article

"Race, Class, and Gender: Prospects of an All-Inclusive Sisterhood," the development of female solidarity remained elusive. Thornton Dill notes that "Black, Hispanic, Native American and Asian-American women of all classes, as well as many working-class women, have not readily identified themselves as sisters of the white middle-class women who have been in the forefront of the [contemporary women's] movement." Over the last three decades, scholars have demonstrated the critical feminist initiatives and achievements of women of color, individually and collectively, but that work, too, accentuates the different priorities, tactics, and ideologies advocated by women from different racial and ethnic communities, and especially between women of color and white women. Thornton Dill argues that these differences are deeply rooted in black and white women's distinct experiences of racial oppression, class exploitation, and patriarchy. Although her work highlights the problematic aspects of the concept of sisterhood, it also provides critical historical perspectives that can serve as the foundation for building interracial and cross-class alliances in the present.[18]

The final two essays in this collection illuminate similarities and differences among women voters through analyses of voting behavior in recent decades. The "gender gap," a term coined by Eleanor Smeal of the National Organization for Women following the 1980 presidential election, "has been used to describe differences between women and men in vote choice, voter turnout, other types of political participation, policy preferences, and public opinion differences." The claims for a significant gender gap in politics has been a source of contention, even among feminist scholars, in part because most studies have focused solely or primarily on white women and men. In chapter 11, Leonie Huddy, Erin Cassese, and Mary-Kate Lizotte use sophisticated quantitative methods to assess "Sources of Political Unity and Disunity among Women," using data from 1980 to 2000 that allows them to assess economic, demographic, and religious factors that affect the gender gap in specific subgroups. In the final chapter, M. Margaret Conway, relying on survey data from 1990 to 2000, focuses explicitly on the gender gap *within* racial and ethnic communities: white, African American, Hispanic, Asian American, and Native American. Huddy, Cassese, and Lizotte conclude that "women are more divided than united politically but they also display some limited political commonality." However, Conway warns that the variables used to test the gender gap have far less explanatory value for African Americans, Latino/as, Asian Americans, and Native Americans than for white

Americans. Without data that reflects "the life experiences of racial and ethnic minorities," it will be impossible to know the extent of a political gender gap and the forces that are most likely to drive it.

Like other contributors to this collection, the authors studying the gender gap make clear that without greater attention to race, ethnicity, class, religion, and other critical variables, we cannot draw general conclusions about "women's" political beliefs and behavior before or after ratification of the Nineteenth Amendment. By examining the ideological, spectacular, racial, and statistical dimensions of women's campaigns for enfranchisement, *100 Years of Women's Suffrage* captures the complex and enduring struggle to recognize all women and all Americans as first-class citizens.

## Notes

1. One of the first articles to reconceptualize the chronology of the U.S. women's suffrage narrative by focusing on the experiences of women of color is Darlene Clark Hine and Christine Anne Farnham, "Black Women's Culture of Resistance and the Right to Vote," in Christine Anne Farnham, ed., *Women of the South: A Multi-Cultural Reader* (New York: New York University Press, 1997): 204–17.

2. This scholarship includes Mary Hershberger, "Mobilizing Women, Anticipating Abolition: The Struggle against Indian Removal in the 1830s," *Journal of American History* 86(1990):15–40; Rosalyn Terborg-Penn, *African American Women and the Struggle for the Vote* (Bloomington: Indiana University Press, 1999); Susan Zaeske, *Signatures of Citizenship: Petitioning, Antislavery and Women's Political Identity* (Chapel Hill: University of North Carolina Press, 2003); Martha S. Jones, *All Bound Up Together: The Woman Question in African American Public Culture, 1830–1900* (Chapel Hill: University of North Carolina Press, 2007); Michael D. Pierson, *Free Hearts and Free Homes: Gender and American Antislavery Politics* (Chapel Hill: University of North Carolina Press, 2003); Judith Wellman, *The Road to Seneca Falls: Elizabeth Cady Stanton and the First Woman's Rights Convention* (Urbana: University of Illinois Press, 2004); Lori Ginzberg, *Untidy Origins: A Story of Woman's Rights in Antebellum New York* (Chapel Hill: University of North Carolina Press, 2005); Stacey M. Robertson, *Hearts Beating for Liberty: Women Abolitionists in the Old Northwest* (Chapel Hill: University of North Carolina Press, 2010); Bonnie S. Anderson, *The Rabbi's Atheist Daughter: Ernestine Rose, International Feminist Pioneer* (New York: Oxford University Press, 2017); and Nancy A. Hewitt, "Feminist Friends: Agrarian Quakers and the Emergence of Woman's Rights in America," *Feminist Studies* (Spring 1986): 27–49, and *Radical Friend: Amy Kirby Post and Her Activist Worlds* (Chapel Hill: University of North Carolina Press, 2018), chs. 4–7.

3. The Fifteenth Amendment was approved by Congress in 1869 and ratified in 1870. The debates over the amendment are analyzed in Ellen DuBois, *Feminism and Suffrage: The Emergence of an Independent Women's Movement in America* (Ithaca, N.Y.: Cornell University Press, 1978); Nell Irvin Painter, *Sojourner Truth: A Life, A Symbol* (New York: W.W. Norton, 1996), ch. 15: Faye Dudden, *Fighting Chance: The Struggle Over Woman Suffrage and Black Suffrage in Reconstruction America* (New York: Oxford University Press, 2011); and Lisa Tetrault, *The Myth of Seneca Falls: Memory and the Women's Suffrage Movement, 1848–1898* (Chapel Hill: University of North Carolina Press, 2014), ch. 1.

4. On western women's suffrage campaigns, see Joan M. Jensen, "'Disfranchisement Is a Disgrace': Women and Politics in New Mexico, 1940–1960," *New Mexico Historical Review* 56, no. 1(1981): 5–35; Wendy Wall, "Gender and the 'Citizen Indian,'" in Elizabeth Jameson and Susan Armitage, eds. *Writing the Range: Race, Class and Culture in the Women's West* (Norman: University of Oklahoma Press, 1997): 202–209; Gayle Gullett, *Becoming Citizens: The Emergence and Development of the California Women's Movement, 1880–1911* (Urbana: University of Illinois Press, 2000); Sarah Barringer Gordon, *The Mormon Question: Polygamy and Constitutional Conflict in Nineteenth-Century America* (Chapel Hill: University of North Carolina Press, 2001); Allison Sneider, *Suffragists in an Imperial Age: U.S. Expansion and the Woman Question, 1870–1929* (New York: Oxford University Press, 2008); Mary Chapman, "A 'Revolution in Ink': Sui Sin Far and Chinese Reform Discourse," *American Quarterly* 60 (December 2008): 975–1001; Tetrault, *Myth of Seneca Falls*, ch. 3.

5. Terborg-Penn, *African American Women*, pp. 42–45.

6. Ibid. See also Ellen Carol DuBois, "Taking the Law into Our Own Hands: Bradwell, Minor, and Suffrage Militance in the 1870s," in *Visible Women: New Essays on American Activism*, eds. Nancy Hewitt and Suzanne Lebsock (Urbana: University of Illinois Press, 1993), pp.19–40; and Nancy Hewitt, "From Seneca Falls to Suffrage: Re-Imagining a 'Master' Narrative," in Hewitt, ed., *No Permanent Waves: Recasting Histories of U.S. Feminism* (New Brunswick, N.J.: Rutgers University Press, 2010), pp. 26–29. For a nearly complete list of women who participated in the New Departure and related efforts to register and to vote in this period, see Ann D. Gordon, ed. *The Selected Letters of Elizabeth Cady Stanton and Susan B. Anthony*, vol. 2, *Against an Aristocracy of Sex* (New Brunswick, NJ: Rutgers University Press, 2000): Appendix C.

7. Tetrault, *Myth of Seneca Falls*, ch. 3, charts the importance of these state campaigns and their efflorescence in the Midwest and Far West.

8. On militancy in the United States, see Ellen DuBois, "Working Women, Class Relations, and Suffrage Militance: Harriet Stanton Blatch and the New York Woman Suffrage Movement, 1894–1909," *Journal of American History* 74:1(June 1987): 34–58; and Mary Walton, *A Woman's Crusade: Alice Paul and the Battle for the Ballot* (New York: St. Martin's Press, 2010). For Britain and

Europe, see Barbara Winslow, *Sylvia Pankhurst: Sexual Politics and Political Activism* (New York: Routledge, 1996); and Lucy DeLap, *The Feminist Avante-Garde: Transatlantic Encounters of the Early Twentieth Century* (Cambridge: Cambridge University Press, 2009).

9. For a similar memoir from the United States, see Doris Stevens, *Jailed for Freedom* (New York: Bone and Liveright, 1920).

10. For studies of black suffragists' activism after 1920, see Liette Gidlow, "The Sequel: The Fifteenth Amendment, the Nineteenth Amendment, and Southern Black Women's Struggle to Vote," *Journal of the Gilded Age and Progressive Era*, v. 17(2018): 1–17; Gordon, et al, eds. *African American Women and the Vote*, chs. 6–9; and Lisa Materson, *For the Freedom of Her Race: Black Women and Electoral Politics in Illinois, 1877–1932* (Urbana: University of Illinois Press, 2009), chs. 3–5.

11. On the importance of black women's activism in southern civil rights movements from the 1920s to the 1940s, see, for example, Gidlow, "The Sequel"; and Kathyrn L. Nasstrom, "Down to Now: Memory, Narrative, and Women's Leadership in the Civil Rights Movement in Atlanta, Georgia," *Gender and History*, v. 11(1999): 113–44.

12. The Chinese Exclusion Act of 1882, in addition to prohibiting the immigration of Chinese into the United States, also prohibited Chinese already in the country from becoming citizens, thereby denying them the right to vote. This Act was finally repealed in 1943, which allowed Chinese women and men to gain citizenship and voting rights.

13. On the white primary, see Darlene Clark Hine with Merline Pitre and Steven Lawson, *Black Victory: The Rise and Fall of the White Primary in Texas* (Columbia: University of Missouri Press, 2003); and Merline Pitre, *In Struggle Against Jim Crow: Lulu B. White and the NAACP, 1900–1957* (College Station: Texas A & M University Press, 2010). On the Voting Rights Act, see Steven F. Lawson, *Running For Freedom: Civil Rights and Black Politics in America Since 1941*, 4th edition (Malden, Mass.: Wiley Blackwell, 2015), chs. 1–4.

14. On possibilities in the South, see Gidlow, "The Sequel," and Nasstrom, "Down to Now." For possibilities in the North, see Materson, *For the Freedom of Her Race*; and Julie A. Gallagher, *Black Women and Politics in New York City* (Urbana: University of Illinois Press, 2012).

15. On the importance of black beauticians in voting rights and other civil rights activities, see Tiffany M. Gill, *Beauty Shop Politics: African American Women's Activism in the Beauty Industry* (Urbana: University of Illinois Press, 2010).

16. The literature on women and civil rights is large and growing. For four critical starting points, see Vicki Crawford, Jacqueline Anne Rouse, and Barbara Woods, eds., *Women in the Civil Rights Movement: Trailblazers and Torchbearers, 1941–1965* (Brooklyn, N.Y.: Carlson Publishing, 1990); Steven F. Lawson, "Black Liberation and Civil Rights," in Nancy A. Hewitt, ed., *A Companion to*

*American Women's History* (Malden, Mass.: Blackwell Publishing, 2002), pp. 397–413; Christina Greene, *Our Separate Ways: Women and the Black Freedom Struggle in Durham, North Carolina* (Chapel Hill: University of North Carolina Press, 2005); and Faith S. Holsaert, Martha Prescod Norman Noonan, Judy Richardson, Betty Garman Robinson, Jean Smith Young, and Dorothy M. Zeller, eds., *Hands on the Freedom Plow: Personal Accounts By Women in SNCC* (Urbana: University of Illinois Press, 2010).

17. In addition to the civil rights citations above, on Puerto Rican and Filipina women's struggles for enfranchisement, see Yamila Azize-Vargas, "The Emergence of Feminism in Puerto Rico, 1870–1930," in Vicki L. Ruiz and Ellen C. DuBois, eds., *Unequal Sisters: A Multi-Cultural Reader in U.S. Women's History*, 2nd ed. (New York: Routledge, 1994): 260–67; and Sneider, *Suffragists in an Imperial Age*, ch. 5 and Epilogue.

18. The Center for American Women and Politics at Rutgers University, New Brunswick, New Jersey, provides both historical and current information on the voting patterns of women by race and place: www.cawp.rutgers.edu/facts.

# PART I

## THE CULTURAL AND POLITICAL STRUGGLES FOR ENFRANCHISEMENT

# 1

# THE RADICALISM OF THE WOMAN SUFFRAGE MOVEMENT

## Notes toward the Reconstruction of Nineteenth-Century Feminism

### ELLEN CAROL DUBOIS

From *U.S. Women in Struggle: A* Feminist Studies
*Anthology*, edited by Claire Goldberg Moses
and Heidi Hartmann (1995)

In this essay, I would like to suggest an interpretation of nineteenth-century suffragism that reconciles the perceived radicalism of the woman suffrage movement with the historical centrality of the family to women's condition. My hypothesis is that the significance of the woman suffrage movement rested precisely on the fact that it bypassed women's oppression within the family, or private sphere, and demanded instead her admission to citizenship, and through it admission to the public arena. By focusing on the public sphere, and particularly on citizenship, suffragists demanded for women a kind of power and a connection with the social order not based on the institution of the family and their subordination within it.

Recent scholarship has suggested that the sharp distinction between public and private activities is a relatively modern historical phenomenon. In his work on the evolution of the idea of childhood in Western Europe, Phillipe Ariès demonstrates that there was considerable overlap between family life and community life in the premodern period. He traces a gradual separation of public and private life from the sixteenth century to the nineteenth century, when "family" and "society" came finally to be viewed as distinct, even hostile, institutions.[1] This development seems to have been clear and compact in U.S. history. In seventeenth-century New England, all community functions—production, socialization, civil government, religious life—presumed the family as the basic unit of social organization.[2] The whole range of social roles drew on familial roles. The adult male's position as producer, as citizen, as member of the church, all flowed from his position as head of the family. Similarly, women's exclusion from church and civil government and their secondary but necessary role in production coincided with their subordinate position within the family.[3] A few women enjoyed unusual economic or social privileges by virtue of their family connections, but, as Gerda Lerner has pointed out, this further demonstrated women's dependence on their domestic positions for the definition of their roles in community life.[4]

By the nineteenth century, this relationship between family and society had undergone considerable change. Although the family continued to perform many important social functions, it was no longer the sole unit around which the community was organized. The concept of the "individual" had emerged to rival it. In the nineteenth century, we can distinguish two forms of social organization—one based on this new creature, the individual, the other based on the family. These overlapping but distinct structures became identified, respectively, as the public sphere and the private sphere. The emergence of a form of social organization not based on the family meant the emergence of social roles not defined by familial roles. This was equally true for women and men. But because women and men had different positions *within* the family, the existence of nonfamilial roles had different implications for the sexes. For women, the emergence of a public sphere held out the revolutionary possibility of a new way to relate to society not defined by their subordinate position within the family.

However, only men emerged from their familial roles to enjoy participation in the public sphere. Women on the whole did not. Women were of course among the first industrial workers, but these were overwhelmingly unmarried women, for whom factory work was a brief episode before marriage. Adult women remained almost entirely within the private sphere, defined politically, economically, and socially by their familial roles. Thus, the public sphere became man's arena; the private, woman's. This gave the public/private distinction a clearly sexual character. This phenomenon, canonized as the nineteenth-century doctrine of sexual spheres, is somewhat difficult for us to grasp. We are fond of pointing out the historical durability of sexual roles into our own time and miss the enormous difference between the twentieth-century notion of sexual roles and the nineteenth-century idea of sexual spheres. The difference is a measure of the achievements of nineteenth-century feminism.

The contradiction between the alternative to familial roles that activity in the public sphere offered and the exclusion of women from such activity was particularly sharp with respect to civil government. In seventeenth-century New England, citizenship was justified on the basis of familial position; the freeholder was at once the head of the household and a citizen. By contrast, nineteenth-century citizenship was posed as a direct relationship between the individual and her or his government. In other words, patriarchy was no longer the *official* basis of civil government in modern industrial democracy. However, in reality, only men were permitted to become citizens. The exclusion of women from participation in political life in the early nineteenth century was so absolute and unchallenged that it did not require explicit proscription. It was simply assumed that political "persons" were male. The U.S. Constitution did not specify the sex of citizens until the Fourteenth Amendment was ratified in 1868, after women had begun actively to demand the vote. Prior to that, the equation between "male" and "person," the term used in the Constitution, was implicit. The same, by the way, was true of the founding charter of the American Anti-Slavery Society. Written in 1833, it defined the society's membership as "persons," but for six years admitted only men into that category.

The doctrine of separate sexual spheres was supreme in the nineteenth century and even suffragists were unable to challenge certain basic aspects of it. Most notably, they accepted the particular suitability of women to domestic activities, and therefore their special responsibility for the private sphere, and did not project a reorganization of the division of labor within the home. Antoinette Brown Blackwell, pioneer suffragist and minister, asserted that "the paramount social duties of women are household duties, avocations arising from their relations as wives and mothers. . . . The work nearest and clearest before the eyes of average womanhood is work within family boundaries—work within a sphere which men cannot enter."[5] No suffragist of whom I am aware, including the otherwise iconoclastic Elizabeth Cady Stanton, seriously suggested that men take equal responsibilities with women for domestic activities. "Sharing housework" may be a more specifically twentieth-century feminist demand than "smashing monogamy." To nineteenth-century feminists, domestic activities seemed as "naturally" female as childbearing and as little subject to social manipulation.

Although suffragists accepted the peculiarly feminine character of the private sphere, their demand for the vote challenged the male monopoly of the public arena. This is what gave suffragism much of its feminist meaning. Suffragists accepted women's "special responsibility" for domestic activity but refused to concede that it prohibited them from participation in the public sphere. Moreover, unlike the demand that women be admitted to trades, professions, and education, the demand for citizenship applied to all women and it applied to them all of the time—to the housewife as much as to the single, self-supporting woman. By demanding a permanent, public role for all women, suffragists began to demolish the absolute, sexually defined barrier marking the public world of men off from the private world of women. Even though they did not develop a critical analysis of domestic life, the dialectical relationship between public and private spheres transformed their demand for admission to the public sphere into a basic challenge to the entire sexual structure. Thus, although she never criticized women's role in the family, Stanton was still able to write: "One may as well talk of separate spheres for the two ends of the magnet as for man and woman; they may have separate duties in the same sphere, but their true place is together everywhere."[6]

Suffragists' demand for a permanent, public role for all women allowed them to project a vision of female experience and action that went beyond the family and the subordination of women which the family upheld. Citizenship represented a relationship to the larger society that was entirely and explicitly outside the boundaries of women's familial relations. As citizens and voters, women would participate directly in society as individuals, not indirectly through their subordinate positions as wives and mothers. Mary Putnam Jacobi identified this as the revolutionary core of suffragism. The American state, she explained, is based on "individual cells," not households. She went on: "Confessedly, in embracing this conception as women, we do introduce a change which, though in itself purely ideal, underlies all the practical issues now in dispute. In this essentially modern conception, women also are brought into direct relations with the State, independent of their 'mate' or 'brood.'"[7] Without directly attacking women's position within the private sphere, suffragists touched the nerve of women's subordinate status by contending that women might be something other than wives and mothers. "Womanhood is the great fact in her life," Stanton was fond of saying; "wifehood and motherhood are but incidental relations."[8]

On one level, the logic behind the demand for woman suffrage in a country professing republican principles is obvious, and suffragists made liberal use of the tradition and rhetoric of the American Revolution. Yet this is not sufficient to explain why suffrage became the core of a *feminist* program, why enfranchisement was perceived as the key to female liberation. I hypothesize that because enfranchisement involved a way for women to relate to society independent of their familial relations, it was the key demand of nineteenth-century feminists. It was the cornerstone of a social movement that did not simply catalog and protest women's wrongs in the existing sexual order but also revealed the possibility of an alternate sexual order. Unlike the tradition of female protest, from the moral reformers of the 1830s to the temperance women of the 1880s, which was based in the private sphere and sought to reinterpret women's place within it, suffragism focused squarely on the public sphere.

In part, the feminist, liberating promise of enfranchisement rested on the concrete power that suffragists expected to obtain with the vote. Suffragists expected women to use the ballot to protect themselves and to impose their viewpoint on political issues. They anticipated that by strategic use of their political power women would break open new occupations, raise the level of their wage scales to that of men, win strikes, and force reforms in marriage and family law in order to protect themselves from sexual abuse, the loss of their children, and the unchecked tyranny of their husbands. The demand for suffrage drew together protest against all these abuses in a single demand for the right to shape the social order by way of the public sphere. No longer content either with maternal influence over the future voter's character or with an endless series of petitions from women to lawmakers, suffragists proposed that women participate directly in the political decisions that affected their lives. "Like all disfranchised classes, they began by asking to have certain wrongs redressed," Stanton wrote. But suffragism went beyond what she called "special grievances" to give women's protest "a larger scope."[9]

In evaluating suffragists' expectations of the power that the vote would bring women, it is important to keep in mind the structure of political power in the nineteenth century. Political decisions were less centralized in the federal government and more significant at the local level than they are now. Herbert Gutman's analysis of the assistance which local politicians gave labor activists in nineteenth-century Paterson, New Jersey, suggests that Susan B. Anthony's prediction that woman suffrage would win women's strikes had some basis in reality.[10]

Even granted the greater power of the individual voter over political decisions that would affect her or his life, suffragists did not understand the ballot as merely a weapon with which to protect their interests in the political process. They also expected enfranchisement to transform woman's consciousness, to reanchor her self-image, not in the subordination of her familial role but in the individuality and self-determination that they saw in citizenship. This was a particularly important aspect of the political thought of Elizabeth Cady Stanton, the chief ideologue of nineteenth-century suffragism. It is developed most fully in "Solitude of Self," the speech she thought her best. She wrote there: "Nothing strengthens the judgment and quickens the conscience like individual responsibility. Nothing adds such dignity to character as the recognition of one's self-sovereignty."[11] Elsewhere, she wrote that from the "higher stand-point" of enfranchisement, woman would become sensitive to the daily indignities which, without due appreciation for her own individuality, she ignored and accepted.[12] She developed the theme of the impact of enfranchisement on women's self-concept most fully in a speech simply titled "Self-Government the Best Means of Self-Development."[13]

Given the impact on consciousness that suffragists expected from the vote, they generally refused to redirect their efforts toward such partial enfranchisements as municipal or school suffrage. Although these limited suffrages would give women certain political powers, they were suffrages designed especially for women and justified on the basis of women's maternal responsibilities. Their achievement would not necessarily prove women's right to full and equal participation in the public sphere. Suffragists did not simply want political power; they wanted to be citizens, to stand in the same relation to civil government as men did. As a result, it was primarily clubwomen who worked for school and municipal suffrage, while those who identified themselves as suffragists continued to concentrate on the admission of women to full citizenship.[14]

An important index to the nature and degree of suffragism's challenge to the nineteenth-century sexual order was the kind and amount of opposition that it inspired, especially from men. Male opponents focused on the family, its position vis-à-vis the state, and the revolutionary impact of female citizenship on that relation. In response to suffragists' demand that modern democracy include women, opponents tried to reinstate a patriarchal theory of society and the state.[15] The family, they contended, was the virtual, if not the official unit of civil government, and men represented and protected the women of their families in political affairs. Male opponents regularly charged that the enfranchisement of women would revolutionize the relations of the sexes and, in turn, the character and structure of the home and women's role within it. The 1867 New York Constitutional Convention expressed this fear for the future of the family when it rejected suffrage because it was an innovation "so revolutionary and sweeping, so openly at war with a distribution of duties and functions between the sexes as venerable and pervading as government itself, and involving transformations so radical in social and domestic life."[16]

Most suffragists were much more modest about the implications of enfranchisement for women's position within the family. They expected reform of family law, particularly of the marriage contract, and the abolition of such inequities as the husband's legal right to his wife's sexual services. They also anticipated that the transformation in woman's consciousness which enfranchisement would bring would improve the quality of family relations, particularly between wife and husband. Stanton argued that once women were enfranchised they would demand that democracy be the law of the family, as well as of the state.[17] Her comment suggests that by introducing women into a form of social organization not based on patriarchal structures, she expected enfranchisement to permit women a much more critical perspective on the family itself. However, suffragists regularly denied the antisuffragists' charge that woman suffrage meant a revolution in the family. Most would have agreed with Jacobi that if antisuffragists wanted to argue that familial bonds were mere "political contrivances," requiring the disfranchisement of women to sustain them, suffragists had considerably more faith in the family as a "natural institution," able to survive women's entry into the public sphere.[18]

Suffragists worked hard to attract large numbers of women to the demand for the vote. They went beyond the methods of agitational propaganda which they had learned as abolitionists, and beyond the skills of lobbying which they had developed during Radical Reconstruction, to become organizers. As suffragists' efforts at outreach intensified, the family-bound realities of most women's lives forced more and more domestic imagery into their rhetoric and their arguments. Yet suffrage remained a distinctly minority movement in the nineteenth century. The very thing that made suffragism the most radical aspect of nineteenth-century feminism—its focus on the public sphere and on a nonfamilial role for women—was the cause of its failure to establish a mass base. It was not that nineteenth-century women were content, or had no grievances, but that they understood their grievances in the context of the private sphere. The lives of most nineteenth-century women were overwhelmingly limited to the private realities of wifehood and motherhood, and they experienced their discontent in the context of those relations. The enormous success of the Woman's Christian Temperance Union (WCTU), particularly as contrasted with the nineteenth-century suffrage movement, indicates the capacity for protest and activism among nine-teenth-century women and the fact that this mass feminism was based in the private sphere. The WCTU commanded an army in the nineteenth century, while woman suffrage remained a guerrilla force.

Unlike the woman suffrage movement, the WCTU took as its starting point woman's position within the home; it cataloged the abuses she suf-fered there and it proposed reforms necessary to ameliorate her domestic situation. As the WCTU developed, its concerns went beyond the family to include the quality of community life, but its standard for nonfamilial relations remained the family and the moral values women had developed within it. The WCTU spoke to women in the language of their domestic realities, and they joined in the 1870s and 1880s in enormous numbers. Anchored in the private realm, the WCTU became the mass movement that nineteenth-century suffragism could not.

The WCTU's program reflected the same social reality that lay beyond suffragism—that the family was losing its central place in social organi-zation to nondomestic institutions, from the saloon to the school to the legislature, and that woman's social power was accordingly weakened. Yet the WCTU, Luddite-like, defended the family and women's traditional but fast-fading authority within it. Its mottoes reflected this defensive goal: "For God and Home and Native Land"; "Home Protection." In 1883, the WCTU formally endorsed the demand for female enfranchisement but justified its action as necessary to protect the home and women within it, thus retaining its family-based analysis and its defensive character. The first resolutions introduced by Frances Willard in support of suffrage asked for the vote for women in their roles as wives and mothers, to en-able them to protect their homes from the influence of the saloon.[19] This was the woman suffrage movement's approach to female oppression and the problem of spheres stood on its head—women entering the public arena to protect the primacy of the private sphere and women's position within it. Yet, the very fact that the WCTU had to come to terms with suffrage and eventually supported it indicates that the woman suffrage movement had succeeded in becoming the defining focus of nineteenth-century feminism, with respect to which all organized female protest had to orient itself. Even though the WCTU organized and commanded the forces, the woman suffrage movement had defined the territory.

Suffrage became a mass movement in the twentieth century under quite different conditions, when women's position vis-à-vis the public and private spheres had shifted considerably. Despite, or perhaps because of, the home-based ideology with which they operated, the WCTU, women's clubs, and other branches of nineteenth-century feminism had introduced significant numbers of women to extradomestic concerns.[20] Charlotte Perkins Gilman noted the change among women in 1903: "The socialising of this hitherto subsocial, wholly domestic class, is a marked and marvellous event, now taking place with astonishing rapidity."[21] Similarly, Susan B. Anthony commented at the 1888 International Council of Women: "Forty years ago women had no place anywhere except in their homes, no pecuniary independence, no purpose in life save that which came through marriage. . . . In later years the way has been opened to every avenue of industry—to every profession. . . . What is true in the world of work is true in education, is true everywhere."[22] At the point that it could attract a mass base, suffragism no longer opened up such revolutionary vistas for women; they were already operating in the public world of work and politics. The scope and meaning of twentieth-century suffragism requires its own analysis, but the achievement of nineteenth-century suffragists was that they identified, however haltingly, a fundamental transformation of the family and the new possibilities for women's emancipation that this revealed.

## Notes

I wish to thank Amy Bridges, Mari Jo Buhle, Ann D. Gordon, Linda Gordon, Carolyn Korsemeyer, and Rochelle Ruthchild for their comments and suggestions on earlier versions of this article.

1. Phillipe Ariès, *Centuries of Childhood: A Social History of Family Life* (New York: Vintage Books, 1962), esp. 365–407.

2. Edmund Morgan, *The Puritan Family: Religion and Domestic Relations in Seventeenth-Century New England* (New York: Harper & Row, 1966), esp. chap. 6; John Demos, *A Little Commonwealth: Family Life in Plymouth Colony* (New York: Oxford University Press, 1970), 2–11.

3. Morgan, chap. 2. Demos, 82–84.

4. Gerda Lerner, "The Lady and the Mill Girl: Changes in the Status of Women in the Age of Jackson," *Midcontinent American Studies Journal* 10 (1969): 6.

5. Antoinette Brown Blackwell, "Relation of Woman's Work in the Household to the Work Outside," reprinted in Aileen S. Kraditor, *Up from the Pedestal: Selected Writings in the History of American Feminism* (Chicago: Quadrangle Books, 1968), 151.

6. Elizabeth Cady Stanton, "Speech to the 1885 National Suffrage Convention," in *History of Woman Suffrage,* ed. Elizabeth Cady Stanton, Susan B. Anthony, and Matilda Joslyn Gage (Rochester, N.Y.: Susan B. Anthony, 1889), 4:58.

7. Mary Putnam Jacobi, *"Common Sense" Applied to Woman Suffrage* (New York: Putnam, 1894), 138.

8. Stanton, Introduction, *History of Woman Suffrage,* 1:22.

9. Ibid., 15.

10. Herbert Gutman, "Class, Status, and Community Power in Nineteenth-Century American Industrial Cities-Paterson, New Jersey: A Case Study," in *The Age of Industrialism in America,* ed. Frederic C. Jaher (New York: Free Press, 1968), 263–87. For Anthony's prediction on the impact of woman suffrage on women's strikes, see "Woman Wants Bread, not the Ballot," reprinted in *The Life and Work of Susan B. Anthony,* ed. Ida Husted Harper (Indianapolis and Kansas City: Bower-Merrill, 1898), 2:996–1003.

11. Elizabeth Cady Stanton, "Solitude of Self," reprinted in *History of Woman Suffrage,* 4:189–91.

12. Stanton, Introduction, *History of Woman Suffrage,* 1:18.

13. Stanton, "Self-Government the Best Means of Self-Development," reprinted in *History of Woman Suffrage,* 4:40–42.

14. See Lois B. Merk, "Boston's Historical Public School Crisis," *New England Quarterly* 31 (1958): 196–202.

15. See, for instance, Orestes A. Brownson, "The Woman Question," reprinted in *Up from the Pedestal,* 192–94.

16. "Report on the Committee on Suffrage," reprinted in *History of Woman Suffrage,* 2:285.

17. Elizabeth Cady Stanton, "The Family, the State, and the Church," unpublished manuscript speech, Elizabeth Cady Stanton Papers, Manuscript Division, Library of Congress, Washington, D.C.

18. Jacobi, 108.

19. Mary Earhart, *Frances Willard: From Prayers to Politics* (Chicago: University of Chicago Press, 1944), chap. 10.

20. This process is described in Anne Firor Scott, *The Southern Lady: From Pedestal to Politics, 1830–1930* (Chicago: University of Chicago Press, 1970), chap. 6.

21. Charlotte Perkins Gilman, *The Home: Its Work and Influence* (New York: McClure, Phillips, & Co., 1903), 325.

22. Susan B. Anthony, "Introductory Remarks," *Report of the International Council of Women* assembled by the National Woman Suffrage Association (Washington, D.C.: Rufus H. Darby, 1888), 31.

Reprinted, with changes, from *Feminist Studies* 3, nos. 1/2 (Fall 1975): 63–71.
©1975 by Feminist Studies, Inc.

# 2

# MORMON WOMEN, SUFFRAGE, AND CITIZENSHIP AT THE 1893 CHICAGO WORLD'S FAIR

## ANDREA G. RADKE-MOSS

From *Gendering the Fair: Histories of Women and Gender at World's Fairs*, edited by TJ Boisseau and Abigail M. Markwyn (2010)

> Never before has the name Mormon met with a general respectful courtesy. . . . Everywhere, in cars, in hotels, in any and all of the buildings and resorts in the fair if one dropped a word about Utah, there was immediate and what was more remarkable, kindly attention. What could have wrought this marvelous change?
>
> —Susa Young Gates (editor), *The Young Woman's Journal*, 1894

On Saturday, May 20, 1893, while representing Utah territory at the World's Congress of Representative Women, Mormon leader Emmeline B. Wells was invited to preside over the proceedings for one day. Considering how nineteenth-century Americans looked down upon the polygamous and culturally isolated Mormon women as objects of pity and even contempt, Wells appreciated the significance of the invitation as "an honor never before accorded to a Mormon woman." Indeed, the presence of women of the Church of Jesus Christ of Latter-day Saints (Mormons, or LDS) at the Congress was in itself a great achievement. However, Wells lamented, "If one of our brethren had such a distinguished honor conferred upon them, it would have been heralded the country over and thought a great achievement."[1] This comment highlights the central irony of the Chicago World's Columbian Exposition of 1893 for the women who benefited from the unprecedented attention to women's rights and contributions that the fair offered, but who still found themselves excluded from the masculine achievements of the White City.[2] Indeed, it was just this gender segregation that permitted Mormon women's presence at the fair to outshine Mormon men's that summer. Taking advantage of an invitation to participate in the World's Congress of Representative Women, Mormon women attempted to fashion a new image for themselves as liberated representatives of a rapidly Americanizing church. The World's Congress, held in conjunction with the fair, proffered Mormon women an unparalleled public opportunity to assert their identity as modern women who were moral, progressive, patriotic, and stood on the cutting edge of suffrage activism.

The Chicago World's Fair of 1893 marked a major crossroads for Mormon women, poised exactly midpoint between the passage of the 1890 Manifesto that ended polygamy for the Utah-based church, and the achievement of Utah statehood in 1896. Since the 1860s, federal antipolygamy legislation had fed persecution and misunderstanding of the Mormons and had also resulted in numerous failed attempts by Utah to achieve statehood. The Manifesto signaled the Church's decision to eschew polygamous practice in favor of more acceptable monogamous marriages. Utah's statehood was the ultimate reward for accepting federal authority, but it also represented a major step for Utah's Mormon majority to prove their assimilation within American society. Significantly, statehood also came with full suffrage rights for women, a move that surprised many who had viewed Mormon women as subjugated and degraded.[3]

The challenge that lay before Mormon women during the exposition was to shift the popular view of themselves away from an association with backward- ness that had clung to Mormons since the founding of their religion in 1830, and especially since they began the open practice of polygamy in 1852. As the World's Fair opened, Mormon women were perceived at best as oddly religious, and at worst as freakish curiosities who lived in harem-style marriages. In 1893, through a concerted de-emphasis on the peculiarity of polygamy and religious isolation, Mormon women sought to shed their lingering stereotype of "oppressed" plural wives while also showing themselves as progressive women who would soon lead the way in a major state women's suffrage victory. The high profile and public organizing experience that LDS women achieved through the Congress of Women and other fair efforts helped them to focus their energy toward later successful efforts to expect and demand suffrage as a facet of statehood when it came three years later.[4]

## Choosing an Experienced Leadership

It should be no surprise that the women chosen to direct Utah's participation in the World's Congress were those who already held other important leadership positions, especially through the Relief Society and the Young Ladies Mutual Improvement Association (YLMIA), the Church's two organizations for adult and adolescent women. Further, many of these women also brought with them previous experience in organized suffrage activism, political involvement, and charitable work. In June 1892, Governor Arthur L. Thomas appointed Emily Richards as President of Utah's Board of Lady Managers for the fair. Richards represented Utah well. She had served in the Relief Society with other high-ranking Mormon women and, as the wife of nonpolygamist church attorney Franklin S. Richards, she was a politic choice to speak for the territory's women in 1893. Free of the taint adhering to a plural-wife status, she could better speak on broader women's issues without drawing unwanted attention to her personal life. For the same reason, Richards had been chosen as Utah's first delegate to the National Council of Women (NCW) meeting in Washington, D.C., in 1888.[5] Her performance was a great success, portraying a positive view of Mormons, and she brought that experience of powerful self-representation to her preparations for the Chicago exposition in 1893.[6] Richards's vice-president was Jane S. Richards, who was Emily's mother-in-law and the wife of apostle Franklin D. Richards. That so many of Utah's women leaders were married to high-ranking church officials guaranteed important institutional connections, especially as they sought and gained support for suffrage.[7]

Not all of Utah's fair leadership came from among Mormon circles. Governor Thomas appointed Margaret Salisbury as the chair of Utah's Lady Commissioners and Alice J. Whalen as her assistant—both noteworthy as non-LDS women.[8] This leadership displayed a united front of Mormon and non-Mormon women, which was especially important in light of the history of religious tensions in Utah.[9] Other women worked tirelessly in World's Fair work. Zina D. H. Young was one of Brigham Young's surviving widows, a staunch suffrage activist and the Relief

Society president for the church.[10] Emmeline B. Wells was Young's Relief Society secretary and the widow of apostle Daniel H. Wells. She served as the chair of the Salt Lake County Board of Lady Managers and as a Utah Lady Commissioner. A staunch advocate of woman's suffrage and journalism, Wells enthusiastically promoted women's participation in the World's Congress by publishing reports of the exposition in her pro-suffrage newspaper, *Woman's Exponent*. This paper served as a medium of interconnection among Mormon women by keeping them informed of Relief Society news, local and national suffrage activities, and other club work.[11]

Utah women's preparation for World's Fair leadership was a natural extension of their previous experiences in other progressive work. Every member of the board was also involved in suffrage activism, journalism, public welfare, or the Church's women's organizations. In fact, a sampling of Utah's most elite female leadership shows the interconnections between their positions on fair organizing committees and their past contributions to reform. Many women had cut their teeth on suffrage activism through local Relief Societies, and women's leadership often overlapped with participation in other categories of organizational club work. Not only were these women experienced organizers and speakers, but they were also contemporary with their national sisters in many areas of progressive action. For example, in 1891, Wells had founded the Utah Women's Press Club (UWPC) for the progress of women in literature and journalism. Wells intended the club to act as another vehicle for organizing world's fair work, especially because she planned to attend a conference of press women during the congresses in May.[12]

Perhaps the best example of Utah women's efforts toward reform was the Salt Lake Deseret Hospital. Founded in 1882 as an institution where "the sick and afflicted can receive equal care and attention, regardless of race or denomination," the hospital was the first truly significant charitable project administered almost entirely by Utah women.[13] Most of its financial support came from the Relief Society and the YLMIA, which showed the intersections of women's religious and public welfare work.[14] Much like the UWPC, the hospital's board of directors included many women who would later stand for Utah's women at the World's Congress, where they consciously chose to highlight these activities as examples of their progressive spirit.

Utah women's desires to overcome unfair prejudice fed a subtle undercurrent of all their fair efforts but were felt most keenly in their preparations for the World's Congress. In April 1893, Susa Young Gates reviewed

Figure 2.1: Deseret Hospital Board of Directors, 1882. *Front row, left to right:* Jane S. Richards, Emmeline B. Wells. *Middle row:* Phoebe Woodruff, Isabelle M. Horne, Eliza R. Snow, Zina D. H. Young, Marinda N. Hyde. *Back row:* Dr. Ellis R. Shipp, Bathsheba W. Smith, Elizabeth Howard, Dr. Romania B. Pratt Penrose. Used by permission, Utah State Historical Society.

the negative stereotypes that had long followed Mormon women: "We, the women of Utah, have been considered slaves and fools, have been looked upon as without mind or intelligence. That we are true to our husbands and families has been accounted to us as a sure mark of vile inferiority of intellect."[15] In spite of these negative images, Gates celebrated the great possibilities for Mormons to improve their image, especially through interactions with national women's leaders at the congress: "And now we are met by these wide-minded, deep-thoughted women in Chicago as equals, as women with at least mind enough to speak for ourselves." Gates also recognized a spiritual mandate for Mormon women to represent their religion in a public forum. Because of that religious connection, she saw LDS women's presence at the fair as a fulfillment of divine prophecy for the advancement of women. "I heard President Joseph F. Smith say about five years ago that the time was close at hand when the women of this Church would be required to stand in public places and give a reason for the hope within them. The prediction begins to be fulfilled."[16]

With this sense of providential calling that women's work at the exposition would lead Mormon women to greater rights, Gates called for young women all over Utah to "daily remember in our earnest prayers our beloved leader, Sister Elmina S. Taylor, that wisdom and great power may be given her." Indeed, Taylor and her YLMIA presidency went to Chicago as "mouthpieces"—worthy of the divine help of heaven through fasting and prayer. The unification of secular and sacred for Mormon women shows how the fair also became a venue for negotiations of faithful purpose and righteous devotion, ultimately leading to the achievement of women's equal rights, or for Gates, the "unlatching of a door that shall soon be flung wide between the women of this gospel and the women of the world."[17]

One of the final tasks for recruiting Mormon women's support for the exposition and the World's Congress was to highlight an increasing sense of belonging to the national American culture. For a people who had just a few years earlier endured persecution by the federal government through antipolygamy legislation, a reemphasis on patriotism was necessary for a new public image. Mormons sought to unify themselves with the nation, especially by sharing the meaning of common cultural and patriotic symbols. In front of a Chicago audience, Chairman R. C. Chambers of Utah's Board of Commissioners contrasted Mormons' newfound emphasis on patriotism with past accusations of their disloyalty and separation: "the people of Utah . . . love the Union and the Union's flag, and, no matter what may have been said of them in the past, to-day they are marching in harmony with the men and women of this great nation."[18]

Utah's women leaders also pursued this renewed rhetoric of patriotic devotion, usually by emphasizing associations with Columbus and Queen Isabella as inspired leaders. Wells called for women to organize "Queen Isabella Circles" and "Columbian Clubs," in affiliation with Relief Societies.[19] That Isabella received so much acclaim showed a significant women-centered take on Columbus's discovery, that his voyage was sponsored by a female monarch. Wells asked, "Who is there among the patriotic women of America whose heart does not bound with enthusiasm at the name of Isabella of Castile?"[20] Mormon leaders consciously applied these symbols toward a greater association with American providence and patriotism, especially in light of invitations for women to participate in the World's Congress.

## World's Congress of Representative Women

Mormon women began preparing for the World's Congress of Representative Women as early as 1891. With the intent of demonstrating the articulate nature of Mormon women, Emmeline Wells's strategies for her own Salt Lake Columbian Club included teaching women "facts and current events," especially to "help some of us to be come [sic] better speakers and more intelligent on all general subjects."[21] Employing their experience in public speaking and organizing, women participated throughout the congress both as speakers and as panel discussants. Zina Young joined with six panelists in a discussion entitled "Charity, Philanthropy, and Religion," and she successfully held her own with "fourteen women ministers of different denominations, conversing freely with them."[22]

The most anticipated day for Utah was Friday, May 19, at a morning session for the National Woman's Relief Society.[23] On this important day when Mormon women would present themselves to the world, Wells admitted to some jitters: "This was the morning of our own meeting and of course it was natural that we should feel the greatest anxiety." However, the women were well prepared and came with the support of some high-ranking church leaders. In spite of the nerves, the women performed excellently, and they later attended a gathering in their honor. Wells, Young, and Salisbury enjoyed many receptions with national women's leaders and newspaper reporters; these associations added further to the public attention Mormon women received.[24]

The speeches remained consistent to Utah women's intended messages, that Mormons were patriotic, moral, and progressive. Zina Card's speech emphasized that Utah children "are taught lessons of patriotism and purity." Then, perhaps to invoke audience sympathy for the church as a persecuted group, Isabella Horne spoke of the many hardships Mormons had to endure on their 1847 exodus from Illinois to Utah. Nellie Little reemphasized this image of persecution by recounting the federal army's 1857 invasion of Utah to "quell an insurrection," but she added that the Mormons were "listening to a reading of the declaration of Independence" at the time.[25]

Two of Utah's female medical doctors spoke, including Ellis R. Shipp, who discussed Utah women's great successes in medicine; Shipp later gave another talk, "Medical Education of Women in Great Britain and Ireland," which made it into the final publication of the World's Congress.

Dr. Martha Hughes Cannon spoke on the types of women "who represent the Mormon faith."[26] Utah women "are of distinct New England type of character . . . [who] did not forget the principles for which so much had been sacrificed to establish religious toleration on the free soil of America." Cannon reminded the audience that these women often "proved their patriotism and loyalty by rallying around their husbands and sons while they raised the Stars and Stripes."[27] These repeated references to Utah's patriotism added to Mormon women's message of their loyal integration within the national community.

Electa Bullock concluded the meeting with a talk that celebrated the industrial successes of women. Directing her speech outside of Mormon circles to include all men and women, Bullock warned against taking away women's influence from government, industry, and education. If women were confined only "to the narrow sphere of house-wife and maid-servant, [then] the wheels of progress would turn backward."[28] By demanding an inventory of legal and professional equality for women, Bullock transcended her status as a so-called degraded Mormon woman, and successfully stood out as a bold spokesperson for all women's rights.

Emmeline Wells gave perhaps the most important talk of the morning, which discussed how Utah women developed their literary and journalistic talents as a strategy for responding to the hardships of frontier life. As president of the Utah Women's Press Club, Wells used her speech to promote the *Woman's Exponent* and the *Young Woman's Journal*, both on display at the fair.[29] She also published a special edition of the *Exponent* and encouraged her readers that "[d]uring the Columbian exposition, thousands of copies should be given away." Showing off the paper would help in defending Mormon women, for, as she said, "It is still very generally believed that women in this Church are ignorant and in subjection, [so] one copy of the *Exponent* . . . is tangible proof to the contrary." In fact, she suggested with some surety, the *Exponent* "enters where no Mormon elder would be permitted."[30]

Fairgoers could access other publications by Utah women, including Wells's compilation, *Songs and Flowers of the Wasatch*, and the *World's Fair Ecclesiastical History of Utah*, edited by Sarah Kimball.[31] Wells also promoted her pamphlet, *Charities and Philanthropies and Woman's Work in Utah*, which celebrated Utah women's longstanding commitment to public welfare and charity. By emphasizing the Deseret Hospital and the Relief Society's efforts in wheat cultivation, Wells consciously fashioned an image that was repeated throughout the fair, that Mormon women were examples of Christian charity and progressive club work.

Following the successful morning program, the Young Ladies' Mutual Improvement Association held its own proceedings Friday night, again to much acclaim. The participants "compared favorably with the women of the east, and were real artists."[32] Emily Richards earned even more attention by having her speech printed in the official publication of the congress. She firmly outlined a history of women's rights in Utah, from the earliest granting of the franchise (and the unfair removal of that right by the federal government's antipolygamy legislation) to married women's rights to own property and obtain divorces on equal terms with men. She also emphasized Utah's progressive dower and custody laws, along with other rights women enjoyed: "all our educational institutions are open to [women]. They are encouraged to practice law, medicine, and all the other professions. They are at liberty to preach the gospel, speak at public gatherings, visit the sick and officiate at funerals."[33] These advancements came not in spite of men's oppression but because of their support, for, she said, "The efforts and achievements of our women are appreciated by the men, who give them every encouragement and assistance in their various enterprises."[34] Richards's talk represents Utah women's two chief aims—to defend themselves against unfair stereotyping and to show the strong connections between fair participation and women's broader hopes for legal and political rights.

The Congress of Women presented Utah women with a unique opportunity, one that had no parallel among Utah's male leadership. There was no official venue for LDS men to single out their successes. Utah Day—held later on September 9—provided the only significant occasion for male leaders to speak to a national audience. President Wilford Woodruff's speech was brief and lackluster due to his illness during the fair, and both he and Cannon generally stuck to stories of Mormons' past persecutions and trials, rather than looking ahead to commonalities and national progress, as Utah's women had done.[35] The World's Congress of Women may have provided the perfect venue for Utah's women to leave a mark on the fair, but it was Utah women's preparation and organizing skills that permitted them to make the most of it.

## Woman's Suffrage and the World's Fair

Utah women interpreted the potential benefits of the fair for changing the perceptions of Mormon women, but also for achieving woman's suffrage for all. In fact, Wells noted that "really the woman suffrage question was one of the most popular themes of discussion presented" at the World's

Congress.[36] Utah's world's fair leadership saw little or no difference between women's work at the exposition and their orchestrated campaign for attaining the vote.

Perhaps the strongest indicator of Mormon women's prosuffrage attitudes was that so many Lady Managers were suffrage leaders at home and nationally, especially through their beneficial associations with the National Council of Women and International Council of Women (ICW). Wells had the special privilege of being Utah's editor-activist for suffrage, and she often corresponded with national suffrage leaders.[37] She added her voice to Utah's suffragists who also spoke in Chicago, including Sarah Kimball, Electa Bullock, and Emily Richards. In preparation for the congress, these leaders used special meetings of Utah's Woman's Suffrage Association (WSA) and the UWPC for endorsing suffrage ideologies. And county world's fair organizations and Relief Societies worked in tandem toward suffrage goals, by holding joint discussions of the suffrage question and by sharing organizational and ideological experience.[38]

Utah's women leaders saw a direct correlation between overcoming past prejudice against Mormon women and the ultimate achievement of woman suffrage. Regarding the 1892 presidential election, Wells insisted that "the women of this Territory should have had the same privilege in this Presidential election . . . as the women of Wyoming." Wells made a clear connection between the world's fair and suffrage goals, since "the Columbian Exposition will do more to bring about the enfranchisement of women than all other causes put together."[39] Emily Richards recognized the same correlation and wanted to "see every woman come here as intelligent beings ready to receive the ballot, that we should prepare ourselves to join hands with the women of the world and be honorably noted as women of Utah." With that in mind, she "urged all to go to the World's Fair that could."[40]

Much of the success of these suffrage leaders came because they did not put themselves at odds with Utah's male politicians. Utah women earned the support of men who saw a definite connection between woman's suffrage and their hope that statehood would bring political equality for all. One ex-mayor of Provo hoped that statehood would bring suffrage, and for that purpose he encouraged women toward "taking an interest in the World's Fair."[41] In the months before the exposition, LDS church leaders gave public statements in support of suffrage, with an appeal for women to continue their organizational efforts. Because so many prosuffrage LDS leaders were the husbands and fathers of Utah's suffragists, these women therefore exerted even greater influence toward legalizing the vote.[42]

Utah's suffrage victory directly stemmed in part from the experiences Utah women had gained at the World's Fair. The improved harmony between Mormon and non-Mormon women after the 1890 Manifesto was further reinforced through their unified efforts in preparation for the World's Congress of Women. Utah women also enjoyed the support of the NCW, ICW, and National American Woman's Suffrage Association, whose associations brought Mormon women greater public respect for their charitable work, journalism, and political action. Most important, the fair's positive exposure helped to foster support for women's rights among Utah's male leaders, national women's groups, the press, and Utah women themselves.[43] Because Utah's women had already enjoyed the right to vote between 1870 and 1882, suffrage support came more easily in 1896, especially in the wake of a stunningly successful showing by Utah women at the Chicago World's Fair.

## Outsiders' Responses

Utah women received the public attention that they had expected at the fair. Many visitors attended the congresses and Utah's exhibits out of curiosity more than anything else. The *Deseret News* reported: "People come in to see what Utah had. They don't expect much. In fact, many of them come in more to 'see a Mormon' than anything else, but they go away praising our display and congratulating Utah people on their enterprise."[44] Mormon women also benefited from many complimentary remarks made by sympathetic spectators, including Elizabeth Lisle Saxon, who had visited Utah in years past, and reported her observations at the World's Congress. As a non-Mormon speaking positively about Mormons, she gave "perhaps the most important impression effected during the morning session." She "paid high compliments to the purity and intelligence of the Mormon women and declared the prevailing opinion and prejudice regarding the social life of women in Utah to be totally unmerited."[45] Utah's women met many notable leaders during the Congress, including May Wright Sewall, Anna Howard Shaw, Rachel Foster Avery, Isabella Beecher Hooker, and other authors, activists, reporters, and national club presidents. Bertha Palmer herself received Wells, Young, and Richards at a reception in her home.[46] Because Utah women achieved such a presence—especially through the

Figure 2.2: Columbian Exposition, Chicago, 1893. Distinguished Mormon visitors to the Utah Building. Used by permission, Utah State Historical Society.

World's Congress of Women—they earned the most attention, not always accurately, but often positively.

The public relations campaign seemed to work desired results among the press. The *Chicago Daily Tribune* attended the session on May 19 and then published a positive report of the speeches, which Wells reprinted in the June 15 *Exponent* for Utah readers. Etta Gilchrist, an Ohio reporter and friend of Wells and Young, who had previously "written a book against [the Mormons'] institutions," attended the May 19 meeting and was moved to reverse some of her past opinions. She recounted that "Mrs. Wells called me to the platform and I went and sat by Brigham Young's wife [Zina Young] and took by the hand each of those women with whom my sympathy had been so long." In a moment, her sympathy turned to admiration: "Truly their forbearance and kindness is saint-like. This one meeting was to me worth coming to Chicago for."[47]

Some reactions bordered on shallow, as when one Chicago newspaper remarked, "All of the Mormon delegates are fine looking women. It is said that Utah will rival Kentucky in its pretty women."[48] The favorable responses continued with more substance, although at times with some dramatic exaggeration. On June 18, Augusta Prescott of the *Chicago Inter Ocean* declared to her readers: "MORMON WOMEN Who Will Take Part in the Fair Congresses ARE NOT POLYGAMISTS," and highlighted Emily Richards and Electa Bullock as examples of progressive Utah women.[49]

Prescott met with May Wright Sewall, president of the World's Congress and also a friend of Wells, and asked her to tell her "something new and interesting about the work which is going on in Chicago for the benefit of women." Of all of the hundreds of women speakers and topics that she could have mentioned, Sewall chose to single out Mormon women's presence at the fair: "Have you heard that we are to have Mormon women to take part in all our congresses this summer?" Then, perhaps disappointing the taste for the exotic, Sewall added, "And do you know that these Mormon women represent some of the finest women clubs and women organizations that are to be found in America?" Here Sewall reinforced the exact message that her Mormon friends had intended for the fair. Not completely convinced, Prescott pressed Sewall further, inquiring, "Do you allow polygamists to address your meetings? And do you countenance polygamy in any of its forms, even though its representatives be pretty women and even club women and woman suffragists?"

"Why, no," said Mrs. Sewall. "We do not countenance polygamy. We were spared the trouble of deciding whether we would allow it to be represented at our congresses by the fact that none of the women who come to Chicago from Utah were of that belief."[50]

It seems unlikely that Sewall was not aware of the continuing polygamist sympathies of many of her Mormon friends. Perhaps the statement that "none of the women . . . were of that belief" indicated the church's 1890 Manifesto renouncing polygamy, which allowed her an ambiguous but technically accurate defense of Utah women. But it also indicates the power to which Mormon women could affect such a publicity miracle, when some of them still did believe in plural marriage. Upon further investigation, Prescott discovered more complexities of polygamy, that while some still kept their plural marriages, "there are many who belong to the Mormon church who have never liked the idea of taking several wives." Prescott described Mormon women as overwhelmingly relieved at the laws abolishing plural marriage, and she argued that they had only progressed and thrived since the abolition of polygamy. Her impressions of Utah women prior to the Manifesto employ the exotic associations of Turkish harems: "Young girls were given no advantages at all. They were kept in great ignorance. They were scarcely sent to school [and] girls were taught nothing at all. . . . They were as ignorant as Turkish women or Japanese girls waiting for a sweetheart. But they had to work from morning until night, scrubbing, sweeping, baking and sewing."[51]

So while the reporter recognized the progress of Mormon women as portrayed at the fair, she attributed it entirely to their being free of the oppression of polygamy. It is interesting that she failed to notice how such grand advancements among the women delegates could have been accomplished in a mere three years. Nor did she mention the extent of Utah women's suffrage activism, charitable work, education, and journalism *prior to* 1890. But still she admitted, "All of the Mormon delegates are fine looking women. . . . They are becoming intelligent, and intelligence makes beauty." She seems particularly smitten with Emily Richards, "an ardent woman's suffragist [who] is interested in many forms of club and charitable work," and also with Mary Romney, who is "determined never, no never, to be a polygamist."[52]

How did Mormon women perceive their own public-relations success at the Chicago World's Fair? Susa Young Gates reported in December 1893 that "Henry Ward Beecher's sister . . . said that if half she had heard was true, she wanted to come to Utah and remain. . . . This is a new day, a new era for Utah!"[53] Wells also noted those comments by Isabella Beecher Hooker, who "spoke up for our people and mentioned what Mrs. Salisbury had said about our women."[54] These compliments did not go unnoticed by Wells, who declared, "Great results are expected from the Woman's Congress."[55] Gates also reported with optimism that "never before has the name Mormon met with a general respectful courtesy. . . . Everywhere, in cars, in hotels, in any and all of the buildings and resorts in the Fair if one dropped a word about Utah, there was immediate and what was more remarkable, kindly attention. What could have wrought this marvelous change?"[56] Much of the credit must go to Utah's women— Mormon or not—who actively used the Chicago World's Fair of 1893 as a venue for reinventing their public image. Working autonomously and demonstrating real innovation and imagination in their organizational strategies, Utah women completed their fair work almost entirely without the assistance, monetary support, or instruction of male church leaders.

Indeed, Mormon male leaders failed to enact a concerted public relations effort at the fair. In part, their integration into the main space of the fair worked, ironically, against their efforts. Most of Utah's masculine pursuits were not highlighted as successes unique to Mormon men but were couched within the Utah Board of Commissioners' larger, nonsectarian exhibits on mining, industry, and agriculture. However, Mormon men's relatively unspectacular impact on the fair was largely a matter of their own failures relative to their female counterparts. Mormon men did not benefit from associations with any national organizations or "cause," as Utah women enjoyed with national suffrage organizations. Utah women had spent the 1880s networking with notable women's leaders, while men had spent that same time in hiding from prosecution or trying to recoup their financial and political losses during the time of federal antipolygamy action. In fact, the First Presidency had requested access to the World's Parliament of Religions in 1893 but had been soundly rejected. Still, in a "remarkable incident," Emily Richards was invited to appear "before the woman's branch of the Parliament of Religions," where she spoke on the "Women of Mormondom."[57] Annie Wells Cannon noted the significance of this event, "for though the Parliament of Religions had refused admission to the male representatives of the Church, yet this gracious lady found opportunity for a hearing through the auxiliary." Richards's experience shone through, for her speech was "carefully prepared, and . . . she gave a fine and sincere talk which carried its truths to the hearts of her audience."[58]

Utah's Mormon women consciously and successfully planned and carried out a public-relations miracle, whereby they gained power over their own message and recreated a new image. Emmeline Wells had drawn a hasty and cynical conclusion about the fact that her appearance at the World's Congress did not receive the same attention as if she had been a man. Contrary to that image, Emily Richards's singular performance at an event where Mormon men were not welcome showed how Mormon women surpassed all expectations in 1890s America for their gender and their religion. These female leaders took advantage of the opportunities that the fair and the congress afforded for women and added to those their own experiences as women of thought, substance, and action.

Perhaps at no other event than the Chicago World's Columbian Exposition of 1893 could the gendered forces of organization, publicity, energy, and talent have merged to favor Utah's LDS and non-LDS women. In 1893, Mormon women went from oppressed and silenced plural wives to patriotic, intelligent, and moral women of political success and progressive benevolence. They had met America and the world, and they were now ready to meet the twentieth century.

## Notes

1. Emmeline B. Wells, Typescript Diary, May 20, 1893, vol. 16 (1893), 22 (L. Tom Perry Special Collections, Lee Library, Brigham Young University, Provo, Utah).

2. Gail Bederman, *Manliness and Civilization: A Cultural History of Gender and Race in the United States, 1880–1917* (Chicago: University of Chicago Press, 1996).

3. By 1896, Utah was one of only four states that had granted full suffrage to women—Wyoming (1890), Colorado (1893), and Idaho (1896)—while a national constitutional amendment was still a generation away. On Utah's battle for woman suffrage, see Lola Van Wagenen, *Sister-Wives and Suffragists: Polygamy and the Politics of Woman Suffrage, 1870–1896* (Provo: Joseph Fielding Smith Institute for Latter-day Saint History and BYU Studies, 2003).

4. See Richard Van Wagoner, *Mormon Polygamy: A History* (Salt Lake City: Signature, 1986).

5. Jean Bickmore White, "Women's Suffrage in Utah," *Utah History Encyclopedia*, found at http://www.media.utah.edu/UHE/w/WOMANSUFFERAGE.html (accessed August 10, 2007). See also Van Wagenen, 130–31.

6. Annie Wells Cannon, "Emily Sophia Tanner Richards," in "In Memoriam: Emily Sophia Tanner Richards, 1929," 20 (archives of the Church of Jesus Christ of Latter-day Saints, Salt Lake City, Utah). See also Van Wagenen, 131.

7. *Woman's Exponent*, March 1, 1892, 126; and October 1, 1892, 52.

8. Carol Cornwall Madsen, *An Advocate for Women: The Public Life of Emmeline B. Wells, 1870–1920* (Provo: Brigham Young University Press, 2006), 387.

9. On the tensions between Mormon and non-Mormon women throughout Utah's suffrage activism, see Van Wagenen.

10. A spiritual and charitable organization for Mormon women, the Relief Society was headquartered in Salt Lake City as the umbrella organization for smaller stake and ward Relief Societies throughout the territory. In Mormon lexicon, a stake is an organizational unit made up of small congregations called wards or smaller units called branches. Each stake consisted of anywhere from ten to thirty wards or branches, each with its own Relief Society. See Janath R. Cannon, Jill Mulvay Derr, and Maureen Ursenbach Beecher, *Women of Covenant: A History of Relief Society* (Salt Lake City: Deseret, 1991).

11. *Woman's Exponent*, May 1, 1892, 159; on Wells and the Exponent, see Madsen.

12. *Woman's Exponent*, March 15, 1892, 136. See Linda Thatcher and John R. Sillito, "'Sisterhood and Sociability': The Utah Women's Press Club, 1891–1928," *Utah Historical Quarterly* 53 (1985): 144–56.

13. Quoted in Martha Sonntag Bradley and Mary Brown Firmage Woodward, *4 Zinas: A Story of Mothers and Daughters on the Mormon Frontier* (Salt Lake City: Signature, 2000), 235.

14. *Woman's Exponent*, February 15, 1893, 127.

15. Susa Young Gates, ed., *Young Woman's Journal* (April 1893), 326.

16. Ibid. Joseph F. Smith was a counselor to numerous church presidents, including Wilford Woodruff during the fair, and Smith himself was president from 1901 to 1918.

17. Gates, 326–27.

18. E. A. McDaniel, *Utah at the World's Columbian Exposition* (Salt Lake City: Lithographing, 1894), 51. On the transition of the LDS Church from isolation and polygamy to patriotism and assimilation, see Thomas G. Alexander, *Mormonism in Transition* (Urbana: University of Illinois Press, 1986).

19. *Woman's Exponent*, June 15, 1891, 186.

20. *Woman's Exponent*, November 1, 1892, 65.

21. Wells, Transcript Diary, July 26, 1892, vol. 15 (1892), 68.

22. Bradley and Woodward, 356.

23. *Woman's Exponent*, April 15 and May 1, 1893, 157.

24. Wells, Typescript Diary, May 19, 1893, vol. 16 (1893), 21.

25. *Woman's Exponent*, June 15, 1893, 177.

26. *Deseret Evening News*, May 27, 1893, quoted in "The World's Fair: Utah at the Fair," *Lesson for September 1993: A Century Ago*, comp. Beatrice B. Malouf, 19 (Salt Lake: Daughters of the Utah Pioneers, 1993).

27. *Woman's Exponent*, June 15, 1893, 179.

28. Electa Wood Bullock, "Industrial Women," in *The Congress of Women: Held in the Woman's Building, World's Columbian Exposition, Chicago, U.S.A., 1893*, ed. Mary Kavanaugh Oldham Eagle, 510–11 (Chicago: Monarch, 1894).

29. *Woman's Exponent*, June 15, 1893, 178.

30. *Woman's Exponent*, July 1 and 15, 1893, 188.

31. Madsen, 387–88.

32. *Woman's Exponent*, June 15, 1893, 179.

33. Emily S. Richards, "The Legal and Political Status of Woman in Utah," in *The World's Congress of Representative Women*, ed. May Wright Sewall, 913 (New York: Rand McNally, 1894).

34. Ibid.

35. McDaniel, 54–57. The World's Fair was significant for bringing national, positive attention to Utah's legendary Mormon Tabernacle Choir—a topic too large for discussion here.

36. *Woman's Exponent*, June 1, 1893, 172.

37. *Woman's Exponent*, May 1, 1892, 158.

38. Sarah M. Kimball, "The Woman Suffrage association of Utah," quoted in Malouf, 42; and "Constitution of San Pete County World's Fair Association," p. 11, Mss 566, L. Tom Perry Special Collections and Archives, Lee Library, Brigham Young University, Provo, Utah.

39. *Woman's Exponent*, November 15, 1892, 76. Utah's Mormon women had enjoyed the vote between 1870 and 1882, when it was revoked by a federal law

that disfranchised polygamists. The 1887 Edmunds-Tucker Act revoked suffrage for *all* Utah women. By 1893, Utah women maintained a hope that suffrage would return with statehood. See Van Wagenen.

40. *Woman's Exponent*, October 15, 1892, 61.

41. Ibid., 61–62.

42. *Woman's Exponent*, March 15, 1892, 133. The Church's first presidency and many apostles all favored woman's suffrage. See Madsen, 280–88.

43. On Utah's statehood and suffrage, see Van Wagenen.

44. *Deseret Evening News*, June 2, 1893, quoted in Malouf, 21–22.

45. *Deseret Evening News*, May 27, 1893, quoted in Malouf, 21–22.

46. Wells, Transcript Diary, May 22, 1893, vol. 16 (1893), 23.

47. *Woman's Exponent*, June 15, 1893, 178–79.

48. Cannon, 24.

49. *The Chicago Inter Ocean*, June 18, 1893, in Charles E. Johnson Collection, P0011, Box 11, Newspaper Clippings, Utah State University Archives and Special Collections.

50. Ibid.

51. Ibid.

52. Ibid.

53. *Young Woman's Journal* (December 1893), 164–65.

54. Wells, Transcript Diary, May 21, 1893, vol. 16 (1893), 22.

55. *Young Woman's Journal* (December 1893), 164–65.

56. *Young Woman's Journal* (January 1894), 212–13.

57. Cannon, 25.

58. Ibid.

# 3

# SUFFRAGE AND SPECTACLE

## MARY CHAPMAN AND BARBARA GREEN

From *Gender in Modernism:*
*New Geographies, Complex Intersections,*
edited by Bonnie Kime Scott (2007)

In increasing numbers, literary and cultural critics have read the Anglo-American twentieth-century suffrage movement in relation to the development of the various cultures of modernity (democratic, aesthetic, visual, advertising, and commodity cultures), and the existence of a feminist literary culture in relation to the emergence of literary modernism.[1] The suffrage movement predates the modernist period, and was characterized throughout by a wide variety of strategies, tactics, and arguments: some radical, some peaceable, some militant, and some constitutionalist.[2] Literary and cultural critics have been struck by the ways in which the dramatic and complex cultural contributions of the last phase of the suffrage movement challenge our understanding of the formation of high modernism and contribute greatly to current efforts to rethink the "great divide" between modernism and mass culture. Much suffrage literature espoused radical politics through the vehicles of the dominant cultural forms of popular culture (the romance, for example); other literary and cultural experiments of the movement borrowed from or contributed to the experimental techniques generally associated with modernism. In both its vibrant print culture and its innovative spectacular politics, the modern suffrage movement in both Britain and America developed new and varied forms of persuasion. The dynamic print culture of the modernist suffrage movement composed a feminist "counter-public sphere" characterized by the creation of a number of women's presses, the establishment of successful oppositional periodicals, the cultivation of feminist speech in a variety of literary genres and popular forms, and the cultivation of feminist work through associations like the Women Writer's Suffrage League in England. At the same time, suffrage offered a challenging visual culture through spectacular activism: sensational publicity stunts; political theatricals and street theater of various sorts; and militant actions. Suffrage organizations capitalized on and helped to shape new understandings of femininity through the new forms of media and visual culture that were defining the new century: especially advertising, cartoons, the accelerated use of photographs in newspapers, and an enhanced desire for sensational journalism. These activities demand to be read in relation to one another, for suffrage activists imagined ways of turning spectacle into print—through media coverage—and making print into a spectacle—through very public creative displays of suffrage banners, petitions, voiceless speeches, and manifestoes.

Though the differences between and within suffrage groups—British and American, constitutional and militant—were immense during the complex period of heightened activism from 1905 to 1920 (roughly from the beginning of militancy in England to the passage of the Nineteenth Amendment in the United States), all embraced the new opportunities that came with modern innovations in print and visual media and developed a wide range of strategies to engage public attention.[3] Large-scale displays of feminist bodies in public spaces worked to announce collectivity and civic participation; the pageant, march, and parade were especially popular vehicles in both countries. And as feminist texts and activists crossed the Atlantic, the cross-pollination of modern political strategies flourished.[4] In both countries new organizations were formed out of frustration with the lack of progress or were revitalized by innovative approaches to lobbying. In Britain, the three major Edwardian suffrage organizations—the non-militant National Union of Women's Suffrage Societies formed in 1897 and led by Millicent Fawcett, and the militant organizations the Women's Social and Political Union (WSPU) formed in 1903, led by Emmeline and Christabel Pankhurst, and the Women's Freedom League (WFL), which broke from the WSPU in 1907, led by Charlotte Despard—participated in the large-scale marches and pageants that composed some of the period's most dramatic street theater.[5] In America, college graduates like Marianne Moore joined with trade unionists and society women to form radical associations like the Collegiate Equal Franchise Society, the Women's Political Union (WPU), the Congressional Union (CU), and the National Woman's Party (NWP), which advocated a radical strategy of symbolic expression.[6] All of these groups organized colorful parades, pageants, and other entertainments that packaged threatening ideas of women's political role within visually pleasing, media-friendly forms, presenting suffrage as, at once, part of a progressive platform and the logical extension of nineteenth-century womanly influence. Initially considered radical, the parade form quickly became "the most characteristic form of activism during the final years of the campaign" (Goddard 250), and could command audiences of nearly 250,000 and involve tens of thousands of women marching according to profession, association, nationality, or branch organization. Suffrage organizations staged a variety of spectacular performances: professional and amateur productions of propaganda plays like Hamilton and St. John's *How the Vote Was Won, tableaux vivants,* debates and speeches, screenings of suffrage newsreels and docu-melodramas, balls and street meetings, cross-country tours by car, train, trolley, or on foot, and other publicity stunts. These spectacles asked spectators to rethink gender by complicating the universal ideal and demonstrating women's fitness for governing through a display of their ability to organize, negotiate conflicts, and achieve solidarity among diverse groups of women.[7]

Figure 3.1: National Woman's Party pickets carried banners quoting President Woodrow Wilson's and other politicians' wartime democracy slogans throughout 1917. In this photograph, party members carry a banner that ironically quotes from Wilson's April 1917 war message. Courtesy of the Library of Congress.

In addition to the pleasing spectacles of street pageantry and exhibitions, members of the militant organizations, England's WSPU and WFL and America's CU and NWP, staged acts of political protest. The WSPU began to gain national attention in October 1905 when Christabel Pankhurst and Annie Kenney disrupted an election meeting at the Free Trade Hall, leading to their arrests. The militancy of this phase of the suffrage campaign consisted largely of the disruption of political meetings through the "interruption of male political discourse" and the strategic courting of imprisonment.[8] Newspapers eager for sensational stories and photographs gave these tactics a great deal of public attention.[9] A shared interest in commanding public attention, insisting upon a right to protest, and manipulating constitutionalist rhetoric made for richly textured forms of radical activity produced by both the WSPU and the WFL: for example, Grille Protests where feminists chained themselves to a metal screen in front of the Ladies' Gallery commented upon women's exclusion from political life as did numerous deputations such as the one fictionalized by Evelyn Sharp.[10] Increasingly, especially after 1912, the WSPU engaged in more violent forms of protest—from window-smashing to the destruction of private and public property through arson and other methods. The strategy of courting imprisonment continued throughout the campaign, but after the first feminist hunger strike in prison in 1909, the story of suffragettes' sacrifice for the cause took on a grimmer aspect as hunger-striking activists were forcibly fed and, after 1913, subject to the Cat and Mouse Act that released them only to re-imprison them once they resumed activism.

American suffragists borrowed militant tactics from their British sisters but eschewed the violent methods. They staged spectacles that attracted media attention, but they also turned their manipulation of "print" itself into a spectacle, through the colorful display of collectively authored banners, placards, and picket signs in public places. Rather than recalling the feminine, decorative, Arts & Crafts banners fashioned by British suffragists that Lisa Tickner has examined, the sleek functional typeface of American suffrage banners responded in many respects to male modernist accusations that feminine decoration was to blame for cultural stasis and decay and anticipated the design of modernist journals like *BLAST*. From about 1907 on, American suffrage activists utilized these and other forms of print cultural spectacle to criticize the government's failure to respond to women's demands for the franchise. Throughout the next twelve years, silent, peaceable women made spectacles of themselves delivering, presenting, and carrying suffrage print culture: they unfurled banners from the Senate Gallery, ceremonially presented four-mile-long petitions to legislators, and delivered voiceless speeches in shop windows.

In 1917, when President Wilson, preoccupied by the war, refused to meet with lobby groups, the NWP picketed the White House, displaying banners that quoted Wilson's empty rhetoric (e.g., "Liberty is a Fundamental Demand of the Human Spirit"). Jailed for obstructing traffic because picketing was in fact legal, suffragists hunger struck while demanding political prisoner status, a strategy that culminated in beatings and force-feedings. Responding to popular stereotypes of women as garrulous, and suffragists as "lantern-jawed harridans" or "iron-jawed angels," stereotypes that foreground the mouth as a site of women's strength and potential unattractiveness, all of these print cultural spectacles visualized women as temporarily and strategically silent. Performing their political voicelessness through print was a key tactic of their campaign.

More conventional suffrage literature was an integral part of this complex strategy of suffrage spectacle, even, as Sowon Park has claimed, an "event" in its own right best understood within a context of production and circulation that included the creation of organizations for women writers and artists, fund-raising events, the interactive nature of some feminist theater, and the role that novels and other literary forms played to convert a mass readership to the cause.[11] In Britain, suffragists and suffragettes created organizations for feminist artists of various sorts: among them, the Women Writers' Suffrage League (WWSL), Artists' Suffrage League, Suffrage Atelier, and Actresses' Franchise League. The WWSL was formed in 1909 by Cicely Hamilton with Elizabeth Robins elected the first president; members included Sarah Grand, Olive Schreiner, Evelyn Sharp, Violet Hunt, May Sinclair, Alice Meynell, and Ivy Compton-Burnett (Park 92). The organization brought together "professional" women writers—meaning any writer who had sold a text—to support the cause with the method "proper to writers—the use of the pen" (Robins, *Way Stations* 112). The members of the WWSL contributed to suffrage periodicals like *Votes for Women, Common Cause,* and *The Vote,* wrote letters to newspapers, and published fiction, plays, burlesques, manifestoes, oratory, autobiographies, diaries, histories, poems, sketches, polemical essays, and songs.[12] Many of these literary works were published through feminist presses like the WSPU's Women's Press and were sold in shops like the Women's Press Shop. The existence of an active feminist readership together with new avenues for the publication and circulation of feminist texts also worked to keep key works in print, for example the classic New Woman novel among suffrage readers, Olive Schreiner's *The Story of an African Farm*.[13]

In the United States, suffragists also produced an unprecedented amount of creative material directed at converting people to the cause— from conventional literary genres to songs, films, cartoons, and slogans, although very little scholarship has addressed this.[14] Writers such as Mary Austin, Charlotte Perkins Gilman, Edna Ferber, Zona Gale, and Alice Duer Miller published both in radical periodicals like *The Woman's Journal, The Suffragist, The Forerunner, The Woman Voter, Women's Political World, Crisis* and *The Masses*, and in mainstream journals devoting special issues to suffrage. The National American Woman Suffrage Association formed its own publishing imprint—the National Woman Suffrage Publishing Company—and the Leslie Bureau of Suffrage Education supplied newspapers with suffrage copy and photographs. Although no formal women writers' associations existed as in Britain, writers congregated in suffrage organizations, and feminist groups, like Heterodoxy, participated in fundraising readings and book auctions, and marched together in parades.

Not only because suffrage literature was created to persuade, but also because much of it was intended for a mass readership as Park and Eileen Sypher have shown, the fiction tends toward realism: for example, documentary reportage, and the incorporation of speeches and polemic in literary works like Robins's *The Convert* and local color in works by American regionalists like Ferber, as well as a reliance on stereotypes such as the attractive suffrage heroine and her anti-suffrage lover. Yet, though it has been tempting to locate a "great divide" between suffrage polemic and modernist literary experiment, recent criticism has also noted a number of historical and formal connections between suffrage art and modernism and the value of the cultural work performed by suffrage texts.[15] Jane Miller has suggested that suffrage literature is proto-modernist, and has argued for a modernism of content rather than form in the suffrage novel. Many suffrage works, however, are also formally innovative in their use of dialect and collective authorship; certainly both the use of parody and pastiche in order to disrupt ideology and the "fluid appropriability of imagery and types" favored by suffrage authors sit nicely next to modernist experiment.[16]

In addition, many modernist artists found common cause (or sometimes cause for criticism) with suffragists and suffragettes. In *BLAST*

Wyndham Lewis announced his sympathy for suffragettes while urging them to stop attacks on public property—especially art. Others, like Virginia Woolf in *Night and Day,* noted the labor of suffragists who struggled in offices, meetings, and letter-writing campaigns. Marianne Moore contributed regular unsigned suffrage copy and a letter to the editor to her local newspapers at the same time that her first poems were being published in *The Egoist.* A St. Vincent Millay sonnet celebrates a suffrage martyr; Ford Madox Ford, then Hueffer, wrote pro-suffrage literature; May Sinclair's *The Tree of Heaven* associates radical suffrage with modernist experiment; Djuna Barnes wrote an essay for the *New York World* in which she described her voluntary submission to a forcible feeding; and Rebecca West covered the campaign in periodical articles. Progressive journals too covered the campaign, for example *The Masses* and, as the essays by Beatrice Hastings in *Gender in Modernism* described below show, *The New Age.*

The materials described below are taken from the height of the modern suffrage campaign and sample ways in which modern feminist literary culture tracked and helped produce new forms of modern feminist activism and spectacle.

Evelyn Sharp (1869–1955), an active journalist, editor, and creative writer, published essays and short fiction in journals like *The Yellow Book,* the *Manchester Guardian,* the *Herald,* and the *New Leader,* in addition to publishing novels and children's literature. A member of the WSPU and the Women Writers Suffrage League, she became editor of *Votes for Women* in 1912 when the editors, the Pethick Lawrences, were imprisoned. In 1910 she published *Rebel Women,* vignettes of suffragette life previously published in journals like the *Manchester Guardian* and *Votes for Women.* These suffrage stories chronicled all aspects of activism—from street hawking newspapers to wearing sandwich boards advertising the cause. "The Woman at the Gate" depicts a women's deputation (a feminist attempt to exercise a citizen's right to petition the king or his representative) as both a personal trial for the individual suffragette about to brave a hostile crowd and as an occasion for political debate and discourse in the public sphere of the city's streets. Here, as in other pieces of suffrage literature, the spectator is as important as the militant action itself and slowly the lines between actor and audience are blurred in such a way as to leave open the possibility of political conversion.

Lady Constance Lytton (1869–1923) joined the WSPU in 1909, joined her first deputation that year, and was sentenced to a month's imprisonment. Daughter of Earl Lytton, viceroy of India, Constance Lytton was given special treatment and placed in the hospital ward despite her pleas to be given the same treatment as other suffragettes. To expose these inequities, and the treatment of women in prison in general, Lytton cross-class dressed as "Jane Warton, Spinster" in 1910 to lead a protest demanding the release of suffragette prisoners in Liverpool. "Jane Warton" was arrested and imprisoned in Walton Gaol, where she went on a hunger strike and was subjected to forcible feeding without a medical examination (which would have revealed her weak heart). The story of Lytton's masquerade as Jane Warton circulated in newspaper articles, letters to the editor, and speeches and became a crucial part of a parliamentary debate on the imprisonment and forcible feeding of suffragettes before Lytton published her memoir *Prisons and Prisoners* in 1914. The autobiographical narrative of imprisonment became an important sub-genre of suffrage writing, and Lytton's text, from which this extract is taken, features many of the sub-genre's conventions: a sense of community forged within the prison, and effort to highlight the plight of women in the prison system, and spiritual language of suffering and enlightenment.

Edna Ferber (1885–1968) was one of the greatest American women novelists of her day, best known for her novel *Showboat*. In *Fanny Herself* (1917), Ferber traces the meteoric rise of Fanny Brandeis from unsuccessful small-town Jewish storekeeper's daughter to successful fashion executive. In one scene, Fanny returns to New York City from a productive European business trip and finds herself in the middle of a suffrage parade. Fanny is struck by the hopefulness of a young underfed girl marching with immigrant textile workers, whose figure is a reprimand to Fanny's entire industry, which bases its profits on the exploitation of underpaid workers such as these. In the cartoon she sketches of this Russian Jewish waif, Fanny resurrects her creative side, which her corporate job has nearly obliterated, and comes home to her roots: "These are my people!"

*The Sturdy Oak,* a novel serialized in *Collier's* and then issued in book form, was intended to fundraise for the November 1917 New York State referendum on woman suffrage. Suffrage had been defeated by 195,000 votes in the 1915 referendum; the 1917 victory, in the largest state in the union, was a turning point for the national campaign. Edited by Elizabeth Jordan, coauthor of suffrage leader Anna H. Shaw's autobiography, plotted by regionalist Mary Austin, and collectively authored by fourteen prominent men and women writers, *The Sturdy Oak* models in literary achievement what might be possible politically if women were permitted to collaborate with men. As one character proclaims: "It isn't that women . . . could run the world better. . . . It's that men and women have got to work together to do the things that need doing" (71). The novel follows the romance plot of many contemporary suffrage films, plays, and novels: a conversion narrative, it features an attractive wife whose unexpected support for suffrage (including assuming a cross-class disguise that allows her to address factory "girls") convinces her district attorney candidate husband George to support suffrage and fight political corruption. George's troubles begin when he publishes a naive campaign statement proclaiming men's role as woman's protector, causing disasters on both the home front and the campaign trail: unmarried women cousins take him at his word and move in, and a "voiceless speech" in a downtown storefront dares the chivalric George not to turn a blind eye to violations of legislation protecting women and children workers, as his pro-industry supporters would like. When his wife inspects the horrible conditions of rental properties near the factory and attempts to organize working women, she is mistaken for a suffrage activist and kidnapped by mobsters, leading George to declare himself an independent in support of suffrage. One excerpt from the novel, by by Anne O'Hagan (1869–1934), reporter, editor, and author, depicts a voiceless speech, invented by American suffragists as a canny means of interrogating political candidates without violating Victorian standards of feminine decorum.

### Notes

1. As the inclusion of an assortment of suffrage literature in other sections of *Gender in Modernism* indicates, the women's suffrage movement has come into its own in modernist studies. See Sylvia Pankhurst and Mrs. F. W. Pethick Lawrence [Emmeline Pethick Lawrence], "Women's Social and Political Union: 'Votes for Women' New Movement Manifesto"; NWSPU, "Our Demand: What It Is and What It Is Not"; Beatrice Hastings, "Suffragettes in the Making," "Feminism and the Franchise"; Edna St. Vincent Millay, "Sonnet for Inez Milholland"; and Cicely Hamilton and Christopher St. John, *How the Vote Was Won*.

2. For studies of the ideas of nineteenth- and twentieth-century suffrage movements, see Bolt and Graham.

3. In Britain, the Representation of the People Act (1918) gave women over thirty the right to vote if they were householders, the wives of householders, occupiers of property with an annual rent of £5 or more, or graduates of British

universities. After July 1928 women and men over twenty-one could vote on equal terms. See Purvis and Holton, 3–4. In the United States, the Nineteenth Amendment, ratified in 1920, enfranchised women. See Ford.

4. On connecting links between the United States and British campaigns, see Harrison.

5. For readings of the British suffrage movement, see Eustance et al., Fletcher et al., Garner, Holton, Joannou, Purvis, Kent et al., and Rosen.

6. For readings of the American suffrage movement, see Dubois, Ford, Lumsden, and Lunardini.

7. On suffrage use of theatrical spectacle, see Auster, Glenn, Finnegan, Chapman, and Green.

8. The phrase is Jane Marcus's, from *Suffrage and the Pankhursts,* 9.

9. The *Daily Mail* coined the term "suffragette" to distinguish the militant WSPU from constitutional suffragists in 1906, and the militants embraced it, the WSPU later naming its journal *The Suffragette*. In the United States, suffragists divided over strategy: whether suffrage would be gained most expediently through state referenda or through federal lobbying or both.

10. See Mayhall, 49–52.

11. See Park, 459. For readings of the importance of the manifesto and theater to the suffrage movement, see Lyon and Kelly in *Gender in Modernism*. Also see Lyon, *Manifestoes* and Stowell.

12. Crawford gives useful bibliographies of British suffrage novels, plays, and poems. A number of recent reprints and collections reproduce material from the British campaign. See Colemore, Jorgansen-Earp; Marcus's *Suffrage*, Norquay, Roberts and Mizuta.

13. See Ardis, 190–94.

14. The exceptions are Bardes and Gossett, who examine the "declaration of independence" trope in nineteenth-century fiction, Friedl, who has anthologized pro- and antisuffrage plays, and Chapman, who has examined the suffrage poetry of Alice Duer Miller and co-edited a special issue of *Canadian Review of American Studies* on suffrage print culture. On suffrage periodicals, see Yellin and Finnegan.

15. The phrase "great divide" is Andreas Huyssen's. For recent criticism on suffrage and modernism, see Howlett, Felski, Lyon, Marcus's "Asylums of Anteaus," Park, and Joannou.

16. The last phrase is Murray's, who has claimed that these techniques anticipate postmodernism (202).

## Works Cited

Ardis, Ann. "Organizing Women: New Woman Writers, New Woman Readers, and Suffrage Feminism." In *Victorian Woman Writers and the Woman Ques-*

*tion,* ed. Nicola Diane Thompson. Cambridge: Cambridge University Press, 1999. 189–203.

Auster, Albert. *Actresses and Suffragists: Women in the American Theater, 1890–1920.* New York: Praeger, 1984.

Bardes, Barbara, and Suzanne Gossett. *Declarations of Independence: Women and Political Power in Nineteenth-Century American Fiction.* New Brunswick: Rutgers University Press, 1990.

Barnes, Djuna. "How It Feels to Be Forcibly Fed." In *New York/Djuna Barnes,* ed. Alyce Barry. Los Angeles: Sun and Moon Press, 1989. 174–79.

Bolt, Christine. "The Ideas of British Suffragism." *Votes for Women.* Edited by June Purvis and Sandra Stanley Holton. New York: Routledge, 2000. 34–56.

Chapman, Mary. "Women and Masquerade in the 1913 Suffrage Demonstration in Washington." *Amerikastudien* 44.3 (Fall 1999): 343–55.

———. *"Are Women People?* Alice Duer Miller's Poetry and Politics." *American Literary History* 18.1 (2006): 59–85.

Chapman, Mary, and Angela Mills, eds. Special "Suffrage" Issue, *Canadian Review of American Studies* 36:1: 1–128.

Colemore, Gertrude. *Suffragette Sally.* London: Stanley Paul & Co., 1911; rpt. as *Suffragettes: A Story of Three Women.* London: Pandora Press, 1984.

Crawford, Elizabeth. *The Women's Suffrage Movement: A Reference Guide, 1866–1928.* London: Routledge, 1999.

Dicenzo, Maria. "Gutter Politics: Women Newsies and the Suffrage Press." *Women's History Review* 12.1 (2003): 15–33.

Dubois, Ellen. *Harriot Stanton Blatch and the Winning of Woman Suffrage.* New Haven: Yale University Press, 1997.

Eustance, Claire, Joan Ryan, and Laura Ugolini, eds. *A Suffrage Reader: Charting Directions in British Suffrage History.* London: Leicester University Press, 2000.

Felski, Rita. *The Gender of Modernity.*

Ferber, Edna. *Fanny Herself.* New York: Frederick A. Stokes Company, 1917. Urbana: University of Illinois Press, 2001.

Finnegan, Margaret. *Selling Suffrage: Consumer Culture and Votes for Women.* New York: Columbia University Press, 1999.

Fletcher, Ian Christopher, Laura E. Nym Mayhall, and Philippa Levine, eds. *Women's Suffrage in the British Empire: Citizenship, Nation, and Race.* London: Routledge, 2000.

Friedl, Bettina. *On to Victory: Propaganda Plays of the Woman Suffrage Movement.* Boston: Northeastern University Press, 1987.

Ford, Linda G. *Iron-Jawed Angels: The Suffrage Militancy of the National Woman's Party, 1912–1920.* Lanham, Md.: University Press of America, 1991.

Gale, Zona. "Folks" [1914]. In *Peace in Friendship Village.* New York: Macmillan, 1919.

Garner, Les. *Stepping Stones to Women's Liberty: Feminist Ideas in the Women's Suffrage Movement, 1900–1918*. London: Heinemann, 1984.

Gilman, Charlotte Perkins. *Selections from Suffrage Songs and Verses*. New York: Charlton, 1911.

Glenn, Susan A. *Female Spectacle: The Theatrical Roots of Modern Feminism*. Cambridge: Harvard University Press, 2000.

Goddard, Leslie. "'Something to Vote For': Theatricalism in the United States Women's Suffrage Movement." Ph.D. diss., Northwestern University, 2001.

Graham, Sara Hunter. *Woman Suffrage and the New Democracy*. New Haven: Yale University Press, 1996.

Green, Barbara. *Spectacular Confessions: Autobiography, Performative Activism, and the Sites of Suffrage, 1905–1938*. New York: St. Martin's Press, 1997.

Harrison, Patricia Greenwood. *Connecting Links: The British and American Woman Suffrage Movements, 1900–1914*. Westport, Conn.: Greenwood, 2000.

Heilmann, Ann, ed. *Words as Deeds: Literary and Historical Perspectives on Women's Suffrage*. Special issue of *The Women's History Review* 11:4 and 12:1 (2002–3).

Holton, Sandra. *Feminism and Democracy: Women's Suffrage and Reform Politics in Britain, 1900–1918*. London: Cambridge University Press, 1986.

Howlett, Caroline J. "Writing on the Body? Representation and Resistance in British Suffrage Accounts of Forcible Feeding." In *Bodies of Writing: Bodies in Performance*, ed. Thomas Foster, Carol Siegel, and Ellen E. Berry. New York: New York University Press, 1996.

Hueffer, Ford Madox. *This Monstrous Regiment of Women*. London: Women's Freedom League, 1913.

Huyssen, Andreas. *After the Great Divide: Modernism, Mass Culture, Postmodernism*. The Macmillan Press for St. Anthony's College, 1988.

Joannou, Maroula. "Suffragette Fiction and the Fictions of Suffrage." In *The Women's Suffrage Movement*, ed. Joannou and Purvis, 101–16.

Joannou, Maroula, and June Purvis, eds. *The Women's Suffrage Movement: New Feminist Perspectives*. Manchester: Manchester University Press, 1998.

Jorgansen-Earp, Cheryl, ed. *Speeches and Trials of the Militant Suffragettes: The Women's Social and Political Union, 1903–1918*. Madison, N.J.: Fairleigh Dickinson University Press, 1999.

Kent, Susan Kingsley. *Sex and Suffrage in Britain, 1860–1914*. London: Routledge, 1990.

Lewis, Wyndham, ed. *BLAST* 1 (June 20, 1914).

Liddington, Jill, and Jill Norris. *One Hand Tied Behind Us: The Rise of the Women's Suffrage Movement*. London: Virago, 1978.

Lumsden, Linda J. *Rampant Women: Suffragists and the Right of Assembly*. Knoxville: University of Tennessee Press, 1997.

Lunardini, Christine. *From Equal Suffrage to Equal Rights: Alice Paul and the National Woman's Party, 1910–1928.* New York: New York University Press, 1986.

Lyon, Janet. *Manifestoes: Provocations of the Modern.* Cornell University Press, 1999.

Marcus, Jane. "The Asylums of Antaeus: Women, War, and Madness—Is there a Feminist Fetishism?" In *The New Historicism,* ed. H. Aram Veeser. New York: Routledge, 1989. 132–51.

———, ed. *Suffrage and the Pankhursts.* London: Routledge and Kegan Paul, 1987.

Mayhall, Laura E. Nym. *The Militant Suffrage Movement: Citizenship and Resistance in Britain, 1860–1930.* New York: Oxford University Press, 2003.

Miller, Jane. *Rebel Women: Feminism, Modernism, and the Edwardian Novel.* London: Virago, 1994.

Murray, Simone. "'Deeds *and* Words': The Woman's Press and the Politics of Print." *Women: A Cultural Review* 11.3 (2000): 197–222.

Norquay, Glenda. *Voices and Votes: A Literary Anthology of the Suffrage Campaign.* Manchester: Manchester University Press, 1995.

Park, Sowon S. "'Doing Justice to the Real Girl': The Women Writers' Suffrage League." In Eustance et al., eds., *A Suffrage Reader,* 90–104.

Purvis, June, and Sandra Stanley Holton, eds. *Votes for Women.* London: Routledge, 2000.

Roberts, Marie Mulvey, and Tamae Mizuta, eds. *The Militants: Suffragette Activism.* London: Routledge/Thoemmes Press, 1994.

Robins, Elizabeth. *Way Stations.* London: Hodder and Stoughton, 1913.

———. *The Convert.* 1907. New York: Feminist Press, 1980.

Rosen, Andrew. *Rise Up, Women! The Militant Campaign of the Women's Social and Political Union, 1903–1914.* Routledge, 1974.

Sinclair, May. *The Tree of Heaven.* London: Cassell and Co., 1917.

Stowell, Sheila. *A Stage of Their Own: Feminist Playwrights of the Suffrage Era.* Ann Arbor: University of Michigan Press, 1992.

Sypher, Eileen. *Wisps of Violence: Producing Public and Private Politics in the Turn-of-the-Century British Novel.* London: Verso, 1993.

Tickner, Lisa. *The Spectacle of Women: Imagery of the Suffrage Campaign, 1907–14.* University of Chicago Press, 1988.

West, Rebecca. *The Young Rebecca: The Writings of Rebecca West, 1911–17.* Viking Press, 1982.

Winkiel, Laura. "Suffrage Burlesque: Modernist Performance in Elizabeth Robins' *The Convert.*" *Modern Fiction Studies* 50.3 (2004): 570–94.

Woolf, Virginia. *Night and Day.* 1919. New York: Harcourt Brace, 1973.

Yellin, Jean Fagin. "Documentation: Du Bois' *Crisis* and Woman's Suffrage." *Massachusetts Review* 14.2 (1973): 265–75.

# 4

# FROM *PRISONS AND PRISONERS*

LADY CONSTANCE LYTTON

From *Gender in Modernism:*
*New Geographies, Complex Intersections,*
edited by Bonnie Kime Scott (2007)

I lay in my bed most of the day, for they did not disturb me, and I tried to keep warm, as I felt the cold fearfully. They brought me all my meals the same as usual, porridge in the morning at 7, meat and potatoes mid-day at 12, porridge at 4:30. When they were hot I fed on the smell of them, which seemed quite delicious; I said "I don't want any, thank you," to each meal, as they brought it in. I had made up my mind that this time I would not drink any water, and would only rinse out my mouth morning and evening without swallowing any. I wrote on the walls of my cell with my slate pencil and soap mixed with the dirt of the floor for ink, "Votes for Women," and the saying from Thoreau's *Duty of Civil Disobedience*— "Under a Government which imprisons any unjustly, the true place for a just man (or woman) is also a prison"; on the wall opposite my bed I wrote the text from Joshua, "Only be thou strong and very courageous." That night I dreamt of fruits, melons, peaches and nectarines, and of a moonlit balcony that was hung with sweetest smelling flowers, honey-suckle and jessamine, apple-blossom and sweet scented verbena; there was only the sound of night birds throbbing over the hills that ranged themselves below the balcony. On it there slept my sister-in-law, and on the balustrade, but making no noise, was a figure awake and alert, which was my brother. My dream was of a land which was seen by my father in his poem of "King Poppy," where the princess and the shepherd boy are the types etherealised. I woke suddenly. I could sleep a little in detached moments, but this dream had made the prison cell beautiful to me; it had a way out.

The strain was great of having to put on my shoes, which were too small, every time I was taken out of my cell to empty slop or to see the Governor. The Matron was shocked that I did not put the right heel in at all and every day I was given another pair, but they were all alike in being too small for my right foot.

The next day, Monday (January 17), the wardress took my bed and bedding away because I would not make it up, but lay on it in the day-time. I told her if she wished she must roll me off, but that I did not intend voluntarily to give it up. She was quite amiable, but rolled me towards the wall and took the bed and bedding from underneath me. There was a little table in my cell which was not fastened to the wall. I turned it upside down and was able to sit in it with my body resting against one of the legs. It was very uncomfortable, but I felt too ill to sit up in the chair, and the concrete floor was much too cold without the bed. Every now and then I got up and walked backwards and forwards in the cell to get a little warmth into me. The Chaplain came in for a moment. He was a tall, good-looking man, of the burly, healthy sort. It seemed to me, from his talk, that he would be very well suited to be a cricket match or football parson, if there were such a thing, but he was totally unsuited to be the Chaplain of a prison, or anyhow of a woman's prison. He thought it wise to speak to me as a "Suffragette." "Look here, it's no good your thinking that there's anything to be done with the women here—the men sometimes are not such bad fellows, and there are many who write to me after they've left here, but the women, they're all as bad as bad can be, there's absolutely no good in them." I did not answer, but I felt inclined to say "Then good-bye to you, since you say you can do no good with the women here."

Presently an officer came and led me out. The manner of nearly all the officers was severe; one or two were friends but most of them treated me like dirt. I was shown along the gangway of the ward, which seemed to me very large, much larger than the D X at Holloway, and went in various directions like a star. I was shown into the Governor's room, which lay at the end of the gangway. It was warm, there were hot pipes against which I was made to stand with my back to the wall, and for a moment, as I put my feet to rest on the pipes, I could think of nothing else but the delight of their heat. The Governor was very cross. I had decided not to do the needlework which constituted the hard labour, for this he gave me three days on bread and water. He would not let me speak to him at all and I was led out, but, before I had got to my cell, I was called back into his presence. "I hear you are refusing to take your food, so it's three days in a special cell." I was taken out and down a staircase till we reached the ground floor. I think my cell was two stories above, but I am not sure; then down again and into a short passage that looked as if it was underground, with a window at the top seemingly only just level with the ground. The door of a cell was opened, I was put inside and the door locked. It was larger than the cell upstairs, and the jug, basin, etc., were all made of black guttapercha, not of tin, placed on the floor. This would have been bad for the ordinary prisoner, as it was quite impossible to tell whether the eating things were clean or not and, in any case, it smelt fairly strong of guttapercha; but as the rule for me was neither to eat nor drink, I was able to put up with it well. The bed was wider than an ordinary plank bed and nailed to the ground, so that I was able to lie on it without being disturbed. Best of all was the fact that it was nearer to the heating apparatus and so seemed quite warm when I was led in. I did not notice at first that the window did not open, but when I had been there six or seven hours it became wonderfully airless. I only left my cell for minutes at a time, when I was allowed to draw water, and the air of the corridor then seemed fresh as mountain air by comparison. I had an idea that Elsie Howey or some of the others would have been put into a punishment cell too. I called, but in vain, my voice had grown weak and my tongue and throat felt thick as a carpet, probably from not drinking anything. I tried signalling with raps on the wall, "No surrender—no surrender," Mrs. Leigh's favourite motto, but I was never sure of corresponding raps, though sometimes I thought I heard them. I could not sleep for more than about an hour at a time, my legs drew up into a cramped position whenever I went off and the choking thickness in my mouth woke me.

Tuesday, January 18, I was visited again by the Senior Medical Officer, who asked me how long I had been without food. I said I had eaten a buttered scone and a banana sent in by friends to the police station on Friday at about midnight. He said, "Oh, then, this is the fourth day; that is too long, I shall have to feed you, I must feed you at once," but he went out and nothing happened till about 6 o'clock in the evening, when he returned with, I think, five wardresses and the feeding apparatus. He urged me to take food voluntarily. I told him that was absolutely out of the question, that when our legislators ceased to resist enfranchising women then I should cease to resist taking food in prison. He did not examine my heart nor feel my pulse; he did not ask to do so, nor did I say anything which could possibly induce him to think I would refuse to be examined. I offered no resistance to being placed in position but lay down voluntarily on the plank bed. Two of the wardresses took hold of my arms, one held my head and one my feet. One wardress helped to pour the food. The doctor leant on my knees as he stooped over my chest to get at my mouth. I shut my mouth and clenched my teeth. I had looked forward to this moment with so much anxiety lest my identity should be discovered beforehand, that I felt positively glad when the time had come. The sense of being overpowered by more force than I could possibly resist was complete, but I resisted nothing except with my mouth. The doctor offered me the choice of a wooden or steel gag; he explained elaborately, as he did on most subsequent occasions, that the steel gag would hurt and the wooden one not, and he urged me not to force him to use the steel gag. But I did not speak nor open my mouth, so that after playing about for a moment or two with the wooden one he finally had recourse to the steel. He seemed annoyed at my resistance and he broke into a temper as he plied my teeth with the steel implement. He found that on either side at the back I had false teeth mounted on a bridge which I did not take out. The superintending wardress asked if I had any false teeth, if so, that they must be taken out; I made no answer and the process went on. He dug his instrument down on to the sham tooth, it pressed fearfully on the gum. He said if I resisted so much with my teeth, he would have to feed me through the nose. The pain of it was intense and at last I must have given way for he got the gag between my teeth, when he proceeded to turn it much more than necessary until my jaws were fastened wide apart, far more than they could go naturally. Then he put down my throat a tube which seemed to me much too wide and was something like four feet in length. The irritation of the tube was excessive. I choked the moment it touched my throat until it had got down. Then the food was poured in quickly; it made me sick a few seconds after it was down and the action of the sickness made my body and legs double up, but the wardresses instantly pressed back my head and the doctor leant on my knees. The horror of it was more than I can describe. I was sick over the doctor and wardresses, and it seemed a long time before they took the tube out. As the doctor left he gave me a slap on the cheek, not violently, but, as it were, to express his contemptuous disapproval, and he seemed to take for granted that my distress was assumed. At first it seemed such an utterly contemptible thing to have done that I could only laugh in my mind. Then suddenly I saw Jane Warton lying before me, and it seemed as if I were outside of her. She was the most despised, ignorant and helpless prisoner that I had seen. When she had served her time and was out of the prison, no one would believe anything she said, and the doctor when he had fed her by force and tortured her body, struck her on the cheek to show how he despised her! That was Jane Warton, and I had come to help her.

When the doctor had gone out of the cell, I lay quite helpless. The wardresses were kind and knelt round to comfort me, but there was nothing to be done, I could not move, and remained there in what, under different conditions, would have been an intolerable mess. I had been sick over my hair, which, though short, hung on either side of my face, all over the wall near my bed, and my clothes seemed saturated with it, but the wardresses told me they could not get me a change that night as it was too late, the office was shut. I lay quite motionless, it seemed paradise to be without the suffocating tube, without the liquid food going in and out of my body and without the gag between my teeth. Presently the wardresses all left me, they had orders to go, which were carried out with the usual promptness. Before long I heard the sounds of the forced feeding in the next cell to mine. It was almost more than I could bear, it was Elsie Howey, I was sure. When the ghastly process was over and all quiet, I tapped on the wall and called out at the top of my voice, which wasn't much just then, "No surrender," and there came the answer past any doubt in Elsie's voice, "No surrender." After this I fell back and lay as I fell. It was not very long before the wardress came and announced that I was to go back upstairs as, because of the feeding, my time in the punishment cell was over. I was taken into the same cell which I had before; the long hours till morning were a nightmare of agonised dread for a repetition of the process.

---

Lady Constance Lytton and Jane Warton. *Prisons and Prisoners: Some Personal Experiences*. London: William Heinemann, 1914; rpt. London: Virago, 1988. 264–71.

# 5

## "WHETHER WE VOTE OR NOT— WE ARE GOING TO SHOOT"

Women and Armed Defense on the Home Front

KIMBERLY JENSEN

From *Mobilizing Minerva:*
*American Women in the First World War,*
by Kimberly Jensen (2008)

If American women are ever called upon to defend
their homes, their children, and themselves, they will
not be helpless as were the Belgian women.

—Lurana Sheldon Ferris of the Women's Defense Club,
1916

[Women] are in the munitions shops, in the mines, in the field,
and in various branches of manual and military service.
Why not the battlefield?

—June Haughton, markswoman, 1916

As Europe became embroiled in the horrors of occupation and trench warfare after the autumn of 1914, Americans watched and debated the question of their own military readiness. This debate about preparedness included much more than a discussion of armaments and "manpower." Within the preparedness rhetoric was a stark discussion of some of the core issues of gender relationships and the gender conventions of the Protector and the Protected. From this perspective, some Americans believed that the "failure" of Belgian men and men in northern France to repel invading German armies led directly to rape and violence against women in these regions. And as the conflict progressed, there were increasing reports of soldiers who reacted to the horrors of the trenches with the "effeminate" male hysteria of "soldier's heart" or "shell shock." These men had also "failed" as Protectors. Would this happen in the United States, or were American men "man enough" to fulfill their roles as Protectors and male citizens? On the home front, some women claimed the citizen's obligation to defend the state as part of the fulfillment of complete citizenship, and some sought to bear arms to do so. What would happen if they became the Protectors rather than the Protected? Others wondered if the wartime conditioning of soldiers to use "violent solutions" would mean increased violence on the home front as a result. Could the women who had taken on the role of Protectors wield the weapons of war in peacetime to defend themselves against violent behavior that men had learned in soldiering? This chapter will examine some women's claims to armed military service and also self-defense as part of more complete female citizenship and a new construction of violence against women on the war front and home front. It will also consider the gendered categories of Protector and Protected that they disrupted.

## Masculinity and Military Preparedness

In her study of the impact of the German invasion and occupation of Belgium and northern France in 1914 and after, Ruth Harris demonstrates that one effect of the rape of Belgian and French women by enemy soldiers was the humiliation of the men of their communities. By "failing" in their role as protectors of women, the men of these regions became "impotent victims rather than . . . heroes defending hearth and home." Racialized discussions of the invasion "voiced the fear of French male impotence" and the ultimate conquest of France by virile Germans.[1] Harris reads in these representations a perceived contrast between Germany as a masculine nation of aggressive power and Belgium and France as passive, feminized states.

For many, the news of Allied soldiers suffering from "shell shock" or "soldier's heart" underscored the supposed failure of masculinity in the wartime generation. Soon after the war began, British medical officers began to report that men in the trenches were suffering from "mental breakdown" and symptoms of hysteria such as numbness, amnesia, the inability to speak, uncontrollable nightmares, crying, and shaking. By

1915 this "war neurosis" created a medical emergency due to shortages of facilities and staff for treating soldiers suffering from its effects. The next year medical officers estimated that cases of shell shock accounted for 40 percent of casualties at the front. As Elaine Showalter illustrates, many believed that shell shock was nothing short of a failure of men to be manly, to "bear up" under the conditions of war. The threat of "wholesale mental breakdown among men," she writes, was a "shocking contrast to the heroic visions" of soldierly masculinity. Military and medical personnel struggled to understand "soldier's heart" in the context of psychology but were influenced by ideas of masculinity and gender roles. Many associated male war neurosis with weakness, effeminacy, or homosexuality—everything that was not "masculine" in soldiers or their behavior. When research could not demonstrate an organic cause, Showalter writes, "many military authorities refused to treat victims as disabled and maintained that they should not be given pensions or honorable discharges." Some suggested that shell-shock sufferers should be shot for cowardice.[2]

This fear of demasculinization was particularly acute because "hysteria" had been a "woman's disease" in the generations before the First World War in Britain and the United States. When men exhibited symptoms of "nervousness," Michael Kimmel notes, medical and social commentators agreed that it was a sign of effeminacy to be cured by bracing visits to the western frontier or other masculine endeavors.[3] If the "Great War" gave men the chance to be manly heroes, it also raised the stakes for proving masculinity.[4] And if that masculinity was vulnerable, as Kimmel suggests, having to be proved over and over again with prescribed behavior, the "failure" of men in Belgium and northern France to repel invasion and "soldier's heart" suggested massive, visible failures on the part of the male citizen Protectors. That sense of failure, as Sandra M. Gilbert has demonstrated in her analysis of literary responses to the war, lasted well beyond the Armistice at the conclusion of the conflict.[5]

In the United States some who observed these "failures" of European masculinity worked to make certain that America would have a record of virility, not impotence. They linked masculinity, military training and service, and active citizenship in the "preparedness" movement. The most prominent supporters of this movement were Theodore Roosevelt and the army's General Leonard Wood. In their view, the primary purpose for military training and preparedness in the United States was the reinvigoration of manhood in the nation. This drive was part of a decades-long preoccupation with proving and shoring up masculinity in crisis. In this context, the fear of masculine failure at the beginning of the European war took on a heightened urgency, and those who offered the solution of military training for manliness became a vocal part of the debate. Roosevelt linked masculinity to citizenship and military service in his call for the training of citizen soldiers and increased military preparedness in the United States as Europe went to war. In his book *America and the World War* (1915), Roosevelt advocated the strengthening of the army and navy and also military training for every young man in the country. "No man is really fit to be the free citizen of a free republic unless he is able to bear arms and at need to serve with efficiency in the efficient army of the republic," he wrote. America's future depended on the citizen soldier who would not shrink from his manly duty.[6]

General Leonard Wood formulated concrete plans for training these citizen soldiers as chief of staff of the army from 1910 to 1914 and commander of the Army Department of the East from Governors Island, New York, from 1914 to 1917. Wood began his military career as a contract surgeon on the western frontier, was a Rough Rider with Roosevelt in the Spanish-American War, and then served as governor-general of Cuba and as military governor in the Philippines.[7] Wood took one side in the debate about military preparedness and the role of the citizen soldier that had been of concern to military planners since the American Revolution. Rather than favoring a large, professional standing army, Wood had faith in the male citizen soldier. He urged that a large-scale program of rifle practice be implemented throughout the country and advocated such instruction in arms as part of the public school education of young men.[8] He believed that young men should then undertake a two-year term of military service after which they would become part of a large national military reserve, making the army a "great mill through which the population is passed and trained to bear arms."[9] Wood spearheaded a program that created summer military training camps for college-age men in 1913, 1914, and 1915. The popularity of the camps led to a greatly expanded program that enrolled other men wishing to prepare themselves in the use of arms and the military life. The core camp was located in Plattsburg, New York, and expanded to camps throughout the country from 1915 to 1917. This Plattsburg Movement, as the training camps came to be called, was an important expression of the remasculinization deemed so necessary by many leaders and reflected in the popular culture of the period.

This aspect of the preparedness movement often focused on rifle and pistol training for citizen soldiers who would then have the power and skills to defend the nation and their communities. Gun practice, its advocates proclaimed, was "a man-maker" and would help to convert the present generation of "effeminates" who would "surprise and shock" America's military fathers, George Washington and Ulysses S. Grant, if they could see them in their current weak condition.[10] In this view, expertise in marksmanship would enable men to recommit to their role as Protectors. And it would save the United States from the embarrassing "failures" of Belgian and French men should the war expand across the Atlantic or should America enter the European conflict.

## Women, Military Preparedness, and Self-Defense

Erman J. Ridgway, editor of the *Delineator*, one of the most popular mainstream women's magazines of the period, introduced the "woman question" in military preparedness in the magazine's February 1915 issue. Ridgway believed that the United States needed to strengthen its military and train a citizen army to avoid Belgium's fate. The "rape of Belgium" was indeed on his mind when, in addition to his call for military instruction for boys and young men in the public schools, he cautiously introduced a proposal for training young women as well. "Why is it necessary to leave our homes defenseless?" he wrote. "Why can not women be taught to take care of themselves just as men are?" Hoping that his readers would not consider him "a wholly uncivilized brute," he continued, "I know some very wonderful women who tramp and fish and hunt as well as any man. What's the harm? What do you think of the whole idea?" Invoking the "frontier heritage" of America ("pioneer women all knew how to defend themselves") and lauding the physical benefits of marching, drilling, and shooting for women's health, Ridgway called for readers' opinions on the proposal.[11] The essay was illustrated at the left margin with an endless column of schoolgirls in military formation shouldering guns, complemented on the right margin by a column of schoolboys in the same attitude.

Ridgway, writing six months after the start of the war in Europe, based his article on the assertion that women should be taught "to take care of themselves" and set the discussion in the context of the invasion of Belgium. Armed women would be empowered to resist physical and sexual assault. Although Ridgway did not specifically state it, this proposal could

Figure 5.1: Illustration for Erman J. Ridgway, "Militant Pacifism" (1915).

be read as an implicit acknowledgement that American men might not be able to fulfill their roles as Protectors. By the June issue of the *Delineator*, 204 readers had responded. According to Ridgway's summary, their responses were split almost evenly, with 97 readers in favor of his proposition and 107 opposed. Those who wrote in favor of his proposal for military training for young women and men favored the implications for equal training while expressing the hope that militarism and war could be avoided. Most of the women who wrote letters against the proposition opposed it regardless of the gender of those to be trained. Many of those in opposition made it clear that they supported the proposal of equal physical training and opportunity for women and men but resisted the militarism embodied in the use of guns.[12]

The *Delineator* article was only one expression of the debate concerning women's self-defense in the context of national defense and preparedness in this period. At rifle ranges and armories around the country in the war years women joined existing rifle clubs and formed their own rifle and gun organizations in what contemporaries considered dramatic numbers. Thousands joined women's paramilitary organizations designed to promote women's defense and military skills. Many of these women were motivated by a belief in the importance of women's equal rights and the need for equal opportunities with men. Their activities were part of the negotiation for women's full citizenship rights in the context of the suffrage campaign. They hoped to become an official part of the citizens' preparedness army or the military itself and in so doing would perform the citizen's obligation to defend the state. For some women, claiming the right of preparedness was also an assertion of their right to defend themselves against male violence, whether in the context of war or in a broader definition of "home defense" against domestic violence or other assault.

In February 1916, the *New York Times* reported that a group of prominent suffragists in Old Orchard, Maine had formed the Women's Defense Club to teach American women "to shoot, and shoot straight." The club was formed, according to the *Times* report, to provide expert instruction in the use of firearms "so that if American women are ever called upon to defend their homes, their children, and themselves, they will not be helpless as were the Belgian women." The concept of "a woman using a gun in defense of her home, her child, or herself is new to many," wrote club organizer Lurana Sheldon Ferris, "but American women do not intend history to repeat itself—where they are concerned." Rather than wait to be raped or killed by "madmen," Ferris explained, women will be "prepared to kill" if "necessity" requires. "Our men, with all their bravery, cannot protect us all." In letters to the editor of the *New York Times* in 1916 and 1917, Ferris also emphasized the link between the activities of the club and women's responsibilities as citizens. "We are teaching patriotism and courage," she wrote. "Certainly patriotism, with efficiency in shooting, or even the ability to load a gun, is a combination that makes either a man or a woman a national asset in time of trouble." As a suffrage activist, Ferris made it clear that armed patriotism was part of the fabric of female citizenship: "Whether we vote or not—we are going to shoot." Due to expressions of interest from women from all parts of the country, Ferris and her colleagues made the organization open to any woman who signed a pledge to "improve every opportunity for learn-ing how to use firearms as weapons of defense." In the summer of 1917 Ferris personally taught "scores" of women how to handle firearms, and thousands of other members throughout the country received instruc-tion from qualified teachers. Ferris believed that "if every State would aid this equipment of its women we might eventually have a citizen soldiery worth while."[13]

In New York City markswoman June Haughton supervised the forma-tion of several women's rifle clubs that practiced on the rooftops of the Hotel Vanderbilt and the Hotel Majestic and in her own indoor studio rifle range. Here she installed the latest equipment, including new "moving picture" technology that simulated various targets in motion. Haughton specifically linked women's use of firearms to military service and ex-panded the concept of female citizen soldiery for defense to also include women's presence on the battlefield. Three months before the United States entered the war, she told the *New York Times* that she was orga-nizing women and training them to shoot because women's proficiency on the rifle range might prove to be "the foundation of a great woman's army." For Haughton, the war in Europe was proof that such an army could be organized and would be needed. Women, she said, "are in the munitions shops, in the mines, in the field, and in various branches of manual and military service. Why not the battlefield?"[14]

The American Women's League for Self-Defense (AWLSD) organized a more extensive program of women's rifle-drill and military prepared-ness. Based in New York City, the group launched a campaign in March 1916 "for women to arm and drill in the use of firearms" in the same spirit as the Women's Defense Club and June Haughton's American De-fense Rifle Club. The *New York Times* reported that the women were "stirred by atrocity tales" from Belgium and other areas of the German occupation. Executive officer Mrs. Leo Boardman emphasized that the league was organizing women all across the country to perform military drills to strengthen their bodies and to handle a gun for defense.[15] In a month the AWLSD had more than three hundred women recruits in New York City alone, including "dentists, lawyers, surgeons, heads of depart-ments, teachers, private secretaries, and stenographers," as well as society women, horsewomen, and "two women with aero pilot licenses." Some members of the league conducted infantry drills at the Ninth Regiment Armory in New York, and others were part of a cavalry corps that drilled in the streets adjacent to the First Field Artillery at Sixty-seventh and Broadway.[16] The league sponsored a variety of other activities to promote

Figure 5.2: "American Women Ready to Fight alongside of Russia's Brave Legion of Death. Members of the American Women's League for Self-Defense" (1917). (Photo no. 165-WW-600-B-2, National Archives, Washington, D.C.)

women's military skills and the defense of American homes. In May 1916 AWLSD members made an expedition to the shoreline of the New York Palisades and conducted "exercises in map drawing of the terrain, with a view to its possibilities for attacking troops," so they could anticipate enemy invasion strategies for the New York coastline.[17] During the summer of 1916 members sponsored a number of camps for women's military preparedness on the Plattsburg model, and uniformed members conducted outdoor drills near the military installations on Governors Island, New York, in the spring of 1917.

The American Women's League for Self-Defense also made efforts to extend its programs nationwide. The *Delineator* began a monthly "Women's Preparedness Bureau" in July 1917, and featured the AWLSD prominently in this series. Editors featured the Cavalry Corps of the AWLSD in "Going in for Military Training and How to Set Up a Camp," in the Preparedness Bureau's section in the August 1917 issue. In later issues editors encouraged readers to write to the AWLSD in New York for more information on women's military camps.[18] Individuals formed local camps for women's rifle-drill and military preparedness following the example of the AWLSD. Candace Hewitt organized a summer camp

Figure 5.3: "Cavalry Corps of the American Women's League for Self-Defense" (1918). (Photo no. 165-WW-143-B-4, National Archives, Washington, D.C.)

in New Jersey for "fifty young women, daughters of well-to-do New York families." The camp included "shooting, care of weapons, swimming, first aid to the injured, rowing, canoeing, riding, cavalry drill and regular military drills."[19]

Following the U.S. entry into the war, groups of American women followed the example of Russian women who formed a regiment known as the Russian Women's Battalion of Death to fight in the world war and defend the Kerensky government in the Russian Revolution. The *Woman Citizen* reported in October 1917 that women from Oklahoma and Texas, "wives of soldiers in the Regular National Army and National Guard," were organizing their own Battalion of Death "to serve in any way the War Department asks—in trenches if necessary." The *Suffragist* reported in that same month that women's regiments were being formed in Texas, Indiana, and Florida.[20]

### Arms and the Woman

These rifle and defense groups and the women's regiments are only the most visible examples of a grassroots movement of American women to promote the female use of guns during the First World War. A close reading of the journal of the National Rifle Association, *Arms and the Man*, from 1914 to 1919 reveals that thousands of women nationwide joined rifle and revolver clubs at indoor and outdoor ranges and for trapshooting (firing at clay targets). The editors of the journal and various contributors linked these activities with the war and preparedness activities and with women's self-defense. For example, in 1915 more than five hundred women participated in special "Beginners' Day Shoots" around the country, and by 1916 there were 193 separate Beginners' Day competitions in various parts of the country specifically for women.[21] These reports emphasized that women's shooting "on a big scale" was a recent development, that women demonstrated an "unusual amount of enthusiasm in learning to use firearms" and were becoming "more and more identified with the sport," and listed women's accomplishments at various tournaments with praise. "Several years ago there wasn't a handful of women trap shots," remarked the writer of a special article, "Feminine Trap Shots," in October 1916. "Now we have thousands of them."[22]

By the time of America's involvement in the war in 1917 and 1918, *Arms and the Man* provided solid documentation of women's participation in gun practice and competitive shooting and linked these activities to the war. "Not many years ago women were conspicuous by their absence in trapshooting matters," one editorialist commented, "but such is not the case today." Many "fair Dianas" were out on the practice ranges and would be competing in tournaments. "Trapshooting Attracts Both Sexes," another editorialist affirmed. In "About Women Shots" another asserted that there were thousands of women who "frequent the traps and shoot regularly," and women were part of the large contingent of newcomers to trapshooting whose interest seemed to be "stimulated by the U.S. entrance into the war."[23] The journal featured articles by two women championship shots in July and October 1917. Elizabeth (Mrs. Adolph) Topperwein of San Antonio, Texas, "the peer of all woman shooters and as good as the male experts with the shotgun," invited all women to join the "standing army of over 500 women" who competed at official trapshooting events. Many of these women, she contended, "hold their own with the best shooters of the sterner sex."[24] Harriet D. Hammond, the Delaware women's champion, "strongly recommended" trapshooting to all women: it helped to develop self-reliance and made women "better able to cope with the affairs of life." After telling of a woman who used a shotgun to protect herself and her home, Hammond concluded, "It makes me wonder why more women have not learned to shoot."[25]

Advertisers were quick to notice the trend. The production of weapons for the army enriched American arms manufacturers during the war years,[26] and the popularity of shooting provided a potential audience of civilian men and women. Women-at-arms were a potential gold mine for gun manufacturers, who catered to this expanding new audience. In some advertisements manufacturers used the tried-and-true method of linking women's sexuality with their product. The Marlin Company, for example, praised the "beauty of build and balance" of the Marlin Repeating Shotgun in an ad featured in *Arms and the Man* in 1915. Potential owners could "double the charm and pleasure in shooting" with "exactly

Figure 5.4: Marlin Firearms Company advertisement, *Arms and the Man* (July 29, 1915): 357.

the right gun." A smiling, shapely woman seems to have great pleasure in holding the weapon. Here the woman's sexuality is part of the sale, targeting men as much as women consumers. The advertisers assured women and men consumers of guns that female shots would not lose their femininity and sexual appeal if they took up a rifle; indeed, they might even enhance it.

But gun manufacturers also highlighted gun use for women and featured guns in women's hands that made them their own Protectors. In an ad featured in 1916 we see a woman who is obviously a skilled shot, wearing a field hat and belt, sighting with her Ross rifle. This is a woman who knows her business and wants to have the best equipment to "paralyze with a single shot." No man would wish to be at the other end of her barrel.

The Colt Firearms Manufacturing Company ran an ad featuring a woman shooter in various issues of *Arms and the Man* in 1916 and 1917. A woman with a pistol is shooting at a target in a small indoor cellar range, getting advice from a man over her shoulder. The ad copy for the Colt Target Revolver reads: "Its *small caliber* makes it the ideal revolver for home practice—the ammunition is inexpensive and gives but little noise or recoil." Colt encouraged women to form "cellar clubs" for shooting practice at home. To support this message, *Arms and the Man* printed an article in its January 1917 issue with specific information on "how to construct an indoor or cellar range."[27]

The Colt Company went as far as any manufacturer to encourage women to use pistols to protect themselves from violence in its ad campaign for 1917, the year that the United States entered the war in Europe. Here the Colt pistol becomes the "Home Protection Colt." Illustrated

Figure 5.5: "Paralyzes with a Single Shot," Ross Rifle Company advertisement, *Arms and the Man* (July 27, 1916): 360.

Figure 5.6: "A Unique Field: Form a Cellar Club—Buy a Colt and Learn to Shoot," Colt Firearms Manufacturing Company advertisement, *Arms and the Man* (September 7, 1916): 480.

testimonials from "Colt protected" women who were saved from rape by their use of the pistol emphasize that women and the home are under siege, that women should be their own Protectors, and that self-defense is part of national preparedness. Violence against women "happen[s] every day," the ad copy suggests, and "preparedness, like charity, should begin at home."

Much of the rhetoric concerning women shooters in the editorials and reports in *Arms and the Man* is complimentary, even respectful, of

Figure 5.7: "Teach the Women 'How to Shoot,'" Colt Firearms Manufacturing Company advertisement, *Arms and the Man* (January 4, 1917): 300.

their enthusiasm and expertise. Men of arms were associating with and reading about women who were proving their own in the shooting world. "The idea of leads, angles and distances" held "no mysteries" for Chicago women, claimed one report. The women of the Livermore Falls Rifle Club of Maine were meeting every Thursday evening at the Armory Hall as they had done since 1914 under the direction of "crack shot" Lieutenant Roys of the National Guard. They had become so expert with the rifle that they challenged any team in Maine or the New England states to a competition.[28] Women seemed to be welcome at many ranges. "There isn't any suffrage question at the traps," said one reporter, and the editors of *Arms and the Man* contended, "Today women shoot and vote under the same conditions as their husbands, brothers and sweethearts."[29]

Another indication that women shots were taken seriously is that *Arms and the Man* offered specific advice for women that would help them improve their performance. A question-and-answer column contained information on the best choices of pistols and small firearms for women shooting on an indoor or basement range.[30] In her 1917 article, Mrs. Topperwein included specific information about common problems for women shots, especially finding a gun with a proper fit. "The borrowed gun is almost certain to be too long in the stock and as a rule too heavy; the result is that it is held in an awkward manner, the recoil received from the shot frightens the shooter and she loses all of her enthusiasm then and there." Have "someone who knows 'fit' you with a proper gun," she advised women readers.[31] In an article titled "Guns for Sportswomen," Henry Sharp advised women readers that they should not be content with firing light guns if they were ready for more powerful weapons. He believed that "women's physical powers have been much undervalued," and that the war work of women—"the remarkable way in which farming implements and other tools have been handled during this war time"—proved that women were ready for heavier guns. Sharp offered specific recommendations for women shots and was enthusiastic about their prospects in the "art of shooting."[32]

We must temper this picture of support for women shots, however, by placing it in the context of the separate sphere for women that existed ideologically and institutionally in the shooting world. Some organizations and many regulations barred female participants from official benefits and many opportunities for competition and recognition. As part of the military-preparedness campaign in the summer of 1914, Congress authorized the U.S. chief of ordnance to issue free of charge to each qualifying member of a registered rifle club one Krag rifle and 120 cartridges of ammunition that were then in government storage. In 1915 Congress authorized civilian use of military ranges and the construction of new ranges.[33] Section 113 of the Defense Act of June 3, 1916, strengthened these provisions and provided for initial and annual issues of targets, target materials, and accessories, as well as rifles and ammunition to rifle groups and free instruction for qualifying individuals at rifle ranges.[34] Congress enacted these measures to foster what President Woodrow Wilson called a "citizenry trained in the use of arms" as part of the program of military preparedness and the training of male citizen soldiers advocated by Leonard Wood, Theodore Roosevelt, and their supporters, including the National Rifle Association (NRA).[35] Although there were some restrictions during 1917 and 1918 on the availability of rifles due to war demand, the government continued to subsidize rifle practice in the United States over the entire course of the war.

Such measures, obviously a boon to rifle clubs and the NRA, were designed in part to eliminate the category of class from a "citizenry trained in the use of arms" through free instruction and the free issue of arms and ammunition. The category of gender, however, was emphatically written into the rules, because the "citizenry" to be trained was male. The use of rifle facilities was for the use of "all able-bodied male citizens of the United States capable of bearing arms," and in another provision for targets and practice, "only physically fit males between the ages of 16 and 45, who are citizens of the United States," were eligible.[36] The National Rifle Association ruled that women could be only honorary, auxiliary, or associate members of rifle clubs under its jurisdiction, in part because of these government eligibility requirements. If women associated with clubs and qualified in competition for the NRA grades of marksman, sharpshooter, or expert, they were not entitled to the official title or decoration awarded in recognition of these achievements.[37] Because they were ineligible for free government issue, women had to pay for all of their own equipment and ammunition, a situation that reintroduced class into the equation for women shots, as only those who could finance their practice could participate. In addition, these institutional barriers for women shooters came alongside the strong association of the preparedness movement with remasculinization of American men and boys.

Some women found ways to subvert these ideological and institutional constraints that defined citizen soldiers as male. At some military rifle ranges available for the use of the "citizen army," women simply presented themselves for instruction and practice. Men in the U.S. Navy and Marine Corps received instruction in firearms at the Wakefield Rifle Range in Massachusetts on weekdays, and on weekends the range was available for civilian use. Individuals could come with their own ammunition or purchase it at the canteen at the range, and the facilities and targets were available free of charge. On Saturdays military instructors offered free assistance to civilian patrons.[38] Some revealing photographs from the collection at the National Archives demonstrate that women came to the Wakefield range in 1918 and that despite the rules they were allowed to do so and received instruction. The photographs preserve a visit made to Wakefield by a group of Boston women in June 1918 collectively identified by the captions on file as the "wives and mothers of men at the front." The photographer for the series was Richard W. Sears of Boston, the husband of one of the women shooters.

The first photograph is a group portrait of these women as they begin their instruction from Major Portal and other U.S. Marine Corps personnel on duty at the range. Most members of the group seem unaccustomed

Figure 5.8: "Wives and Mothers of Men at the Front Being Instructed in Shooting at the Wakefield Rifle Range, Wakefield, Mass., by Major Portal and U.S. Marines, 1918." (Photo no. 165-WW-143-B-1, National Archives, Washington, D.C.)

to the rifle and uncertain, especially the woman turning to see how the others are holding their weapons. The scene is framed by a serene backdrop of trees and an expanse of grass, but the viewer's eye is drawn to the cluttered and chaotic array of hats, arms, hands, rifles, and skirts as the women try to make sense of the directions spoken by the instructors and offered by their guiding hands. There are more male instructors than women shooters. The staff has placed tarps on the ground to protect the women's genteel civilian clothing from the grass and dirt of the range.

By contrast, a second photograph shows these same women after they have gained more proficiency with guns. They point their rifles purposefully at the target; even their bodies form a unified, projectile-like triangle, and their faces show confidence and determination. Now only one male instructor stands behind them, and they no longer appear to need his guidance. They are skilled and efficient shots after one day at the range.[39]

Some women collected the necessary funds and formed rifle and gun clubs as auxiliaries to the male clubs sanctioned by the National Rifle Association. Others formed independent clubs, including groups such as the American Women's League for Self-Defense and the Women's

Figure 5.9: "Teaching Women to Shoot at the Wakefield, Mass., Rifle Range. The Women Are Learning the Art under the Direction of a Sergeant of Marines." (Photo no. 165-WW-143-B-6, National Archives, Washington, D.C.)

Defense Club. A reading of *Arms and the Man*, the *New York Times*, and *Stars and Stripes*—the newspaper of the American Expeditionary Force in France—provides evidence for the existence of thirty-nine such groups. Some of these groups, including the Women's Auxiliary of the La Creole Rifle Club of Dallas, Oregon, were able to gain special permission to use the National Guard rifle range in Oregon for their practice.[40]

At least two clubs were formed by groups of women working in factories during the war. Women employees at the Shepard Norwell Company of Boston formed the Shepard Women's Rifle Club. They organized the club according to military discipline, and members earned military titles. In May 1918 the editors of the *Stars and Stripes* in France received a letter from Sergeant Grace M. Brown, an officer of the club and a Shepard worker. Brown wished that she could personally be in France and expressed the solidarity that she and the other women workers at Shepard felt with the soldiers. "We are straight United States through and through," she wrote. *Arms and the Man* reported in March 1917 that nearly two hundred women employees of "a Boston commercial house" were organizing a women's rifle club. It is possible that this was

Rifle and Gun Clubs Formed by Women or Groups with Women's Auxiliaries, 1914–19

Akron Gun Club (Akron)
American Defense Rifle Club (New York City)
American Women's League for Self-Defense (New York City)
Atlantic City Trapshooting School (Atlantic City)
Birmingham Rifle and Revolver Club (Birmingham)
Boston Customhouse Women Yeoman's Rifle Team (Boston)
Bridgeport Remington UMC Women Employees Rifle Club (Bridgeport, Connecticut)
Carondelet Rifle Club (St. Louis)
Centennial Rifle Club (Chicago)
Charleston Women's Rifle Team (Charleston, South Carolina)
Cumberland Women's Rifle Club (Cumberland, Maryland)
Danbury Women's Rifle Club (Danbury, Connecticut)
Engineer's Rifle and Revolver Club (Cleveland)
Gordon—Van Time Rifle Club (Davenport, Iowa)
Iowa State University Women's Rifle Club (Des Moines)
La Creole Rifle Club (Dallas, Oregon)
Laurel House Gun Club (Lakewood, Ohio)
Liberty Rifle and Pistol Club (San Antonio)
Lincoln Park Gun Club (Chicago)
Livermore Falls Women's Rifle Team (Livermore Falls, Maine)
Middletown Women's Rifle Club (Middletown, New York)
Montclair Women's Rifle Club (Montclair, New Jersey)
Mount Pleasant Women's Rifle Team (Mount Pleasant, South Carolina)
Nemours Ladies Trapshooting Club (Wilmington, Delaware)
New York Rifle Club (New York City)
Pahquioque Rod and Gun Club (Danbury, Connecticut)
Parkland Gun Club (Parkland, Maryland)
Portland Gun Club (Portland, Oregon)
Rochester Women's Pistol Club (Rochester, New York)
Salt Lake City Rifle Club (Salt Lake City)
Santa Fe Rifle Club Women's Auxiliary (Santa Fe)
Shepard Women's Rifle Club (Boston)
Soo Gun Club (Sioux City)
South Bend Rifle and Revolver Club (South Bend, Washington)
Warsaw Gun Club (Warsaw, Indiana)
Washington State College Women's Rifle Corps (Pullman)
Women's Defense Club (National headquarters in Old Orchard, Maine)
Women's Military Reserve of the United States (New York City)
Women's Revolver League (Bayonne, New Jersey)

the Shepard Club of which Brown was an officer, or it could have been a separate club formed by another group of working women. The journal reported that this group would probably become an auxiliary of the club organized by the male employees so that the women might benefit from the "free distribution of targets" and other materials the men received. In another case, the "insistent demand" among the women workers at the

Remington UMC ammunition factory at Bridgeport, Connecticut, for the organization of a rifle club resulted in weekly meetings at the Park Rifle Club range beginning in April 1917. Male members of the Park team offered their services as instructors and allowed the women to use the club's "regulation NRA rifles" for their practice at the range.[41] These references emphasize that working women were taking the initiative to form rifle groups and also that they were able to further subvert the regulations against women in the citizen army by gaining the cooperation of some of their male colleagues who had official access to equipment.

Some experienced women shots used their skills to teach other women how to shoot and to emphasize women's capabilities with firearms. As we have seen, June Haughton led the movement to form rifle clubs for women in New York City. Mrs. B. G. Earle of New York, a champion woman shot, was employed by the Laurel House Gun Club in Lakewood, Ohio, in 1917 to teach the growing numbers of "Fair Dianas" who were eager to learn to shoot a rifle with precision. At Iowa State University, thirty-five women students practiced rifle shooting for an hour each day under the direction of Mrs. Jacob Maier. Maier was the wife of a sergeant on the military instructional staff at the university. She had learned to be "a crack shot with the pistol and rifle when her husband was stationed in the Philippine Islands and it was necessary for her to carry a gun at all times for safety." Mrs. Jackson Morris provided instruction in shooting to male soldiers "on the range as an instructor and under orders from Uncle Sam" at Camp Shelby, Mississippi. Morris was "the first woman to qualify as a sharpshooter in the American Army" and was living at the camp as the wife of a major stationed there.[42]

Annie Oakley, the woman most associated in the American popular imagination with the female use of guns, became a shooting instructor for women and made an instructional tour of military camps during the war years. By the First World War Oakley was no longer dazzling audiences in Buffalo Bill's Wild West Show, but her place in popular culture as an expert markswoman remained strong. With her husband and partner, Frank Butler, Oakley came to live permanently in North Carolina in 1915 and became a member of the staff of the Carolina Hotel at the famous Pinehurst resort, giving exhibitions and shooting lessons.[43] The local Pinehurst *Outlook* reported that Oakley had "lost none of her magic with firearms" and that there was great enthusiasm among her women students at Pinehurst for learning the art of shooting.[44] In the summer of 1918 Oakley toured military training camps across the country at her own expense, "spending a day or two in each cantonment shooting the rifle, revolver and shotgun for the benefit of the soldiers, and then giving instruction to any or all who desire same." One report estimated that she visited more than a half-million soldiers on this tour.[45]

Some women who entered the "armed forces" during the First World War joined the women on the periphery of military service in their claims to the female right to bear arms. They had an important incentive to do so, because qualifying "marksmen" received additional pay. Legislation for the U.S. Navy and Marine Corps specified that those who qualified as marksmen received an extra two dollars per month, sharpshooters received three dollars, and expert riflemen received an extra five dollars per month. When monthly paychecks for privates were seventeen dollars per month, the extra money could represent quite a difference in salary.[46] Iona E. C. Myrick, the chief woman yeoman of the U.S. Marine Corps unit at the Boston Customhouse, organized the First Women Yeoman's Rifle Team with fifteen members late in 1917. The women had "a view to qualifying according to the rules and regulations" that governed the men of the navy in their requirements for marksmanship qualification. Captain J. L. Bastey, an official rifle instructor for the War Department, supervised the weekly meetings of the club at a "shooting gallery."[47] It is not clear whether officials allowed the group to qualify under navy regulations and receive additional wages.

Elizabeth Bertram also challenged the issue of firearms qualification for women in the marines. Bertram was working as a legal secretary in Denver when she enlisted as a private to help with U.S. Marine Corps recruiting.[48] She had learned to use a rifle as a young girl, and because she had done "a great deal of target practice" she considered herself "a better than average shot." When she learned that "qualifying on the rifle range added dollars to pay checks" in the marines, she recalled in a later interview, she "asked for permission for a tryout."[49] Bertram's commanding officer refused to send her to the official rifle range located "on the western slope of the Rocky Mountains more than a hundred miles away." He "certainly would not send a female on such a jaunt simply on her say so that she knew how to handle a gun." The major did agree to let her try her skill at the Denver police practice range just outside the city, and he made arrangements for a "one person regulation full course tryout." Bertram recalled that the day of the tryout was cold and windy, "with squalls of icy rain." A corporal from the recruiting office escorted her to the police range, where a number of Denver police officers were waiting under the range shelter to watch what would happen as this woman marine came to shoot. The Enfield rifle provided for Bertram's use was too long in the stock. "I did fairly well on kneeling and sitting, and managed a few good shots prone," she recalled, "but every time I tried rapid fire the result was disaster." She was determined, however, and "stuck it out for the full course." At the end of the day, because of the poor fit of her borrowed rifle, Bertram's shoulder was "pounded almost to jelly," and she was soaked with rain and mud. When she arrived back at the recruiting office, the major sent her home without comment.

The next day the major called her into his office, where her "target sheets were spread over the desk with every bullet hole carefully evaluated." The major told her that she had "qualified unofficially," and she now had permission to be part of the next group going to the official firing range, where, presumably, she could qualify for extra pay as a marine marksman. Then, as she recalled, the major came around the desk to where she was standing, "pinned his own engraved marksman medal on my blouse," and said, "'in the meantime, you may wear this.'" Bertram was grateful but unable to properly salute, she recalled, because of her sore right arm. Before the next group of marines went to the Colorado firing range, however, the Armistice was signed to end the war. All of the marine reservists (F) were transferred to inactive duty. Bertram never received the extra pay of a marksman. The record does not show whether the major let her keep her borrowed medal.

The relationship between women and guns during the First World War became a part of the fabric of popular culture. The first installment of the *Delineator*'s "Women's Preparedness Bureau" featured a picture of a woman with a rifle as a part of a photographic series on women's preparedness, and the caption told readers that "managing a modern rifle" was one aspect of women's service.[50] A U.S. poster from 1918 titled "Feminine Patriotism" represents three avenues of women's wartime service. Against a sky-blue background, one woman, dressed in a uniform and apron, represents "domestic economy"; another, wearing the uniform of a nurse, represents "aid to the suffering." And in the center, backed by the U.S. flag, is a woman dressed in khaki uniform shouldering a gun, who represents "home defense."

In the suffrage journal the *Woman Citizen*, associate editor Betty Graeme reported in the summer of 1917 that "with everybody going in" for "gun practice or manuals of arms," sewing seemed "relegated to the limbo of forgotten arts." Still, a sewing machine was a "good thing to have in the family during war-time," she said with tongue in cheek, "to

Figure 5.10: "Feminine Patriotism" (1918). (National Archives, Washington, D.C., Poster no. 6005)

place alongside of great-grandmamma's spinning wheel and beneath Aunt Jemima's sampler. Just to show that you came from the right sort of stock, you know." *Arms and the Man* reported in 1916 that the "mammoth electric sign" over the Million Dollar Pier at Atlantic City had been changed "to show a man and a woman shooting alternately" and that it was now attracting "more attention than ever."[51]

～ ～

As these examples demonstrate, some American women made their own claims on the preparedness movement, linking self-defense to national defense and to a full expression of the obligations and rights of citizenship. However, as they called for participation in the citizen's army, and some for a place in the military itself, these women defined violence against women on the war front and the home front and exposed the limits of men's power to protect them. Women joined gun clubs and defense groups so that they would not be in the same situation as the women in Belgium and northern France, unprotected and vulnerable to rape and assault. Once opened, this door also led to a critique of the gender convention of men as Protectors and women as the Protected. It also highlighted the stark reality that some men abused the women they were supposed to protect. Groups of women who gained proficiency in the use of guns were a potential threat to the domestic order in more ways than one. Against the backdrop of the urgent call for remasculinizing men through military training to enhance their role as Protectors, these women's claims engendered strong opposition and backlash. The cultural and social debate about the woman soldier that followed was also a debate about these women's redefinition of violence and self-defense.

## Notes

1. Harris, "'Child of the Barbarian,'" 186, 197.

2. See Elaine Showalter, "Male Hysteria," in *The Female Malady: Women, Madness, and English Culture, 1830–1980*, 170.

3. See Kimmel, *Manhood in America*, 134–35.

4. Paul Fussell discusses the British focus on masculinity and war in *The Great War and Modern Memory*. In her study of the slaveholding South, Drew Gilpin Faust concludes that "in failing to protect women or to exert control over insolent and even rebellious slaves, Confederate men undermined not only the foundations of the South's peculiar institution, but the legitimacy of their power as white males, as masters of families of white women and black slaves" (*Mothers of Invention: Women of the Slaveholding South in the American Civil War*, 79).

5. Kimmel, *Manhood in America*, 119–20 and chaps. 3–5; Sandra M. Gilbert, "Soldier's Heart: Literary Men, Literary Women, and the Great War."

6. Theodore Roosevelt, *America and the World War*, 136, 146. Kathleen Dalton emphasizes that TR also saw preparedness as universal service that would foster Americanism and citizenship (*Theodore Roosevelt*, 447–49).

7. For information on General Leonard Wood's career, see John Garry Clifford, *The Citizen Soldiers: The Plattsburg Training Camp Movement, 1913–1920*,

1–29; John G. Holme, *The Life of Leonard Wood*; and Jack C. Lane, *Armed Progressive: General Leonard Wood*.

8. Leonard Wood, "Rifle Practice for Public Schools," 16. See also Clifford, *Citizen Soldiers*, 9–11.

9. Clifford, *Citizen Soldiers*, 10. See also Lane, *Armed Progressive*, for Wood's views. For background on the debate concerning citizen soldiers versus a professional army, see Lawrence Delbert Cress, *Citizens in Arms: The Army and the Militia in American Society to the War of 1812*.

10. See L. E. Eubanks, "Gun Practice a Man-Maker," 485; and "Effeminacy and the Rifle Range," 468.

11. Erman J. Ridgway, "Militant Pacifism," a special column on the regular editorial page titled "You, Us, and Company."

12. See "You, Us, and Company," for both the April 1915 and the June 1915 issues of the *Delineator*, both on p. 1.

13. "Women in a Defense Club," *New York Times*, February 17, 1916, 5; Lurana Sheldon Ferris, "The Women's Defense Club," letter to the editor, *New York Times*, March 31, 1916, 10; Ferris, "Plans of Woman's Defense Club," letter to the editor, *New York Times*, February 18, 1917, 7:4.

14. Quoted in both "Plans Range for Women: Rifle Range for Women," *New York Times*, December 25, 1916, 9; and *Arms and the Man* (January 1917): 293; "Women Form Rifle Corps," *New York Times*, February 10, 1917, 8. See also "Hotel Roof for Women's Rifle Club," *New York Times*, April 8, 1917, 1:2; and *Arms and the Man* (April 28, 1917): 93, for a detailed description of her studio range.

15. "Women Are to Arm and Learn to Drill," *New York Times*, March 10, 1916, 7.

16. See "200 Women Soldiers Give a Public Drill," *New York Times*, March 10, 1916, 8; and "Women Are Bored by Military Drill," *New York Times*, April 2, 1916, 1:24.

17. "Women Scout in the Rain," *New York Times*, May 15, 1916, 9.

18. See "The *Delineator*'s Women's Preparedness Bureau: Going in for Military Training and How to Set Up a Camp," 31; and "The *Delineator*'s Women's Preparedness Bureau: What Can I Do to Help?" 50.

19. See "Fifty Society Girls to Study War's Art," *New York Times*, June 1, 1916, 14; "Lone Dog Guards Girls' Plattsburg," *New York Times*, June 2, 1916, 5; and "Parents See Girl Campers," *New York Times*, June 5, 1916, 8. Barbara Stenson also discusses women and the preparedness movement in *American Women's Activism in World War I*.

20. "American Battalion of Death," 372; "Women May Fight for Democracy Abroad," 3.

21. "Eleven Thousand Beginners Shoot," 517. For an example of one "Beginners' Day Shoot" in Delaware, see *Arms and the Man* (June 29, 1916): 277; and "Twenty-seven Beginners at Greenhill," 337.

22. See "Feminine Trap Shots Real Sportswomen," 77; "Chicago's Lady Trap Shooters," 437; *Arms and the Man* (August 24, 1916), 437; and for tournaments, "Scattering Shot," 37–38. For other examples of this trend, see "Livermore Women Becoming Shots," 492; a report on activities in Birmingham in *Arms and the Man* (February 11, 1915): 397; and the continuing reports throughout these years for the Nemours Ladies Trapshooting Club of Wilmington, Delaware, in *Arms and the Man*.

23. See *Arms and the Man* (August 4, 1917): 378; "Trapshooting Attracts Both Sexes," 458; "About Women Shots," 338; and Peter B. Carney, "Target Smashing Stimulated by Entrance of U.S. in War," 237.

24. Mrs. Adolph Topperwein, "Why I Took Up Trapshooting," 297. Accounts of her tournament wins and other aspects of her shooting career may be found throughout *Arms and the Man* for the period. See, for example, "Nemours [Ladies] Trapshooting Club," 197; *Arms and the Man* (July 27, 1916): 358; and "The Woman Who Broke 1952 Out of 2,000 Clays," 217.

25. Harriet D. Hammond, "Why I Like Trapshooting," 98. Hammond was a member of the Nemours Ladies Trapshooting Club.

26. See DeConde, *Gun Violence in America*, 116.

27. A. L. McCabe, "How to Construct an Indoor or Cellar Range," 313.

28. See "Chicago's Lady Trap Shooters"; and "Livermore Women Becoming Shots."

29. "What One Woman Does," 38; "Trapshooting Attracts Both Sexes."

30. See "Inquiries of General Interest," 316.

31. See Topperwein, "Why I Took Up Trapshooting." I am grateful to Barbara Handy-Marchello for alerting me to the ways in which women who use rifles can be discouraged by improper fit, and how it is often an unrecognized reason for claims that women do not like to shoot or cannot do it well.

32. Henry Sharp, "Guns for Sportswomen," 398.

33. See "Help for Rifle Clubs," *New York Times*, August 23, 1915, 4; "Civilian Rifle Clubs," 66; and "The N.R.A. on the Job," 228.

34. Section 113 of the Defense Act of June 3, 1916, is quoted in its entirety in *Arms and the Man* (January 19, 1918): 332–33.

35. See, for example, "Universal Military Training Urged," 287; and "The National Rifle Association Meeting," 323–26.

36. The limitations for regular military service for men were the ages of eighteen to forty-five. This regulation follows those limits and allows young men of sixteen and seventeen, "potential soldiers," to participate. See Section 113 of the Defense Act of June 3, 1916, pts. 1 and 2.

37. "Decorations for Women," 494.

38. See "Navy Leases Wakefield Range," 453; and "An Open Letter from Wakefield," 68.

39. The photographer is also present in this photograph: his shadow is cast across the female line.

40. "To Have a Ladies' Auxiliary," 73.

41. "Sergeant Miss—Yes, That's Right," 7; *Arms and the Man* (March 22, 1917): 517; "Girls Form Rifle Club," 93.

42. *Arms and the Man* (April 21, 1917): 78; *Arms and the Man* (August 11, 1917): 393–94; *Arms and the Man* (April 6, 1918): 32.

43. *Arms and the Man* (November 16, 1916): 158.

44. See Claude R. Flory, "Annie Oakley in the South," 336. For background on Oakley's life and career, see Glenda Riley, *The Life and Legacy of Annie Oakley.*

45. "Annie Oakley Visits Camps," 215; Flory, "Annie Oakley in the South," 337.

46. These rates were established in an act of May 11, 1908 (35 Stat., 110) (*Laws Relating to the Navy, Annotated: Including the Constitution of the United States, the Revised Statutes of the United States, and the United States Statutes at Large, in Force March 4, 1921*, 947). In 1918 the commandant of the U.S. Marine Corps recommended that since there were no specific regulations for the pay and other benefits of marine reservists (F), the term enlisted men in the appropriate statues for "pay, allowances, gratuities, and other benefits granted by law" should be made applicable to women reservists as well (*Annual Report of the Secretary of the Navy for the Fiscal Year 1918*, 1602).

47. See "Women Yeoman Shoot," 455.

48. The U.S. Marine Corps employed women marine reservists (F) outside of Washington, D.C., in cities such as Denver, San Francisco, and Portland, where recruiting offices were in need of clerical workers.

49. This episode is taken from an interview with Elizabeth Bertram, part of a series of interviews conducted in 1971 and 1972 with women who had served as marine reservists (F) during the First World War. Part of the Bertram interview is reprinted in Linda L. Hewitt, *Women Marines in World War I*, 28–29.

50. "The *Delineator*'s Women's Preparedness Bureau: Let Us Help You toward Greater Self-Dependence in War or Peace," 22.

51. *Woman Citizen* 1 (July 14, 1917): 111; *Arms and the Man* (November 9, 1916): 137.

# 6

# UNSIGHTLY EVIDENCE

### "Female Inversion" and the
### U.S. Woman Suffrage Movement

## LAURA L. BEHLING

From *The Masculine Women in America, 1890–1935,*
by Laura L. Behling (2001)

> Yours it is to determine whether the beautiful order of society . . .
> shall continue as it has been [or] whether society shall break up
> and become a chaos of disjointed and unsightly elements.
>
> —The Reverend Jonathan Stearns, "Female Influence and
> the True Christian Mode of Its Exercise," 1837

In an early-twentieth-century cartoon by H. C. Greening that brazenly announced its politics in its title, "Giving the Freaks a Treat," a dime museum manager shouts to his charges "tuh hustle out an' blow dereselves tuh a look!" (see figure 6.1). From the placards posted around the entrance boasting of the freakish "Octopus Man" and the "Pigheaded Boy," it would seem the carnival barker should be shouting to the passersby on the street, enticing them with promises of the "Human Toad" and other freaks of human and animal nature. Instead, the museum manager calls to his "freaks" to come outside and see creatures more freakish than they, suffragists, holding placards of their own that declare "Votes for Women" and "We Demand Our Rights"—sentiments and possibilities even more outrageous than the "Octopus Man" with four legs and four arms. The suffrage procession causes the inversion of the normal order

GIVING THE FREAKS A TREAT.

*Manager dime museum* (as suffragette procession passes) —·" Hey, Chimmie ! Chimmie ! tell d' bunch tuh hustle out an' blow dereselves tuh a look ! "

Figure 6.1: Cartoon by H. C. Greening, n.d., in *Caricature, Wit, and Humor of a Nation in Picture, Song and Story*, 8th edition. (New York: Leslie-Judge, 1911), n.p.

of events—the freak show exhibits are called to look at the people on the street rather than the people enticed to look at the museum's living collections. Greening's cartoon clearly asserted that women advocating their enfranchisement were organic oddities. The root cause of what had now become a congenital inversion, the viewer can easily infer, was the political novelty of enfranchised women, whose campaign also encompassed some degree (more perceived than real) of economic autonomy and personal independence.

The critic Richard Le Gallienne, in his 1924 *Vanity Fair* article "The Modern Girl—and Why She Is Painted," wondered if "woman herself is losing the feminine virtues" as a result of her new independence. "In short," he queried, "is she becoming more of a man, or less of a woman?" Le Gallienne answered his own question: "No, not less of a woman, I think. She is too shrewd for that. But more of a man, perhaps. . . . It may be that she is thus evolving toward a more complete human being than either man or woman has ever been before. A new sex!" His discovery was not simply androgyny but an altogether new sex, which suggested that the two sexes, male and female, no longer could contain the changes in gender that have occurred. For Le Gallienne, two types of women in particular embodied this confusion of traditional sex and gender pairings: the suffragist and the flapper, both of whom Le Gallienne characterized as the "awful feminine example" and the "menace of the hour" (27).

Although Le Gallienne certainly did not go so far as to label his "new sex" a "third sex," as some sexologists termed homosexuals in those days,[1] his more-than-androgynous conflation of the modern woman with maleness, of her becoming "more of a man," is important, as is the linking of the suffragist with the flapper, who is identified with sexual promiscuity and appropriation of male behaviors—for example, smoking, drinking, driving. Le Gallienne envisioned an entirely new construction since neither the suffragist nor flapper fit comfortably, if at all, into the traditional pairings of sex and gender: female-feminine and male-masculine. In essence, Le Gallienne argued for the creation of a third sex-gender combination, defined by marriage custom and political rights, that was both female and masculine. Le Gallienne's "new sex" was what other writers termed the "masculine woman." A fashion advertisement from *Vanity Fair* in 1914 visually suggested that the female and male gender assignments of feminine and masculine were not absolute, unchangeable pairs but could result in a woman's possessing "the ways of a maid with the modes of a man" (see figure 6.2).

Le Gallienne was not the first to suggest the fluidity of gender. Richard Barry, a journalist writing in *Pearson's Magazine* in March 1910, proposed sex-gender fluidity specifically in relation to the U.S. woman suffrage movement as he attempted to answer "why women oppose woman suffrage" (n.p.). In the present civilization, Barry wrote, a man who is all masculine and a woman who is all feminine do not exist. What is usually called the "normal" man has about 85 percent masculine traits and 15 percent feminine ones; the woman has about 85 percent feminine and 15 percent masculine. Thus, Barry concluded, the "perfect marriages" are formed when the 85 percent men marry the 85 percent women, and "havoc comes when an 85 percent man marries a 60 percent woman, or vice versa." As an unabashedly antisuffrage polemicist, Barry proposed his gender theory to trap the suffragists by their own words and illustrate their "perversity" in order to "discredit the movement as a whole" (Camhi 26). Barry reported that when he asked National American Woman Suffrage Association president Anna Howard Shaw about his theory,[2] she allegedly replied, "I think the ideal person would be 50 percent masculine and 50 percent feminine." Barry concluded from Shaw's remark that she

Figure 6.2: Advertisement in *Vanity Fair*, May 1914, n.p.

"unconsciously made an estimate of her own mentality and her own personality." Since Shaw was one of the leading suffragists, Barry pointed out, her comment was "an exceedingly significant sidelight." For Barry, it proved that the suffrage movement caused an increase in masculinity and a decrease in femininity in women and, thus, was a hindrance to the formulation of a "perfect marriage" because two clearly defined opposites (masculine and feminine) were no longer so secure.

The woman suffrage movement, however, did not so much suggest alternatives to women's gender and sexual behavior as it offered men and women afraid of perceived changes a tangible movement on which to blame their fears.[3] That is, the suffragists themselves did not propose alterations in woman's femininity or appearance, nor did they predict such changes should emancipation be realized. They were ardent defenders of the roles and behaviors traditionally assigned to males and females, as evidenced by Elizabeth Cady Stanton, who more than fifteen years before the ratification of the Nineteenth Amendment, validated women in their domestic and feminine roles. Writing in *Collier's Weekly* in April 1902, Stanton argued that without the vote, a "woman has no voice as to the education of her children or the environments of the unhappy wards of the State." Stanton's argument, reliant on "the love and sympathy of the mother-soul" (9), was consistent with domestic rhetoric, particularly since women were traditionally understood to be the educators of young children. A literate voting population was vital, she explained, to make well-informed decisions about family life, orphans, and charitable organizations—all areas that women were expected to oversee and legislate and where they were presumed to have more expertise than men. The Reverend Anna Garlin Spencer was even more succinct in her reasoning about why women should be given the vote: "The instant . . . the State took upon itself any form of educative, charitable, or personally helpful work, it entered the area of distinctive feminine training and power, and therefore became in need of the service of women" (quoted in Evans 154).

The rhetoric of other suffragists also asserted not the rejection but the validation of femininity if women were to achieve the vote. In 1917, the Federal Suffrage Association published a memorial sketch of Clara Bewick Colby called *Democratic Ideals*. Its purpose, as Olympia Brown, the president of the Federal Suffrage Association, stated in the introduction, was to advance Colby as a hero of the woman suffrage movement, holding her up as a godmother, of sorts, because "[n]o woman was ever more loyal to the cause of woman's suffrage and none ever made greater sacrifices for it" (xi–xii). The glowing tribute honored Colby by assigning her the characteristics of an ideal woman with impeccable motivations: "Even in her advocacy of Woman's Suffrage her chief thought was not so much the practical advantage of the vote to women, as the maintaining of the integrity of our republic, the fulfillment of the promise made by the Founders of our Government" (xi).

Brown asserted that Colby's pedigree also took on typically feminine ideals: "Unassisted and from humble beginnings she became a well known and honored advocate of Woman's Suffrage, a devoted reformer in many lines, a consecrated church worker, a writer of marked ability, and interpreter of poets and philosophers." Then, as unassailable

evidence of character and a clear defense against those who feared enfranchised women would lose their femininity, Brown noted that Colby
was "amid all an exceptionally fine housekeeper and excellent cook. She
was a loyal friend, and always a faithful worker in whatever engaged her
attention" (xi). Elizabeth Cady Stanton received similar accolades from
Lizzie Boynton Harbert in an essay included with her novel *Out of Her
Sphere* (1871). Stanton, she wrote, "reigns a queenly mother of seven
children. Twenty years of her life she devoted to her children, and when
they had outgrown her care, she devoted her maturer years to loving,
maternal care for society, for humanity" (180).

Carrie Chapman Catt, the leader of the National American Woman
Suffrage Association, also addressed many concerns of the antisuffragists in her introduction to *The Woman Citizen: A General Handbook of
Civic Duties, with Special Consideration of Women's Citizenship* (1918).
Using the rhetoric of militarism popularized by World War I, Catt clearly
articulated that a woman was first and foremost "the mother, the wife,"
even before she was a "loyal American," an order solidly fixed since her
"real desire is to protect the interests of [her] sons and husbands." Her
"burning patriotism" was summoned not so that she could voice her
opinions on "principles of government," war, defense strategy, or even
educational policy. Rather, a woman should be involved politically in the
same areas she oversaw in the home. "The housewife's own knowledge
must enter into food conservation," Catt wrote, and "the nurse's own experience must obtain to make the Red Cross do its effective best" (8—9).
Woman's domestic talents were useful "to keep the camp zone clean,"
and her maternity, her "mother's voice," was "above all the one which
will be wanted for deliberation about an increased birth rate to make up
for war's ravages" (9). This philosophy was rendered pictorially by the
National American Woman Suffrage Association's journal, the *Woman
Citizen*, on July 28, 1917 (see figure 6.3). As "Mrs. Voteless Citizen" looks
up to the legislative mountain top and sees wrestling male politicians, she
notices (as does the viewer) that the "food problem" hangs precariously
in the balance. Her political expertise is couched in the language of "responsible" housekeeping by the illustrator Lou Rogers. Manipulating the
domestic agenda requires the talents of those best suited for such tasks,
a married woman who clutches canning jars in her left arm as evidence
of her competence. As this rhetoric of the women suffragists exemplifies,
enfranchisement promised to retain woman's traditional feminine for-
mulations and maintain her not only in the domestic sphere but as the
feminine and heterosexual object of her successful husband.

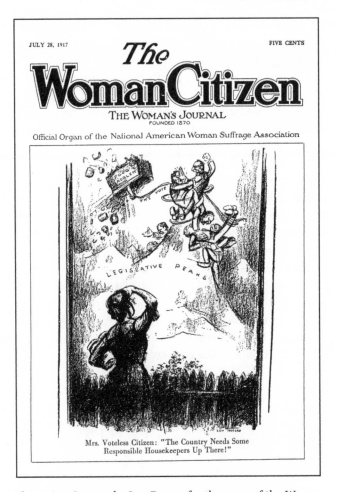

Figure 6.3: Cartoon by Lou Rogers for the cover of the *Woman Citizen*, July 28, 1917.

If it was not the suffragists who proposed radical revolutions in the conceptions of sex, gender, and sexuality, who was responsible? Certainly, the notion of women assuming the masculine prerogative to vote, sanctioned by a constitutional amendment, was novel. Yet unlike the late-twentieth-century women's rights movement in which women's same-sex relationships were proposed as a step toward female independence, the U.S. woman suffragist movement was not campaigning for tolerated sexual "inversion." Susan E. Marshall reports that antisuffragists charged that suffragists were "not seriously interested in political reform" but instead were exercising "selfish ambition, political intrigue, and noisy notoriety"; "in the words of one male opponent," Marshall notes, women were drawn to politics by "monomania" (105). The concern was that women, once enfranchised, would run for public office, leave the home to vote and campaign, and, as a result, neglect the domestic duties to which they had been assigned by virtue of their sex. Even more specific was the worry that woman suffrage would destroy domestic bliss, pictorially rendered by the severe-looking suffragist who aims to kick down the "home" a young girl has constructed (see figure 6.4). "The awards of women's office, which interfered with maternal duties, would put a premium on singleness and childlessness," Aileen S. Kraditor explains. "Women who thus invaded the masculine sphere would forfeit their right of chivalry, that mode of male behavior which enabled society" (23).

Antisuffragists, according to the historian Jane Jerome Camhi, attempted to prevent women's enfranchisement by employing two rhetorical strategies. First, their arguments were "almost all proscriptive—intimating, if not explicitly detailing, the evil consequences that would ensue if woman suffrage were enacted." Second, they were "imputative," presented so that the "suffrage question emerged as a mere symbol of what was assumed to be the real issue, the threat of the spread of feminist ideas" (6). This attempt to confuse suffragism with the wider-ranging

THE HOUSE THAT JILL BUILT

Figure 6.4: Cartoon in *Life*, February 27, 1913, 424.

"feminism" relied on the suffragists' call for equality. Antisuffragists sought to preserve a "separate, but equal" policy, allowing women to retain their uniqueness from men and, indeed, applauding that distinctiveness. "Far from apologizing for the differences between the sexes," Camhi argues, "the Antis looked upon them as not only divinely inspired, but also as the crowning step in an evolutionary process," culminating in the "masculine man" and the "feminine woman" (922). In her "talk to women on the suffrage question," Emily P. Bissell, an active opponent of woman suffrage, succinctly illustrated the Antis' position in 1909: "Biology teaches her the tremendous value of sex. All the way from the one-celled amoeba up to man, the greater differentiation of sex is the mark of higher development. Man and woman are not alike and are not meant to be alike. They become more different the more they perfect their own development, and the development of the race" (n.p.).

These antisuffrage arguments rang hollow against the practical reality of suffrage parades, where suffragists went to great lengths to demonstrate their virtues. As Linda Lumsden details, "A wagon full of babies joined a small torchlight parade on New York's First Avenue in 1915 to show that suffragists were devoted mothers." Not only did these suffragists' babies establish the women were feminine and maternal, but more deeply it showed them as heterosexual and procreative, addressing two fears central to the rhetoric of female inversion. Because their femininity was questioned, "individual marchers also took pains to appear feminine," Lumsden continues. "One Grecian herald in the 1912 parade cooked dinner for her mother before marching to prove that she could be both feminine and a suffragist. The press dependably latched onto parades' 'distinctly feminine points,' such as the pretty girls who tossed a crowd candy wrapped in suffrage messages" (87).

Antisuffragists, however, had an even greater fear than a woman's neglect of her domestic duties and her emphasis on her unique characteristics of her sex.[4] Antisuffragists cautioned against physiological changes, claiming that a woman's physical beauty would be compromised—she would become, using Greening's term, a "freak." In short, the suffragist would become, in the words of Robert Afton Holland, "large-handed, big-footed, flat-chested, and thin-lipped." A California newspaper reporting on a suffrage parade, noted, however, "Judging from the delegation, the square-jawed, short-haired suffragist is a mere creature of a comic weekly, while the real thing is a vision of loveliness" (quoted in Lumsden 87).

Such "loveliness" had its drawbacks, though. If antisuffragists could not criticize suffragists for being less feminine, they could criticize them, as Linda J. Lumsden notes, for "flaunting their sex" (88). In a statement released by the National Association Opposed to Woman Suffrage (NAOWS), the "sex appeal" expressed by suffragists in a 1913 march was "flagrant and the dominant note in the parade" (88). Josephine Dodge, president of NAOWS, contended that the uneasy balance of femininity in the suffrage movement proved that at its heart was a "sex disturbance" (quoted in Lumsden 89). It is, perhaps, not surprising that the Miss America Pageant held in Atlantic City, New Jersey, was started in 1921, only a year after woman suffrage became a reality and that the winner embodied, according to Samuel Gompers of the American Federation of Labor, "the type of womanhood America needs—strong, red-blooded, able to shoulder the responsibilities of home-making and motherhood. It is in her type that the hope of the country resides" (quoted in Banner 269).

Edward Allsworth Ross, writing in his *Changing America: Studies in Contemporary Society* in 1912, sketched the following picture of the social harm an independent woman could cause: "Society can have the kind of woman it wants. Take the women of eastern Prussia, for instance. These peasant women bear a child in the morning; in the afternoon they are out in the field. I have seen them, and what a type they are, squat, splay-footed, wide-backed, flat-breasted, broad-faced, short-necked—a type that lacks every grace that we associate with woman" (74–75). Speaking of women who work in the city, Ross continued:

> Now, there will be a disappearance of the race, if we extend no hand to help these working girls. What will happen will be that the girls of a distinctly feminine type, the girls who have the qualities of finesse, grace and charm will prove too fragile to meet the conditions. They will collapse and go to the bad, they will lose their health, or if they endure until they are married and become mothers, they will not be able to be mothers of full families, of sons and daughters that will endure to the end.
>
> But some there be who would stand the condition. And of what type would they be? They would be of this other type—the type that appears in those peasant women. In three or four generations we would have in this country all through the lower stratum that coarse type replacing the high-strung, high-bred, feminine type which is our pride and which extends up and down through layers of society in this country. (75)

The fear Ross expressed drew on a history of sex role expectations explained by Drs. Jordan and Davieson in a series of lectures delivered at the Museum of Anatomy in Philadelphia in 1871. As a woman becomes sexually mature, they contended, "the bust develops, the eyes sparkle with vividness and expression, indicative of soul and feeling: the periodical indisposition peculiar to her sex commences, girlish playfulness is exchanged for that graceful bashfulnes [*sic*] and retiring modesty which are so pleasing in girls of this age, her mind is occupied with ideas pure, but strange and absorbing; in a word, she is a woman, 'fairest of creation, last and best of all God's works'" (80). If a woman were allowed to work, not only would she fail to achieve this expected physical ideal, "last and best of all God's works," Ross argued, but her maternal ability would be affected.

Fifty years later, Avrom Barnett, in his 1921 *Foundations of Feminism: (A Critique),* continued the argument of Jordan, Davieson, and Ross. Claiming that a "critical appreciation of biological limitations will help the student as nothing else can to an intelligent reading of Feministic literature, throughout which a most surprising ignorance of the modern biological situation is everywhere" (47), Barnett undertook a critical reading of both biological sex differences and sociological expectations. "The ironical Feminist reading this," Barnett claimed, "will regard [Ross's conclusion] as an illustration of the universal masculine self-assumed prerogative of dictating what women shall do and how they must look. . . . Feminists very likely will even laud this 'splay-footed, flat-breasted, broad-faced, short-necked' type" (87—88). "Feminists," he later concluded, "do not seem to be alive to the fact that the working woman who practices self-flagellation by going to work, like the mediaeval monk, attains an ideal but ruins her health" (93).

In June 1907, the *Woman's Tribune,* the "official organ of the International Council" for the National American Woman Suffrage Association, reprinted the following verbal caricature of British suffragists, originally published in the British humor magazine *Punch,* called "A Bit of Fun":

> The context at Hexham appears to have produced some fresh varieties of suffragettes, alias suffragists, namely, "Suffragines," and "Suffragelles." Suffragines, according to the Daily Mail Special Correspondent, are widely differentiated and readily distinguished from the true Suffragettes. Whereas the Suffragette's eye gleams with the light of battle, the Suffragine wears a gloomy look of discontent. The former on political grounds attacks the Government; the latter bears a grudge against the male sex in general. The Suffragelles, again, are a corps of lady suffragists enrolled to skirmish on the Liberal side against the attacks of Miss Fraser's Border

Suffragettes. We do not wish to appear in any way to indulge in suffrajib-ing or suffrajeering. But one is tempted to ask with some apprehension, whether any further liberties on these lines are going to be taken with the English language. Is a harangue, for instance, of the now familiar kind to be described as "a suffrajaw?" Are the militant suffraJills to entangle their suffraJacks in adventure which are calculated to end in suffragaol? The possible upspringing of all these verbal monstrosities is an excessively painful subject with which we dare not further suffrajoke. (44)

That the editors of the *Woman's Tribune* chose to reprint the satiric "bit of fun" may have been an act of appropriating the oppressor's language to defuse its power. It may also have been a show of solidarity with British women, who were struggling to gain their political autonomy at the same time. Of more importance, however, is what the piece revealed about the opposition's fears of women in the suffrage movement.

Suffragists, according to the piece, were divided into distinct groups: the "suffragettes" and "suffragists," and their varieties, the "suffragines" and the "suffragelles." The "suffragettes" were recognized by their mili-tant eyes agleam at the political battle to be waged and their impend-ing attack on the government. The other group, the "Suffragines," was discontentedly gloomy and bore a grudge against males in general. This dichotomy was further strengthened by the implication that the "militant suffraJills" would, presumably by aggressive sexuality, "entangle their suffraJacks in adventures which are calculated to end in suffragaol." The agency ascribed to the militant suffragists was remarkable in its ability to manipulate sexually "calculated" adventures designed to "entangle" the male suffragists.

*Punch*'s characterization of the British suffragists clearly signaled a move toward the construction of a masculine woman, derived particu-larly from woman suffragists. Men were supposed to initiate sex, often cleverly entangling their female prey. In this satirical account, it was the militant "SuffraJills" who were on the sexual offensive, and men were the passive recipients of sexual aggression. Masculinity, at least in terms of sexual prowess, had been transferred from the male to the female. This picture was countered by the grudge-bearing "Suffragines," who were gloomy, presumably, because they were unhappy with their place in life and man's existence in the world. It was easy to infer that these "suffra-gines," since they begrudged men, had no use for men as either platonic or sexual partners. "Suffragettes," as the *Punch* piece declared, were of two types: militant and sexually aggressive "suffragelles" and man-hating "suffragines." Both types, and thus all women who support their right to vote, at the very best, abandoned their femininity since they had abandoned men. At the very worst, they appropriated masculine characteristics, assumed the role of sexual subject and pursuer, reduced men to objects, even emasculated them, and became masculine themselves.

The writer J. George Frederick, however, dismissed this as merely hypothetical. "Woman is now attempting very daring arrangements of her destiny," he warned in the *Woman Citizen,* and man "hardly realized that the athletic ideal for woman necessarily implied certain psychic changes of deep significance—one of them, the unmistakable introduction of virility into female character" (8). James M. Buckley, writing in *The Wrong and Peril of Woman Suffrage* (1909), confessed, "*I believe* that there are two objects in nature alike obnoxious—a mannish woman and a womanish man" (86). Both of Buckley's "objects" were created by the fluidity of sex and gender combinations and the attachments of nontraditional sex-gender pairings. Yet the "womanish man," while certainly an "obnoxious" development, was not nearly as intriguing or inflammatory as the sex-gender opposite, a "mannish woman," whom Buckley traced directly to the woman suffrage movement.[5] An even more pointed critique was Dr. H. W. Frink's remark in *Morbid Fears and Compulsions:* "A certain proportion of at least the most militant suffragists are neurotics who in some instances are compensating for masochistic trends, in others are more or less successfully subliminating sadistic and homosexual ones (which usually are unconscious)" (quoted in Macy 134). "B. V. Moodus," the "first U.S. Suffragette Senator" depicted by the cartoonist Thelma Grosvenor Cudlipp in *Vanity Fair* in 1920, visually epitomized these anxieties: her masculine appearance was directly attributable to her politics (see figure 6.5). In short, the changes in the political status of women would cause aberrant, disruptive psychological and physiological changes.

The antisuffragist crusader Horace Bushnell made the link explicitly organic. Suffrage for women is "radical enough," he wrote, "when time enough is added, to alter even the type of womanhood itself. At first, or for a short time, the effect will not be so remarkable, but in five years, and still more impressively in twenty-five, it will be showing what kind of power is in it." After one hundred years of voting, the changes in women would become "a fact organic" and would become a trait of the race. The physical characteristics Bushnell attributed to political enfranchisement were many: "The look will be sharp, the voice will be wiry and shrill, the

Figure 6.5: Cartoon by Thelma Grosvenor
Cudlipp in *Vanity Fair*, August 1920, 34.

action will be angular and abrupt, wiliness, self-asserting boldness, eagerness for place and power will get into the expression more and more
distinctly, and become inbred in the native habit" (135). Even more omi-
nous, the "race" of these "forward, selfish, politician-women" would be
characterized by "thin, hungry-looking, cream-tartar faces" that would
be "touched with blight and fallen out of luster" (136).

The middle-class women who were active in the suffrage movement,
according to John D'Emilio and Estelle Freedman, formed same-sex ties
"in an age when their society still validated female bonding," but "they
also lived in an era when same-sex relationships came under sharper
scrutiny" (193). Physicians, reflecting the cultural prejudices of their society, were explicit in making the link between the suffrage movement and
female inversion. By the end of the nineteenth century, European writers
such as Richard von Krafft-Ebing "were describing same-sex relationships in medical terms, as signs of mental and physical degeneration"
(D'Emilio and Freedman 193) and were linking "women's rejection of traditional gender roles and their demand for social and economic equality

to cross-dressing, sexual perversion, and borderline hermaphroditism" (Smith-Rosenberg 272). Havelock Ellis, even though he subscribed to a congenital theory of inversion, declared in *Sexual Inversion*, "Having been taught independence of men and disdain for the old theory which placed women in the moated grange of the home to sigh for a man who never comes, a tendency develops for women to carry this independence still farther and to find love where they find work" (262). Their insistence on remaining unmarried, establishing themselves in a career, gaining the franchise, and entering into a relationship with another woman "emerged within Ellis' model as 'unnatural' and selfish" (Smith-Rosenberg 278). The female invert "denied the boundaries that separated the genders and 'unnaturally' inverted traditional femininity both sexually and socially," Smith-Rosenberg concludes (278). One physician succinctly commented, "The driving force in many agitators and militant women who are always after their rights is often an unsatisfied sex impulse, with a homosexual aim" (quoted in D'Emilio and Freedman 193).

In an attempt to explain why "sexual inversion in women" was increasing, that is to say, why women were acting more like men, Ellis connected homosexuality in women to "influences in our civilization today which encourage such manifestations." In particular, he cited "the modern movement of emancipation—the movement to obtain the same rights and duties, the same freedom and responsibility, the same education and the same work"—as responsible for the increase in observed "inversion." Although Ellis noted that the movement was "on the whole a wholesome and inevitable movement," he emphasized that it carried with it certain disadvantages, including an increase in women's criminality and insanity ("Sexual Inversion in Women" 155). Since these two "disadvantages" had been increasing, Ellis's explanation continued, so had homosexuality, "always . . . regarded as belonging to an allied, if not the same, group of phenomena" to which criminality and insanity belong. As a disclaimer, Ellis admitted that these "modern movements" could not be understood to cause sexual inversion directly, but he still assigned them indirect blame, noting that they "promote hereditary neurosis." "They develop the germs of it," Ellis concluded. These "modern movements" like women's emancipation, "probably cause a spurious imitation," Ellis explained, "due to the fact that the congenital anomaly occurs with special frequency in women of high intelligence who, voluntarily or involuntarily, influence others" ("Sexual Inversion in Women" 156).

In 1908, Iwan Bloch made an even more exact connection: "There is no doubt that in the 'women's movement'—that is, in the movement directed towards the acquirement by women of all the attainments of masculine culture—homosexual women have played a notable part" (511).

The physician James B. Weir Jr. argued that the suffrage movement would lead to a demand for a "matriarchy"—reasoning that "the right to vote carries with it the right to hold office, and, if women are granted the privilege of suffrage, they must be given the right to govern" (817). Weir pronounced that this would be a regression for human society, "distinctly, and emphatically, and essentially retrograde in every particular" (818). In his article "The Effect of Female Suffrage on Posterity," published in the *American Naturalist* in September 1895, Weir explored "this atavistic desire [matriarchy] in the physical and psychical histories of its foremost advocates" (815).

"I think," he confidently reasoned, "that I am perfectly safe in asserting that every woman who has been at all prominent in advancing the cause of equal rights in its entirety, has either given evidences of masculo-femininity (viraginity), or has shown, conclusively, that she was the victim of psycho-sexual aberrancy." He followed with examples of "every viragint of note in the history of the world, [who] were either physically or psychically degenerate, or both," and provided Joan of Arc, Catherine the Great, and Messalina, "the depraved wife of Claudius," as historical precedent. Weir added that Messalina was so much a woman of "masculine type, whose very form embodied and shadowed forth the regnant idea of her mind," that her "gross carnality" and "lecherous conduct shocked even the depraved courtiers of her lewd and salacious court" (819).

Not all women in favor of female suffrage, however, belonged to Weir's class of viragints. Some women were motivated by a single, feminine purpose, such as universal temperance or "the elevation of social morals," and thus were not comparable to those women who desired a share in the government, the initial step, Weir reasoned, in the establishment of a "matriarchate." "Woman is," Weir continued, "a creature of the emotions, of impulses, of sentiment, and of feeling" (821). If a duty like suffrage were to be added, he reasoned, a woman's environment would "very materially change" and "would entail new and additional desires and emotions which would be other and most exhausting draughts on her nervous organism" (823). Even greater than the effects of suffrage on the individual woman, however, would be its influence on society. Although Weir admitted that the right to vote carried with it "no immediate danger," he asserted that the "final effect of female suffrage on posterity would be exceedingly harmful." "Probably many years" after suffrage, Weir surmised, the worst effects would be realized, when woman, "owing to her increased degeneration, gives free rein to her atavistic tendencies and hurries ever backward toward the savage state of her barbarian ancestors . . . toward that abyss of immoral horrors so repugnant to our cultivated ethical tastes—the matriarchate" (825).

Clearly, those suffragists to whom Weir attributed matriarchal desires, those women suffering from "viraginity" or "psycho-sexual aberrancy," were most threatening. "The pronounced advocates and chief promoters of equal rights are probably viragints," Weir concluded, "individuals who plainly show that they are psychically abnormal" and whose abnormality is "occasioned by degeneration, either acquired or inherent, in the individual." Weir, however, pushed his discussion of viraginity further, knowingly detailing the "many phases" of the physical and psychological aberrances. The "mild form," Weir wrote, was the tomboy "who abandons her dolls and female companions for the marbles and masculine sports of her boy acquaintances." The "loud-talking, long-stepping, slang-using young woman" was another form, as was "the square-shouldered, stolid, cold, unemotional, unfeminine android (for she has the normal human form, without the normal human *psychos*)." But "the most aggravated form of viraginity," he claimed, was "homo-sexuality" (822). What Weir accomplished by linking suffrage to viraginity and viraginity to homosexuality was to imply that homosexuality was responsible for the woman suffrage movement (later, after 1920, the quest for more expansive women's rights) and that woman suffragists were homosexuals.

Fictionally, these organic changes were most apparent in two texts: Henry James's *Bostonians* (1886) and William Lee Howard's *Perverts* (1901), texts that focus on a variety of women activists who embody, in varying degrees, the sharp looks, eagerness for power, and lusterless complexions that suffragists and feminists were thought to manifest. Both novels provide the crucial fictional link between the woman suffrage movement and the reconstruction of the women in the movement, physically, psychologically, and sexually. Most specifically, the portrayal of the relationship between Olive Chancellor and Verena Tarrant in *The Bostonians* has attracted significant attention as critics have argued over its implied homosexuality. Earlier readings, as Terry Castle relates, dismissed the same-sex attraction (150–51). Hugh Stevens notes that other critics "engage in full character assassination of Olive Chancellor, who emerges as 'unnatural' as opposed to the healthy, life-affirming Basil Ransom" (92). In the face of such duplicitous reaction, Castle wonders how "can James's novel not be a 'a study of lesbianism,' if its central character . . . is in fact a 'horrid' lesbian? What else besides such a character . . . would one need?" (151).

Expanding this debate about sexuality to more than the figure and motivations of Olive Chancellor, to include other female characters in the text, clarifies the vital connection between politics and physiology. Ruth Evelyn Quebe argues the connection between fiction and suffrage history, suggesting that the disagreements among James's reformers reflected the split between the National Woman Suffrage Association and the American Woman Suffrage Association (95).[6] Reading these women activists according to their varying levels of commitment to the cause permits us to see just how women's activity in politics influenced their physical and psychological character—at least according to these authors. Early in the novel, after Basil Ransom has arrived from the South, he attends a meeting with his cousin, Olive Chancellor, where the women's reform orator, Mrs. Farrinder, will speak. Interestingly, it is Mrs. Farrinder who exemplifies the rhetoric of the woman suffragists themselves and whose appearance demonstrates that the activists still embodied femininity, domesticity, and maternity. According to the narrator, Farrinder "was held to have a very fine manner, and to embody the domestic virtues and the graces of the drawingroom; to be a shining proof, in short, that the forum, for ladies, is not necessarily hostile to the fireside." As the final pronouncement of her adherence to womanly characteristics and most specifically to her heterosexuality, the narrator adds, "She had a husband and his name was Amariah" (39). This example of a true, independent-minded female reformer in a clearly feminine body, however, does not assume prominence in the novel.

Rather, the most egregious example of the woman reformer is Dr. Mary J. Prance, the physician who, "[e]xcept for her intelligent eye . . . had no features to speak of" and "looked like a boy, and not even like a good boy" (47). An even more frightful figure than Miss Birdseye, who belongs to the "Short-Skirts League" (36), Prance exemplifies precisely the qualities that antisuffragists had predicted.[7] Physically, she has lost all semblance of femininity—she was even "bored with being reminded . . . that she was a woman" (53)—evidenced by her lack of feminine curves and bobbed hair. "She was a plain, spare young woman, with short hair and an eye-glass" (39). Politically, she embodies an even more radical notion. Although she has little sympathy for the woman suffrage cause, only attending the meeting because she is curious about what is occurring in the apartment above her own, Prance clearly has the most radical views about the social place of women since she remarks that there is no difference between men and women. They "'are all the same to me! . . . I don't see any difference. There is room for improvement in both sexes. Neither of them is up to the standard'" (48). With these words, Prance distances herself from the reformers who, like Mrs. Farrinder, still espoused the domestic and maternal role for women. Instead, she adopts a rhetoric that demands not simply equal enfranchisement and opportunity but no differentiation between the sexes and their social status. Prance does seem to excuse these views by declaring that the women reformers have "'a capacity for making people waste time. All I know is that I don't want any one to tell *me* what a lady can do!'" (53), but she is the manifestation of antisuffrage predictions come alive still decades before the ratification of the Nineteenth Amendment and a warning of what would occur if feminism were expressed in its extreme. Valerie Fulton succinctly declares that Prance is "the best ally in the novel against the woman's suffrage movement" (246). As Ransom witheringly remarks about her, "It was certain that whatever might become of the movement at large, Doctor Prance's own little revolution was a success" (53).

Having established the two extremes of women's reform in Mrs. Farrinder, who espouses suffrage rhetoric but still embodies femininity, maternity, and domesticity, and Dr. Prance, who exemplifies everything the antisuffragists had predicted, the novel then turns to reform-minded Olive Chancellor, whose "union" with Verena Tarrant does not simply dismiss heterosexuality but for a time affirms a same-sex relationship. Ransom, who cynically opposes the reforms women are advocating, delights in the evening because it confirms what he has long believed about political women's disastrous effect on society. Olive Chancellor embodies Ransom's thoughts, as the narrator notes. "What Basil Ransom actually perceived was that Miss Chancellor was a signal old maid. That was her quality, her destiny; nothing could be more distinctly written. There are women who are unmarried by accident, and others who are unmarried by option; but Olive Chancellor was unmarried by every implication of her being. She was a spinster" (29). It is, of course, Chancellor who, immediately upon seeing the young Verena Tarrant, falls in love with her and her speaking talents. Never able to publicly express her own views on women's reform, Chancellor prefers to work behind the scenes, using her social and economic connections to advance the cause. Comfortably affluent on Charles Street, although perhaps a trifle embarrassed by her wealth, Chancellor is a dangerous embodiment of women's independence. Self-supporting (and financially supportive of the movement) and believing in the right of suffrage and equality, she utterly shuns marriage and, for much of the novel, removes the beautiful Verena Tarrant from heterosexual practice.

Verena herself, despite her involvement in reform efforts, does not pose the risk of a woman like Olive Chancellor. A "delicate, pretty girl," according to the narrator, Tarrant warrants the physical accouterments that the other women in the novel are not accorded. "She was strong and supple, there was colour in her lips and eyes, and her tresses, gathered into a complicated coil, seemed to glow with the brightness of her nature. She had curious, radiant, liquid eyes (their smile was a sort of reflection, like the glisten of a gem), and though she was not tall, she appeared to spring up, and carried her head as if it reached rather high" (61–62). Her conventional appearance befits a woman; she is, according to Alfred Habegger, "constituted by the familiar feminine traits, and the commenting author insists that this vulnerable femininity is her greatest triumph" (338). Her young age excuses her from her reliance on her parents, most notably Selah Tarrant, the mesmerist who prepares her to speak by "the mysterious process of calming her down" (62).

At various times throughout this text, Verena Tarrant does serve as the mouthpiece for women's reform, which seems to suggest she is committed to the cause. Yet her feminine appearance and behavior contradict such a reading. Verena Tarrant is no women's rights advocate; she simply speaks its rhetoric. As she prepares for her first speech, after Mrs. Farrinder refuses to address the group, she is "stroked and smoothed" by her father, who glories in the theatrics. Indeed, according to the narrator, Verena is readied for a "performance" (62). When she finally does begin to speak, the narrator remarks of Ransom, "It was not what she said; he didn't care for that, he scarcely understood it." Ransom is not so much impressed with Verena's claims of the "goodness of women" and "universal sisterhood" as he is enthralled by her delivery; he was "delighted to observe that such matters as these didn't spoil" the performance (63). It was, at last, "simply an intensely personal exhibition," and "the argument, the doctrine, has absolutely nothing to do with it" (64).

Selah Tarrant gives way to Olive Chancellor, who now becomes Verena's handler, preparing speeches for her and arranging her public engagements. It is the political world that has united Olive and Verena since that first oration. "'Are they very much united?'" Basil Ransom asks Miss Birdseye. "'You would say so if you were to see Miss Chancellor when Verena rises to eloquence,'" she answers. "'It's as if the chords were strung across her own heart; she seems to vibrate, to echo with every word. It's a very close and very beautiful tie, and we think everything of it here. They will work together for a great good!'" (192). From this description, it is seemingly Olive who is most enamored of Verena, specifically her rhetorical abilities. It is also apparent that their relationship is sanctioned, even cheered, by the other reformers, who look to the union as amenable to the cause.

The two women's relationship, though forged out of the movement, is not based on a shared political viewpoint, however. During their trip to Europe, Verena confesses to Ransom that Olive Chancellor makes her speeches for her, "'or the best part of them.'" "'She tells me what to say—the real things, the strong things. It's Miss Chancellor as much as me!'" she exclaims, apparently oblivious to the strings by which she is controlled (195). Although she holds her own when feminist views are playfully challenged by Ransom, Tarrant obviously does not have an original and independent thought. It should be no surprise, then, that the novel concludes with Verena's forsaking Olive Chancellor and choosing Basil Ransom, acquiescing again to the stronger power, in this case heterosexuality. Chancellor resumes the status she had at the start of the text, that of "spinster" or "old maid," her same-sex "union" with Tarrant thwarted and ultimately destroyed by the man.[8]

The melee that occurs backstage, as Ransom attempts to remove Verena physically from the auditorium and psychologically from the feminist cause, brings the novel and Olive Chancellor to a swift and unforgiving conclusion. Powerless to act in the face of Ransom and the heterosexuality he represents, Chancellor can do nothing but watch as Verena Tarrant's mask of political interest dissolves to reveal her true ambivalence about women's rights. Even though she calls out for Olive as she is violently whisked out of the theater by Ransom and even sheds tears, the indictment is clear. Olive Chancellor's power over the impressionable young woman is no match for the heterosexual status quo; to return the society to its heterosexual norm, the same-sex relationship is not allowed to persist. "The reason he manages to win Verena," Habegger posits, "is that he has nature on his side" (337).

Moreover, as Mrs. Farrinder makes clear when she comes backstage to ascertain why Verena has failed to deliver her address, the blame rests with Olive. "'Well, Miss Chancellor,' [Mrs. Farrinder] said . . . with considerable asperity, 'if this is the way you're going to reinstate our sex!'" (382). Since Mrs. Farrinder is seemingly unaware of the drama surrounding Verena and her choice of love, her denouncement of Olive carries a dual meaning. Her husband, Amariah, remarks on "a want of organisation" (383), clearly the area where Olive has been most success-ful for the movement. But this criticism also emanates from the hetero-sexual and married Mrs. Farrinder and can be read as a condemnation of Olive's "union" with Verena. The way to "reinstate" the female sex into society, in other words, is through the heterosexual status quo, not through same-sex unions and feminist rhetoric.

This fictional rendition of women reformers did not escape their real-life counterparts, who challenged some of the conclusions James's novel offered. Writing a review of *The Bostonians* in the *Woman's Journal,* a magazine devoted to covering the activities of the National American Woman Suffrage Association, Lucia True Ames decided that the novel was "evidently intended as a tremendous satire on the whole 'woman question'" since Olive's "bitter, unnatural antipathy towards marriage and men" was decidedly atypical, as the glowing tributes to Stanton and Colby illustrated (82–83). Nevertheless, James's fiction of the women's movement does provide a valuable glimpse into the rhetoric and public perception of those politics that plagued the quest for woman suffrage. Olive Chancellor may ultimately elicit pity for having to face an impatient Boston audience at the end of the novel; Castle regards her as "English and American literature's first lesbian tragic heroine" (171). Yet pity does not extend to her brief expression of same-sex sexuality. That move, from "old maid" to "lesbian," when coupled with Dr. Prance's "revolution" into gender indeterminacy, signaled that the fear of woman suffrage and political independence had come to pass.

The physician William Lee Howard's 1901 novel *The Perverts* pres-ents an even more frightening possibility than James's Olive Chancellor and Dr. Mary J. Prance. Howard's familiarity with the latest scientific theories regarding heredity and mental health were two subjects that he entwined in his medical work and his writing. In a *New York Medical Journal* article in 1900, he wrote, "The female possessed of masculine ideas of independence, the virago who would sit in the public highways and lift up her pseudo-virile voice, proclaiming her sole right to decide questions of war or religion, or the value of celibacy and the curse of woman's impurity, and that disgusting antisocial being, the female sexual pervert, are simply different images of the same class—degenerates" ("Effeminate Men and Masculine Women" 687).

Howard's novel fictionalizes his medical conclusions by focusing on two fighting siblings with nervous disorders inherited from their parents, who, according to the narrator, were too old to produce mentally healthy children. According to Leigh Newcomber, hero psychologist of the novel, his nervous disorder—"dipsomania," which is successfully controlled through "scientific methods" (35)—was "inherited." He was given, the narrator explains, the "exhausted nervous organism of his immediate progenitors, and all the instability, infirmness, swaying and distorted characteristics belonging to a decaying family." So, too, were his three sisters. Zora, the eldest, shows "no intellectual force, no moral perversion, no mental activity." Marcia, however, is an egotistic, "typical hysteric, whose uncontrollable impulses have been fostered on account of the objective symptoms of her hereditary psychopathic soil." In short, according to Leigh, "this unfortunate woman is so desirous of mating that she is continually on the man hunt" (38). Mizpra is the youngest and "most unfortunate of the family." "Her condition," Leigh writes in his notebook, "appears to be a constant perversion of all the normal womanly attributes." Even "her mind . . . is not the ordinary female kind" since it is, according to Leigh, "a strange mixture of deceit and cunning. She is deep, sinister, and forbidding" (39).

As the novel progresses, traditional sex-gender assignments become even more pronounced. Leigh, who early in *The Perverts* allows his dipsomania to reduce him to a drunken philanderer consorting with prostitutes, slowly regains control of his nerves and becomes not only a faithful husband and father but also a strong, morally superior protector of society from the mentally ill. Mizpra, however, attempts to gain total control of her widowed mother's assets and becomes even more masculine. When Leigh receives a letter from Mizpra, he notices that although her handwriting is familiar, it is "somewhat changed in its character. It was masculine; a masculinity that would have done credit to Catherine de Medici." Furthermore, her "large jaws were now prominent, her muscled neck, small hips, uncomely waist, her black hair and large hands, all make a bold frame from her hard and coarse features." When she tells Leigh that he "'need not attempt to see [his] mother,'" her voice comes from what the narrator characterizes as a "masculine larynx" (49). The physiological effects of Mizpra's "nervous disease" and transgressions are clear: the more evil she becomes, the more masculine. Even more important is the converse: the more masculine she becomes, that is, the more she adopts the nontraditional, unaccepted gender to her female sex, the more evil, or to use Howard's term, the more "perverted," she becomes.

To lend validity to such notions, Howard allows Leigh Newcomber ample opportunities to lend scientific support to Mizpra's dangerous behavior, termed "her latent criminal instincts." Although Leigh does exonerate Mizpra's actions because she lacks the "force or power" to control herself as a result of her unfortunate heredity, even positing that "she had no knowledge of her abnormal condition, of her moral epilepsy" (50), the indictment of Mizpra's criminality and assumption of masculinity is obvious. "What we look for most in the female is femininity," Leigh recalls one of his teachers remarking. "And when we find the opposite in her we must look for some atavistic anomaly, which is generally of a criminal type" (50–51). In Mizpra's case, the anomaly makes her "an enemy to every living thing" (65).

Mizpra's "perversion," however, extends beyond her appropriation of a "masculine" voice and physique. In a conversation with her mother, Mizpra remarks that both of her sisters have married, which prompts Mrs. Newcomber to declare that Mizpra, unless she is careful, will become an "'old maid.'" Mizpra's vehemence at her mother's comment, declaring that marriage is "'disgusting,'" illustrates her even further fall into "perversion" and loss of femininity. "'What poor, weak, helpless creatures women are!'" Mizpra fumes, emphasizing that marriage is "'such a disgusting, vile, humiliating acceptance of the loss of personal freedom'" (87). Still, Mizpra does marry, although she never consummates the relationship. Her husband, Burke Wood, is a weak man; according to the narrator, he "was one of those unfortunate bipeds whom men despise, women hate, and the females of perversive instincts employ as useful adjuncts to their much-scorned skirts" (193). The marriage is strictly one of convenience; Mizpra needs a secretary. Neither does Mizpra accept the female's role of maternity, declaring that there are "'too many babies now,'" or the female's reliance on femininity, pronouncing that with her weak husband, she will use her "'intellect, my power over him,'" not the traditional "'feminine baubles of Eve'" (204).

The scientific issue of genetic inheritance is, at least in terms of Mizpra, displaced by the delineation of psychic and physiological changes caused by her perversion. Mizpra's and Mrs. Newcomber's move to Colorado Springs, presumably to enjoy the benefits of a "Western lung resort," prompts Mizpra to establish a "select young ladies' school." She considers herself to be "an emancipator of female slaves" by teaching the town's young girls to "give up their lives to the slavery of the hearth and home" since "it was beneath the dignity and rights of their sex" (90). Moreover, Mizpra continues her scientific experiments, as she tells her mother, to "prove in the future, without dissent, the strength, the force, and reasoning power of the female mind" (85).

But Mizpra's teaching methods are suspect, as Burke Wood informs her. "'I have heard that you have been instilling some of your brilliant ideas into your pupils' minds,'" Burke tells Mizpra. When Mizpra discovers the daughter of the town's physician, Dr. Camp, wears corsets, she makes her take them off before the whole school. "'Then it is said,'" Burke recounts, "'you stood her on the platform and with your hands on her flesh, marked out the creases formed by the corsets. She told her father your hands were so cold and rough, the treatment so humiliating, that she fainted.'" Dr. Camp, he adds, "'tells everyone that his daughter had a severe nervous shock in consequence of your treatment, and that you ought to be driven out of town'" (92). Mizpra is nonplussed by this account and excuses her actions by saying that Dr. Camp's daughter "'is suffering from the feminine folly of imitating the male in all animal life on the globe—that is, the garnishing of the body to attract the opposite sex. In the animal kingdom such folly is the sole prerogative of the male'" (93).

The psychology and physical manifestations of "perversion" are certainly the focus of Howard's novel. But his characterization of Mizpra, whose actions dismiss femininity and maternity, as "evil" contrasts sharply with his treatment of the male sibling and his "perversions." Leigh, despite initial failings, is able to control his nervous disease and at the end of the novel force Mizpra to her death, thereby saving not only himself but, the worried reader can infer, all of society as well. Yet it is virtually impossible to determine causality in Mizpra's psyche. Is she evil because she has masculine characteristics? Or does her inherited perversion manifest itself physically in masculinity, signaling that a perverse psyche causes a perversity in sex-gender assignment? Leigh's inheritance is of no help in determining blame, since he, despite the narrator's insistence on the irrepressible power of heredity, is able to overcome his dipsomania by scientific method, which, at least for Leigh, is stronger than genetic disposition.

But Mizpra's perversion, more particularly her physical and psychical expression, clearly is meant to be the most important aspect of her being. Even if her "perversion" can be forgiven because it was inherited, the manifestations of such perversion cannot; Mizpra's ultimate "perversion" is located in her denial of marriage and maternity. Even more explicit than the physical same-sex attraction suggested in Mizpra's handling of Dr. Camp's daughter is the passing reference to a "mild sort of fellow-feeling—not womanly—"she experienced with a female physician who was, the narrator knowingly suggests, "one of the big-footed, short-haired kind" (286). Despite Howard's claim that the entire Newcomber family is afflicted with hereditary "perversion," clearly some perversions, those that confuse traditional sex-gender assignments and allow for the possibility of sexual inversion, are more "perverse" than others. Yet it is not simply that there are varying degrees of perversions. Hereditary sources, too, are ascribed different values of perversion in the Newcomber family. Although initial speculation offers both the father and mother as causes, blame finally rests on maternal heredity. Mrs. Newcomber married late, at the age of thirty-six; by this time, the narrator explains, "her maternal and reproductive instincts had been starved and enfeebled by a life of wrong training and misdirected study, augmented by the unphysiologic life of the disappointed *femme sole*." The narrator attributes Mrs. Newcomber's "wrong training" and "misdirected study," which result in her reproductive enfeeblement, and hence Mizpra's evil perversion, to "the false and unhealthy ideas of New England woman suffragists" (205). Mizpra, last-born child of the mistrained mother, "only needed a strong character, a decided maternal and womanly guide and adviser" to give "proper stimulation" to foster the "normal development of the sexual cells in the cortex of the brain" (206–7). But Mrs. Newcomber, the reader is told, because her "physical and mental activities [had] been in channels far removed from anticipation and thoughts of married life," lacks the maternal factors necessary for Mizpra to develop properly. More specifically, Mrs. Newcomber's belief and involvement in the woman suffrage campaign are transformed into a genetic anomaly and become the cause of Mizpra's perversion, her "abnormal pleasures and passions" (206).

Echoing Howard's 1900 article in the *New York Medical Journal*, his scientifically minded narrator elucidates the effects woman suffrage ideas supposedly had on women. "The female possessed of masculine ideas of independence, the viragint who would sit in the public highways and lift up her pseudo-virile voice, proclaiming her sole right to decide questions of war or religion, or the value of celibacy and the curse of woman's impurity" is, the narrator posits, a "degenerate," whose inheritance does not excuse her behavior, even though she is a "victim of poor mating" (207). There is, however, a far worse type of degeneracy. "That disgusting anti-social being, the female sexual pervert," is simply a "different degree of the same class" of "degenerates" to which Mizpra and her mother undoubtedly belong:

> When a woman neglects her maternal instincts, when her sentiment and dainty feminine characteristics are boldly and ostentatiously kept submerged, we can see an anti-social creature more amusing than dangerous. . . . [But] should this female be unfortunate enough to become a mother, she ceases to be merely amusing, and is an anti-social being. She is then a menace to civilizations, a producer of non-entities, the mother of mental and physical monstrosities who exist as a class of true degenerates until disgusted Nature, no longer tolerant of the woman who would be a man . . . allows [her] to shrink unto death. (207–8)

The vitriolic explanations of "perversions" continue, although now the narrator expands the definitions far beyond Mizpra and Mrs. Newcomber to include fictional and nonfictional society:

> The female who prefers the laboratory to the nursery; the mother quick with child who spends her mornings at the club, discussing "Social Statics," visiting the saloons and tenements in the afternoon, distributing, with an innocence in strange contrast to her assumptions, political tracts asking the denizens to vote her ticket, is a sad form of degeneracy. Such females are true degenerates, because they are unphysiologic in their physical incompleteness. The progeny of such human misfits are perverts, moral or psychic. Their prenatal life has been influenced by the very antithesis of what the real woman would surround her expected child with. The child born of the "new woman" is to be pitied. . . . (208)

Finally, the narrator makes the most pointed references to the degenerate "new woman," particularly the challenges she poses to the medical establishment:

> It is this class that clamors for "higher education" for the woman; that crowd the public halls shouting for the freedom of women and demanding all the prerogatives of the men. It is these female androids who are insulted in the dark umbrage of ignorance and delusion regarding their negative nature; who are fadists, 'ismites, and mental roamers. Ideally mobile, they go from the laboratory to the convent, even restless, continuously discontented, morbidly majestic at periods, hysterically forcible at times. They demonstrate their early perverted mental growth by their present lack of reasoning powers. . . . They claim to know more about the science of medicine without study than the men who have devoted their lives to that science. (209)

Howard sought to instill hereditary causes of perversions to bolster his claim in the preface that people suffering from such "nervous diseases" should be confined to a hospital so that their mental illness can be controlled. The literary case exemplifies the medico-scientific theories of the day positing inheritance as a definite influence. Dr. Charles L. Dana, a nineteenth-century neurophysiologist, speculated that "if women achieve the feministic ideal and live as men do, they would incur the risk of 25 per cent more insanity than they have now" (n.p.). Dana excuses his projections by noting that "I am not saying that woman suffrage will make women crazy," but Howard, by locating the source of Mizpra's perversion in her suffragist mother's independent activities and delayed interest in maternity, certainly suggests that perversion is caused by woman's emancipation. If the empirically knowledgeable narrator is to be believed, the politically active woman en route to enfranchisement is the source and cause of "perversion." Or, as Dana explained: "woman suffrage would throw into the electorate a mass of voters of delicate nervous stability . . . [and] add to our voting and administrative forces the biological element of an unstable preciosity which might do injury without promoting the community's good" (n.p.).

This connection of masculinized women to woman suffrage to female inversion persisted through the early decades of the twentieth century, particularly as the woman suffrage movement progressed to its decisive constitutional victory in 1920. Havelock Ellis, Smith-Rosenberg reports, insisted that "the numbers of lesbians had steadily increased since the expansion of women's roles and institutions." According to Smith-Rosenberg, "Feminism, lesbianism, equality for women, all emerge in Ellis's writings as problematic phenomena. All were unnatural, related in disturbing and unclear ways to increased female criminality, insanity, and 'hereditary neurosis'" (279). The marriage reformer J. W. Meagher was explicit in linking women's rights activists to abnormal sexuality: "The driving force in many agitators and militant women who are always after their rights is often an unsatisfied sex impulse, with a homosexual aim. Married women with a completely satisfied libido rarely take an active interest in militant movements" (quoted in Smith-Rosenberg 283). Sigmund Freud also strengthened the connection between masculine gender and inversion in his *Three Essays*. As George Chauncey Jr. points out, "Freud, like Ellis and the whole of turn-of-the-century sexology, continued to assert that 'character inversion' was a regular feature of *female* inversion, although no longer maintaining that this was true of male inversion" (94). After World War I had decimated the number of eligible men, Christine Bolt observes, fears of a declining middle-class birthrate intensified. "Under these circumstances," she concludes, "'deviant' sexual behavior by women, of whatever kind, remained unacceptable on both sides of the Atlantic" (270).

This inversion of enfranchised women, accomplished through scientific theory, popular press illustrations, and fictional predictions of impending sociobiological disaster, was succinctly echoed by Professor Lionel J. Tayler, a nineteenth-century London University lecturer in biology, who was experiencing firsthand the sex-gender confusion of marching suffragists. "It is for the good of all concerned," he wrote, "that the unlikeness between man and woman exists, and . . . any effort to change woman's nature to the end that she may become a female man will and should fail" (quoted in "Woman and Man" 175). Although the success of the woman suffrage movement contradicted Tayler's forecast of failure, the fear of sex-gender confusion embodied in the suffragists remained solidly affixed in the public's mind, clearly articulated by the organic discontent of Greening's "freaks." As a desperate counter to such perverted possibilities, literature and popular press accounts attempted to disenfranchise this masculine woman and the perverted politics she was thought to practice. Authors relied on more subtle means to eradicate the masculine woman and her "freakish sexuality" from the acceptable status quo. A woman who acted contrary to the feminine gender, as the suffragists were thought to have done, needed to be labeled aberrant, seduced, parodied, or removed to maintain social order.

### Notes

1. The sexologist Edward Carpenter attached this term to male and female inverts as an attempt at more fully defining and understanding just what this nontraditional sex-gender combination was.

2. In the early twentieth century, two groups dominated the suffrage movement. The National American Woman Suffrage Association was the largest, with two million members by 1917. Dr. Anna Howard Shaw presided from 1905 to 1915, when Carrie Chapman Catt took over. After 1920, it became the League of Women Voters. The National Woman's Party, headed by Alice Paul, employed more militant tactics, such as picketing the Wilson White House in 1917. For detailed studies of these groups, as well as the entire woman suffrage history, see Kraditor; Lumsden; Marshall; Camhi; and Jablonsky.

3. Linda Lumsden suggests that the members of the National Woman's Party (NWP), who introduced more radical strategies than the conservative National American Woman Suffrage Association (NAWSA), in many ways embodied this fearful perception that suffragists were masculine. In the picketing of the Wilson White House, Lumsden claims that "[t]he pickets came directly to the paramount symbol of American male power. They not only did not care if they were perceived as unwomanly but also hoped to offend and provoke the male establishment" (118). The militancy of the NWP only exacerbated the perceptual conclusions about the women suffragists; the members of both the NAWSA and the NWP provoked the same fearful response—they were acting contrary to their sex.

4. Susan E. Marshall has categorized rhetoric from 214 antisuffrage writings according to gender and political issues. Breaking the movement into three periods—1867 to 1899, 1900 to 1912, and 1913 to 1921—she claims that "male attacks on suffragists' personality," jibes directed at their changing gender roles, "escalated over time" (105). See table 4.2 (101) in her study.

5. Buckley's connection of these nontraditional sex-gender combinations to the woman suffrage movement did not only explain the "mannish woman"; according to Marshall, male antisuffragists "attacked male supporters of women's rights as 'feminine men and mollycoddles,' a 'deplorable spectacle of human weakness'" (105).

6. The National Woman Suffrage Association supported a broad platform of women's causes, whereas the American Woman Suffrage Association sought the franchise within each state. Quebe places Olive and Verena "on the more radical side of the schism" (95).

7. Frederick Wegener reads Dr. Prance as a wholly positive figure who "personifies the ideology of unassisted self-making re-sanctioned so piously in Gilded-Age America" (170). Her placement within the woman's rights movement in relation to the reformers does, however, force a narrower reading of her. The self-made woman was, and still is, a problematic figure.

8. Sara DeSaussure Davis reads this fictional love triangle as based on historical fact. "James was personally acquainted" with various people involved in the suffrage movement, Davis writes, including Anna Dickinson, Susan B. Anthony, and Whitelaw Reid (571). He used Dickinson as the model for Verena Tarrant, while Anthony and Reid became fashioned as Olive Chancellor and Basil Ransom, respectively. "The striking similarity between the triangle of Anthony-Dickinson-Reid and of Olive-Verena-Basil is easily recognizable," although James did alter several important aspects of the historical model. Most notably, according to Davis, James "goes beyond what was known or publicly realized about Anthony and Dickinson. . . . in all likelihood [James] drew additionally from his observations of the friendship between Kate Loring and Alice James" (580).

# PART II

# WINNING AND WIELDING
# THE BALLOT

# 7

## FIGHTING FOR RIGHTS
## IN THE 1910s AND 1920s (Excerpt)

### JULIE A. GALLAGHER

From *Black Women and Politics in New York City,*
by Julie A. Gallagher (2012)

### Black Women and the Struggle for Suffrage

In a chapel just beyond the banks of the Seneca River in the "burned-over" district of New York State, Elizabeth Cady Stanton and Lucretia Mott brought together the nation's first formal gathering dedicated to women's rights in 1848. For the next seven decades, African American women and men, including the towering abolitionist, Frederick Douglass, and white women like Susan B. Anthony and Lucy Stone, fought for women's rights, above all the right to vote. At the end of the Civil War, African American leaders such as Mary Ann Shadd Cary, Charlotte Forten, Josephine St. Pierre Ruffin, and Sojourner Truth worked for suffrage in various Northern and border cities. As part of their efforts, they joined the two principal suffrage organizations, the National Woman Suffrage Association (NWSA) and the American Woman Suffrage Association (AWSA) to push the issue forward.[1] In the early 1870s, determined to exercise what they believed was their fundamental right of citizenship, Cary, Truth, Anthony, and other women attempted to vote. In Battle Creek, Michigan, Truth was denied a ballot; in Washington, D.C., Cary was denied as well; in Rochester, New York, Anthony and more than a dozen other women were arrested.[2]

Throughout the rest of the nineteenth century, efforts to secure women's enfranchisement continued, but they were hardly unified. Fault lines surfaced repeatedly over critical issues like the embrace or rejection of racial equality and over strategies like the targeting of the U.S. Congress or the states. Suffragists' debates regarding support of the Fifteenth Amendment, which enfranchised black men, fractured the movement in the immediate aftermath of the Civil War.[3] It took twenty years for the NWSA and AWSA to merge their efforts in the wake of that conflict and form the National American Woman Suffrage Association (NAWSA). Even when officially welcomed into suffrage organizations led by white women, black women rarely experienced equal treatment; at times they were excluded from or segregated during strategy sessions and public events.[4] The most striking examples of racism went beyond the exclusion of black women from meetings, however. In Southern states the goal was to exclude them from the right to vote itself.[5] Despite the myriad obstacles they faced, black women persevered.

In the Reconstruction South, black women had participated in a kind of family politics whereby they attended civic celebrations, discussed issues, and evaluated candidates with their husbands even though they could not vote. When they moved north to New York, Chicago, and Detroit, they retained their concerns about political and civic life and, despite some class tensions, joined their efforts with those of women, especially clubwomen in these cities who had taken up the suffrage cause.[6] In New York City, for example, Victoria Earle Matthews, a journalist for T. Thomas Fortune's newspaper the *New York Age*, was an ardent champion of women's suffrage. Born into slavery in Georgia and brought north through her mother's efforts, Matthews was a passionate and effective organizer. She co-founded the Women's Loyal Union in the wake of Ida B. Wells's 1892 anti-lynching speaking tour in New York, and she helped secure more than ten thousand signatures in support of a woman's suffrage resolution.

Sarah J. S. Garnet, a native New Yorker, was born twenty years before the Civil War. A teacher by profession and the first African American female principal in the New York City public school system, Garnet was a lifelong activist. In the 1880s, she fought to keep African American schools open and traveled to the state capital to protest against discrimination that black teachers faced. Although the widow of Henry Highland Garnet, the renowned abolitionist, minister, and diplomat, Sarah Garnet was respected in her own right for her breadth of activism. She started the Equal Suffrage League in the late 1880s, which was the only black women's organization in Brooklyn dedicated to the cause, and after the NACW's founding, she headed its Suffrage Department. She died in 1911, just as New York suffragists launched their final rounds of struggle, but her influence on black women was felt across the city and the nation. In keeping with Garnet's vision, Frances R. Keyser, first president of the NACW affiliate Empire State Federation of Colored Women's Clubs, was a dedicated suffragist as well. She guided her organization's racial uplift strategy. Not only did it include the embrace of respectability, but Keyser also ensured that it incorporated the acquisition of full citizenship rights for women, politically as well as socially.[7]

By 1910, Irene Moorman also joined the ranks of suffragists, although, like many women, she maintained a broad political agenda. Not only did she serve as president of the Negro Women's Business League, but she was also an early and enthusiastic Garvey supporter. Moorman became president of the New York UNIA Ladies' Division in 1917. At first Moorman doubted that white America would grant black women full political rights, especially given the devastating effects Jim Crow laws and vigilante violence had had on black men's right to vote in the South. But she was persuaded enough by a conversation she had with Alva Belmont, prominent white socialite and founder of the Political Equality League, that she organized a suffrage meeting at the Mount Olivet Baptist Church on West Fifty-Third Street in February 1910. Under Moorman's leadership, the meeting proved a success. That day more than one hundred women in the audience joined the Political Equality League and harnessed their energy to the suffrage fight.[8]

Historically, black women, like white women, had been denied the full rights of citizenship. But black women had a considerable set of challenges to contend with that white women did not. African Americans' physical safety was jeopardized when white people's racism boiled over into violent, riotous rage, as it did in Manhattan in 1863 and again in 1900. Their access to jobs, education, and decent housing was circumscribed by ideological color lines and restrictive covenants. Time and again, Moorman's and many other black women's skepticism about their attainment of real political power in New York and in cities across the North proved justified. A year after the Mount Olivet Baptist Church meeting, the *New York Times* reminded New Yorkers just how alive and well Jim Crow was in their city. When Harriet Alice Dewey, a white woman and wife of philosopher John Dewey, wanted to host an interracial suffrage meeting in her uptown apartment, the building owners demanded she cancel it, emphasizing that the problem was black women's attendance.[9]

Most often, however, black women met resistance from white women themselves rather than from outside obstacles. As historian Rosalyn Terborg-Penn notes, even Belmont, who helped fund suffrage offices in black neighborhoods in New York, evinced racism. A Southerner by birth, she also gave money to the Southern Woman Suffrage Conference, which fought a federal suffrage amendment because it would enfranchise Southern black women.[10] Racism proved there was no such thing as sisterhood, but black women remained committed to women's enfranchisement and were cautiously willing to work with white women nonetheless.

New Yorkers first voted for a women's suffrage amendment in 1915. In anticipation of the election, black women, like white women, escalated their efforts. Lyda Newman opened the Negro Suffrage Headquarters in Manhattan as part of the coordinated effort with the New York Woman Suffrage Party. Not only did she encourage neighborhood mothers to get involved by providing childcare, but she also canvassed the district and organized street meetings to educate the community about women's suffrage. New Yorkers voted down the amendment in 1915, but suffragists made sure it was on the ballot again in 1917.[11]

Annie K. Lewis, president of the Colored Women's Suffrage Club of New York City, led the final push in Harlem. Yet even as the state's historic vote loomed, black women questioned their status in the suffrage movement in relation to white women. Tensions boiled over weeks before the 1917 election when Mary Sharperson Young, a Colored Women's Suffrage Club member and later leader in the UNIA, charged that she had been discriminated against during the statewide suffrage convention in Saratoga. Lewis called a meeting of the Colored Women's Club to discuss the matter and invited white suffrage leaders Anne Watkins and Annie Matthews to attend.[12] The meeting lasted well past midnight and generated a great deal of debate. Annie Lewis and Helen Christian, both of whom had also been at the Saratoga convention, disputed Young's interpretation of the event, arguing that black women had received equal treatment to white women. Others at the Harlem meeting, including a woman referred to in the meeting minutes only as "Mrs. Goode," shared Young's perspective of black women's lack of equal status. Goode sparked "quite a verbal battle" when she argued that black women should form an independent suffrage organization rather than work through the New York City Woman Suffrage Party. Lewis tried to silence Goode, arguing that she was not a member of the Colored Women's Suffrage Club and therefore not entitled to speak at the meeting. She and Christian wanted to maintain a positive relationship with the white leadership of the New York State Woman Suffrage Party. Interracialism versus black separatism was one of many ideological fault lines that divided black women and men at the same time that the commitment to racial equality united them. As a UNIA member with a strong sense of race pride, Young may have been more willing to forsake niceties to expose racist undercurrents.[13] Young's and Goode's advocacy of separatism did not prevail in this debate, however. By the meeting's end, the majority of participants concluded that black women's status was equal to white women's status in the New York suffrage organization, and they left with a rousing suffrage speech by Harlem's Helen Holman, a Colored Women's Club member and a Socialist, ringing in their ears.[14]

For black women who pursued leadership roles, especially those whose leadership took them face to face with white-led organizations, certain lessons were clear by the 1910s. The first lesson that all American women had to contend with was that at its root, public citizenship was a masculine domain. The Tammany Tiger had been against the enfranchisement of women for years. For example, when a group of white women initially asked Tammany favorite son Assemblyman Al Smith to support women's suffrage, he "shot a stream of tobacco juice at a spittoon and told them that as far as he was concerned a woman's place was at home."[15] In pursuing the franchise, women were hammering away at one of the foundations of male privilege and power, and men were determined to give as little ground as possible. Though hardly new, the second lesson was similarly challenging. White women could not be counted on to stand with black women in the struggle against racism or racialized gender discrimination that black women alone faced.[16] If black women wanted to engage in politics, they would have to wear an emotional coat of armor to fend off outward attacks and more subtle but equally pernicious slights from hostile men, black and white, and from white women.

The third lesson posed a distinct dilemma. Discord among African American women, it was increasingly clear, was draining but often unavoidable. Black women held diverse ideological positions, competed over strategies, and suffered from class tensions. Annie Lewis, for instance, faced criticism from black women outside the Colored Women's Suffrage Club. Her opponents argued, according to the *New York Age*, that Lewis was "not generally known as an educated woman," implying that she was unfit to lead the crusade in Harlem.[17] Moreover, Goode and Young had questioned her suffrage strategies and willingness to work with white women whose commitment to racial equality was thin or nonexistent. Gender, race, class, and ideological issues individually, and as interconnected dynamics, created daunting challenges to black women. The situation was familiar though disheartening. Their growing numbers and impending enfranchisement may have positioned them one big step closer to the levers of political power, but they understood there was much more terrain to cover before they garnered any real capacity to make lasting, structural changes.

At times working across the color line, but more often in separate organizations, suffragists ultimately attained their goal. The Republican-controlled legislature in Albany sent the suffrage amendment to the voters again. In addition to the women's steady efforts, a combination of forces gave the amendment a strong boost between the failed vote in 1915 and the successful vote in 1917. Although the national Democratic and Republican parties were unsupportive of the vote for women, the progressive reform spirit ran high in New York City. Activists had worked assiduously to wear down the resistance of the New York State legislature and that of male voters, especially during the 1910s.[18] In addition, in 1917 the Socialist Party fielded a number of successful candidates for the state assembly and a competitive candidate for mayor. It also actively supported women's suffrage.[19] Finally, although Tammany Hall was nothing if not a man's world, some of its leaders appreciated not only the momentum behind the suffrage amendment but also the possibility of capitalizing on new voters. In a demonstration of Murphy's strategic leadership, it was the vote in New York City—Tammany's stronghold—that gave the suffrage amendment its significant margin of victory.[20] With the amendment's passage, more than a million women in New York were enfranchised.

### Citizenship Education for Women

Immediately after women's suffrage became law, voter education campaigns proliferated. The *New York Times* ran a series titled "The Woman Voter," which detailed numerous aspects of New York City politics, including the function of primary elections and party leaders. The series also explained how political power was determined.[21] The *New York Age* noted that "Colored women . . . have begun to form clubs and are talking politics with zest and enthusiasm." On the eve of the first presidential election after the Nineteenth Amendment's ratification, the editors of the *Age* urged women to "learn all the preliminary steps to voting and to get the practice of marking a ballot." At the same time, they displayed their skepticism that women were fully ready to take on the franchise and argued that "there is no reason why they should not permit men to assist them in it."[22] Women continued to face paternalism and resistance long after they won the vote. Getting the majority of the press to take them seriously as political actors would prove to be a significant and intractable challenge. But that did not keep Harlem's women from moving forward. The YWCA hosted forums on "preparation for citizenship" and the NAACP urged women to learn all about the government and election laws in order to advance the race. *The Crisis*, its monthly publication, contended, "They may beat and bribe our men, but the political hope of the Negro rests on its intelligent and incorruptible womanhood." Though a heavy and intensely gendered burden, black women stood ready to respond.[23]

The significant shifts in the electoral demography that resulted from the Great Migration and women's suffrage posed unprecedented challenges and opportunities to party operatives across New York City. The political culture was both racialized as white and deeply masculine. Tammany Hall had its work cut out if it wanted to attract these untested constituents rather than concede them to the more reform-minded and ostensibly more supportive Republican Party.[24] At the same time, these new voters had to learn the political ropes. They had to determine how and when to participate in formal politics; they also had to cultivate strategies that would not only land them inside party clubhouses but also give them a say in evolving political agendas. The challenges were numerous, and access to political parties and the halls of government, women learned quickly, did not equal power.

## Political Parties Respond

The varying degrees to which the Democrats, Republicans, and Socialists were willing to reconfigure their political structures in response to African Americans' and women's participation in electoral politics emerged over the next few years.[25] In 1918, the first election after women in New York won the right to vote, Tammany Hall courted African Americans and women. The groundwork it had laid with the UCD seemed to be paying off. After a successful stint in the state assembly, Al Smith sought the governorship. The NAACP gave Smith a glowing endorsement, noting that in Albany, Smith had "achieved a record for constructive and progressive legislation unsurpassed by any man."[26] Moreover, after 1917, when Edward A. Johnson, a Republican black man from Harlem, was elected to the New York State Assembly, Tammany began to run black men for the office.[27]

At the same time, in early 1918 a group of men and women formed the Independent Citizens' Committee for Alfred E. Smith. Among them were prominent white progressive reformers Belle Moskowitz and Frances Perkins, who had worked with Smith on safety legislation in the aftermath of the Triangle Shirtwaist fire, and suffragist Harriot Stanton Blatch.[28] Most politicians expected that women would vote as a bloc; Smith was no different. To win women's votes, Smith asked Moskowitz to set up a special Women's Division and advise him about how to speak to women's groups.[29] As a result of Tammany's foundational work courting black men's votes and Smith's cultivation of women's votes (there is no evidence he made overtures to black women specifically), he was elected governor of New York in November 1918.[30] Tammany was back on top in the city and in the state capital in Albany.

Tammany's outreach efforts through the UCD and the Women's Division were typical vote-getting approaches. It simultaneously pursued a second, novel strategy. The Tiger wanted to determine if it could win more women's votes if it ran female candidates, so it fielded a white female candidate in the 1918 election. It was only curious to a point, however. The Democrats ran Mary Lilly in a solidly Republican assembly district in Manhattan against Allen Ellenbogen, the Republican incumbent. Their political curiosity was not so strong as to risk a safe Democratic seat. A progressive reformer, Lilly showed her mettle, beating both Ellenbogen and the Socialist candidate, Robert Vogel, by a few hundred votes. One of the first two women elected to office in New York, Lilly headed to the state capital in Albany to represent the Seventh Assembly District.[31]

The Republicans also competed for African Americans' and women's votes. In 1917 they began to run black men for elected office in predominantly African American districts, and black men won. At the same time nearly seventy-five thousand black women were enfranchised in 1917, a sizable constituency that the party fought to hold. The GOP chose four African American women to serve as delegates and alternates for the New York State Republican convention. This was hardly a radical step, but it created the opportunity for black women officially to weigh in on the party's platform for the first time. Moreover, in the 1920 presidential campaign, the first after the Nineteenth Amendment's passage, Warren Harding made more of an effort to secure black voters in the North than most Republican candidates had in recent elections, and this effort included targeting black women. The party also wanted to secure white women's votes. As part of its strategy, it set up women's divisions at all levels to court the anticipated women's voting bloc, and party bosses selected New York City suffrage leader Mary Garrett Hay, a white woman, to chair the platform committee.[32]

The Republicans wanted also to see how African American and female candidates fared as candidates. The Nineteenth Assembly District was in the heart of Harlem. In 1917, the GOP fought to retain black men in the party by running an African American for office. They fielded Edward A. Johnson, former dean of Shaw University's law school, for the seat. Upon his victory, Johnson became the first black man elected to office in the state of New York. Johnson won with substantial African American support, but he also won at least some white support. A year later, Democratic challenger and Tammany operative Martin J. Healy, a white man, defeated both Johnson in his reelection bid and Socialist Party candidate and labor leader A. Philip Randolph. That the two black men held competing political views helped divide the black vote. But so did the controversial issue of prohibition. Johnson supported it. That may have helped him win over black women who worried about temperance, a central element of their racial uplift strategy. The majority of voters, however, preferred the anti-prohibition candidate, Healy. The extent to which voters, now including thousands of black women, made their decisions based on race or prohibition is impossible to measure, but Healy's victory was narrower than the racial divide, indicating that he won some African Americans' votes.[33] Prohibition may well have been the deciding factor.

Republicans in Manhattan wanted to test the new voters' electoral proclivities further. The Long Island GOP ran a successful female candidate for the State Assembly in the 1918 election. Ida Sammis, a white woman from Suffolk County, served in Albany with Mary Lilly. A year later Harlem Republicans put Marguerite Smith, a white woman, up for office for the Nineteenth Assembly District against the incumbent, Martin Healy. Prior to the primary, the Nineteenth Assembly Republican club negotiated a deal with the local leadership to run a black man for the board of aldermen and a white woman, Smith, for state assembly in an effort to capitalize on both black and female voters. Harlem residents unhappy with the party's strategy, however, wanted African American candidates to run for both, so Rev. R. M. Bolden, a black man from the district, was tapped to run against Smith in the primary election in a direct challenge to the party's wishes.[34] But with strong party backing and the *New York Age*'s endorsement, Smith defeated Bolden in a heated race and headed to the general election, where she also beat Healy. Tammany took a drubbing during the 1919 elections, and Smith was one of many Republicans that year who benefited from its temporary decline.

Because Tammany's losses included its only female assemblywoman, Mary Lilly, Smith's cohort of women in the legislature remained tiny.

In sum, the Democrats and Republicans tried to capitalize on the new constituents flooding the voter rolls in the late 1910s. To win women's support they made small changes to the party structures and ran a handful of white women for the assembly. Fighting to secure black women's votes, the Republicans also selected African American women to represent their districts at the state and national party conventions. The success of even these modest gestures had important lessons to convey to the political parties—namely, that women were not only eager to participate in party politics, but they could win. Nevertheless, these lessons were willfully lost on both the Democrats and the Republicans. Lilly's and Smith's victories and the other work women did for the parties failed to change Democratic or Republican leaders' behavior toward women in any lasting or substantial way. The parties were more attentive to the lessons they learned about running black men for office. At least in predominantly African American districts, after 1917 the Democrats and Republicans fielded black male candidates for office on a fairly consistent basis. The racialized white nature of party politics changed more than its gendered masculine dimensions. For the black women who had shown their commitment to electoral politics and may have wanted to run for office, the interconnected dynamics of racism and gender discrimination kept them off the political parties' radar screens almost completely. No black women got the chance to show either Democrats or Republicans how they would fare at the polls because throughout the 1920s, neither party ran them for office. Resilient in the face of adversity and discrimination, black women pushed forward nonetheless, determined to make a space for themselves in the political arena and to have a say in the social, political, and economic landscapes of Harlem and Brooklyn.

African American men and women as well as white women looking for a more inclusive political home found it in the Socialist Party.[35] Not only had the party actively backed women's suffrage, but between 1917 and 1921, when Socialists in New York had representative presence in both city and state legislatures, they ran a significant number of African American and female candidates, including Grace Campbell, a black woman and head of the Harlem Negro Settlement House. Campbell ran for office at least twice. She ran unsuccessfully for the Twenty-First State Assembly District seat in 1919. The following year, Campbell challenged incumbent Marguerite Smith for the Nineteenth Assembly District seat.[36] Again she lost. Neither Campbell nor any of the other Socialist Party candidates, including the labor leader A. Philip Randolph, received positive coverage in black newspapers like the *New York Age*, which had a staunchly Republican editorial board. Campbell may have been the first African American woman to run for elected office in New York City, but because of her leftist political affiliation and the indifference the press had about women in politics, this historic marker passed without comment from the city's largest black newspaper.[37]

In the years following World War I and the Russian Revolution of 1917, an oppressive climate of intolerance settled upon the nation. Anti-immigrant advocates began a vigorous campaign to close the nation's gateways. In 1921 and even more robustly in 1924 Congress answered their call with a pair of laws that dramatically reduced the number of Europeans allowed into the country. In the wake of an unprecedented strike wave in 1919, labor unions and striking workers, including the Industrial Workers of the World (IWW) and the Boston police, were violently repressed. United States Attorney General A. Mitchell Palmer ordered the raids of radical organizations and labor unions. Over five thousand people were caught up in the dragnet. Anarchist activist Emma Goldman was deported; Socialist labor leader and five-time presidential candidate Eugene Debs was jailed. A near toxic Red Scare spread across the country.

The New York State Assembly was not spared from the witch hunt. In 1920, five state assembly members who had won their elections on the Socialist Party ticket were barred from taking their seats in the state house.[38] Suspicion ran so high that the state assembly passed a bill by a wide margin excluding the Socialist Party from participation in future elections. It was only Governor Smith's veto that kept the bill from becoming law.[39] The repressive environment did not keep Socialist candidates from trying to win elections, however. In addition to Campbell, a number of African Americans and women ran for city, state, and national office, including A. Philip Randolph and Harriot Stanton Blatch. But in the hostile climate, Socialists fared poorly at the polls. More so than the two major parties, third parties remained more supportive of those who had been historically marginalized, especially African American and female candidates; however, they did not lead women to electoral victories.[40] If women were going to win, it would be with the less welcoming Democratic and Republican parties.

In assessing the elections in the late 1910s, it is impossible to definitively identify why voters made the decisions they did. Their affinities with or concerns about candidates' racial or gendered identities likely played a contributing role in how people voted. African American candidates did well in predominantly black districts. Yet if black voters had cared only about racial solidarity, then Johnson would have held their loyalties in his reelection bid against Healy, and Bolden could have defeated Marguerite Smith in the primary campaign. Similarly, Grace Campbell could have beaten or at least seriously challenged Marguerite Smith and the white Democratic candidate. But political ideology was also an important factor in people's voting behavior. New Yorkers generally, and Harlemites particularly, did not support Socialist candidates, especially after 1919. Even Campbell's longstanding and respected community activism did not help her win over large numbers of black voters. At the same time, the gendered culture of clubhouse politics and the "gendered imagination" of the society in which they lived undermined women in electoral politics.[41] Even though organizations like Tammany made room for a handful of powerful white women, men continued to dominate national and state party conventions, clubhouse politics, and campaign slates. Mary Lilly and Marguerite Smith were the only women from New York City elected to the state assembly between 1918 and 1933.[42] During the same period, in contrast, black men not only ran for the state assembly and board of aldermen regularly, but more than a handful won.

While the vote was a significant step for the advancement of women's citizenship rights, it was clear that the Democrats and Republicans had no intentions of running black women for office. After Campbell's failed campaigns black women did not appear on party ballots for more than a decade. Instead, they worked in the limited ways they could to compel the parties, over time, to take them seriously as political actors and to pay attention to the issues they raised. These were very much uphill struggles. As the new decade dawned and the Progressive Era drew to a close with Warren Harding's presidential election, black women employed a variety of political strategies to make advances for their communities and themselves.

### Notes

1. Terborg-Penn, *African American Women*, chapter 3.

2. Terborg-Penn, *African American Women*, 40.

3. Nell Irvine Painter,"Voices of Suffrage: Sojourner Truth, Frances Watkins Harper, and the Struggle for Woman Suffrage," in *Votes for Women: The Struggle for Suffrage Revisited*, ed. Jean Baker, 42–55 (New York: Oxford University Press, 2002).

4. Ellen Carol DuBois, *Harriot Stanton Blatch and the Winning of Woman Suffrage* (New Haven, Conn.: Yale University Press, 1997), 186–87.

5. Terborg-Penn, *African American Women*; Marjorie Julian Spruill, "Race, Reform, and Reaction at the Turn of the Century," in *Votes for Women*, ed. Marjorie Spruill Wheeler, 102–17 (Knoxville: University of Tennessee Press, 1995); Rebecca Edwards, *Angels in the Machinery: Gender in American Party Politics from the Civil War to the Progressive Era* (New York: Oxford University Press, 1997), 142–44.

6. See Materson; Tera Hunter, *To 'Joy My Freedom: Southern Black Women's Lives and Labors After the Civil War* (Cambridge, Mass.: Harvard University Press, 1997), 32–33; Elsa Barkley Brown, "To Catch the Vision of Freedom: Reconstructing Southern Black Women's Political History, 1865–1880," in *African American Women and the Vote, 1837–1965*, ed. Ann Gordon et al., 66–99 (Amherst: University of Massachusetts Press, 1997); White, 40–41, 49–50; Anne Meis Knupfer, *Toward a Tenderer Humanity* (New York: New York University Press, 1996), chapter 3.

7. Hallie Q. Brown, *Homespun Heroines and Other Women of Distinction* (New York: Oxford University Press, 1988, [1926]), 115; Charles Harris Wesley, *The History of the National Association of Colored Women's Clubs, A Legacy of Service* (Washington, D.C.: NACW, 1984), 77; Karen Garner, "Equal Suffrage League," in *Organizing Black America*, ed. Nina Mjagkij, 224–25 (New York: Garland, 2001); Gerda Lerner, *The Majority Finds Its Past* (New York: Oxford University Press, 1979), 86; Terborg-Penn, *African American Women*, 87, 94–95; Gordon et al., *African American Women*.

8. *New York Times*, February 7, 1910; Terborg-Penn, *African American Women*, 100–102.

9. *New York Times*, February 25, 1911. See also Osofsky, chapter 8.

10. Terborg-Penn, *African American Women*, 101.

11. *New York Times*, August 29, 1915; September 2, 1915.

12. *New York Age*, September 20, 1917; September 27, 1917; October 4, 1917; November 1, 1917; Robert Hill, ed., *Marcus Garvey and UNIA Papers* (Berkeley: University of California Press, 1986), vol. 1, 224–25; vol. 3, 698, 700; vol. 4, 941; vol. 5, 785, 834; Terborg-Penn, *African American Women*, 87, 92, 100–101. Anne Watkins was the daughter of Luke Edward Wright of Tennessee, former Confederate general, U.S. Ambassador to Japan from 1906 to 1907, and Secretary of War from 1908 to 1909. She was married to John Humphrey Watkins, former railroad president and Wall Street bond dealer. Available at http://www.tngenweb.org/giles/history/bios/wright.htm (accessed August 31, 2011); *New York Times*, September 21, 1909.

13. *New York Age*, September 27, 1917.

14. *New York Age*, September 20, 1917; *Negro World*, February 24, 1923; Barbara Bair, "'Ethiopia Shall Stretch Forth Her Hands unto God': Laura Kofey and the Gendered Vision of Redemption in the Garvey Movement," in *A Mighty Baptism: Race, Gender, and the Creation of American Protestantism*, ed. Susan

Lester and Lisa MacFarlane, 59 (Ithaca, New York: Cornell University Press, 1996).

15. Elisabeth Israels Perry, *Belle Moskowitz: Feminine Politics and the Exercise of Power in the Age of Alfred E. Smith* (Boston: Northeastern University Press, 2000 [1992]), 114.

16. Aileen Kraditor, *The Ideas of the Woman Suffrage Movement, 1890–1920* (New York: Norton, 1981 [1965]), chapter 7; Terborg-Penn, *African American Women*, chapter 6; Evelyn Brooks Higginbotham, "In Politics to Stay: Black Women Leaders and Party Politics in the 1920s," in *Women, Politics and Change*, ed. Louise A. Tilly and Patricia Gurin, 200–201 (New York: Sage, 1990).

17. *New York Age*, September 27, 1917; November 1, 1917; November 22, 1917.

18. *New York Times*, February 7, 1910; September 2, 1915; April 29, 1917; October 28, 1917; November 5, 1917; Ida Hustead Harper, ed., *History of Woman Suffrage, 1900–1920*, vol. 5 (New York: Arno, 1969), DuBois, *Harriot Stanton Blatch*, chapters 5–7; Freeman, *A Room at a Time*, 60–61; Kristi Andersen, *After Suffrage: Women in Partisan and Electoral Politics before the New Deal* (Chicago: University of Chicago Press, 1996), 77.

19. *New York Times*, November 7, 1917; November 8, 1917. The Socialists won ten seats in the state assembly, an increase of eight from the prior election. Moreover, although Morris Hillquit, the Socialist Party candidate for mayor, came in third behind the victorious Democrat John Hylan and Fusion candidate and incumbent John Purroy Mitchell, he beat the Republican Party candidate Bennett. Election totals were: Hylan, 293,386; Mitchell, 148,060; Hillquit, 138,793; and Bennett, 52,828.

20. *New York Times*, November 8, 1917; November 27, 1917. New York City gave the suffrage amendment a majority of 92,696. The amendment was defeated by 3,856 votes in the rest of the state. Eleanor Flexner, *Century of Struggle: The Woman's Rights Movement in the United States* (New York: Atheneum, 1972 [1959]), 290.

21. *New York Times*, January 6, 1918; January 7, 1918; January 8, 1918.

22. *New York Age*, November 22, 1917; September 18, 1920.

23. *The Crisis*, March 1920, 234. See also Judith Weisenfeld, *African American Women and Christian Activism: New York's Black YWCA, 1905–1945* (Cambridge, Mass.: Harvard University Press, 1997), 178; Higginbotham, "In Politics to Stay"; Terborg-Penn, *African American Women*, chapter 7.

24. Freeman, *A Room at a Time*, 108; Gustafson, *Women*, 3; Higginbotham, "In Politics to Stay," 206–7; Terborg-Penn, *African American Women*, 103–4.

25. *New York Times*, January 18, 1918; February 22, 1918; March 1, 1918; May 19, 1918; August 7, 1919; October 26, 1920. The minutes of the Brooklyn Democratic Party reveal that they began to include women in the Executive County Committee in September 1922 and continued to have women at both the county committee level and executive committee level thereafter. Brooklyn Democratic

Party Papers, series I, box 3, Brooklyn College Special Collections. Andersen, 80–81; Freeman, *A Room at a Time*, chapter 6.

26. *The Crisis*, November 1918, 45. See also Sherman, 133, for mention of Democrats' success in local elections in New York City.

27. Lewinson, 59; Osofosky, 169–74.

28. Matthew Josephson and Hannah Josephson, *Al Smith: Hero of the Cities* (Boston: Houghton Mifflin, 1969), 194; Perry, *Belle Moskowitz*, 117.

29. Perry, *Belle Moskowitz*, 117–18.

30. "A Dozen Reasons Why Women Should Vote for Alfred E. Smith," campaign literature, Brooklyn Democratic Party Campaign Materials, 1898–1927, Metropolitan New York Library Council Digital Collections, available at http://cdm128401.cdmhost.com/cdm/search/collection/bc; Allen, 228; Perry, *Belle Moskowitz*, 168–83; Josephson and Josephson, 197, 287–88; Lewinson, 59.

31. *New York Times*, November 7, 1918. Lilly won 7,572 to Ellenbogen's 7,388 and Vogel's 432 votes.

32. *The Crisis*, September 1918, 240; Lewinson, 63; Sherman, 138; Terborg-Penn, *African American Women*, 142; Elisabeth Israels Perry, "Defying the Party Whip: Mary Garrett Hay and the Republican Party, 1917–1920," in Gustafson, Miller, and Perry, 97–107.

33. *New York Times*, November 8, 1917; November 7, 1918; Lewinson, 59. Healy won 6,977 votes to Johnson's 5,557 and Randolph's 1,078. Healy's plurality over the two men together was just 342 votes.

34. *New York Age*, August 30, 1919; September 6, 1919; *New York Times*, September 2, 1919; September 3, 1919.

35. *Marcus Garvey Papers*, vol. 1, 222; *New York Times*, November 7, 1918; October 26, 1920; October 1, 1922.

36. *New York Times*, November 8, 1917; November 6, 1918; November 7, 1918; August 7, 1919; July 5, 1920; November 3, 1920; July 11, 1921; October 1, 1922.

37. *New York Age*, August 19, 1919; July 10, 1920; September 18, 1920; reviewed *New York Age*, 1919–1920 for references to Grace Campbell.

38. *New York Times*, January 8, 1920; April 2, 1920.

39. *New York Times*, April 21, 1920; May 20, 1929.

40. Among others, A. Philip Randolph, Chandler Owens, Fannie Jacobs, and Mary McVicker ran for the state assembly; Fanny Witherspoon and Pauline Newman ran for Congress. *New York Times*, November 7, 1918; October 26, 1920; November 10, 1921; October 1, 1922; DuBois, *Harriet Stanton Blatch*, 229; *Marcus Garvey Papers*, vol. 1, 222.

41. Andersen, 80–102; Freeman, *A Room at a Time*, 23–24. For a discussion of the "gendered imagination," see Kessler-Harris, *In Pursuit of Equity*.

42. Helene Weinstein, *Lawmakers: Biographical Sketches of the Women of the NYS Legislature (1918–1988)* (Albany, N.Y.: Legislative Women's Caucus, 1989).

# 8

# NEW WOMEN

## NANCY A. HEWITT

From *Southern Discomfort:*
*Women's Activism in Tampa, Florida 1880s-1920s,*
by Nancy A. Hewitt (2001)

On November 10, 1916, women tobacco stemmers from the Lozano and Sidelo Cigar Company walked out, demanding higher wages. They marched to other factories, calling out the workers, and by nightfall some 1,500 cigar makers had left their benches, and another 8,500 threatened to join them. The spontaneity and militancy of the movement was recognized as the work of women. Celestino Vega, the factory owner, sought "protection" for his male rollers when they were accosted by a "disorderly mob of strikers" who "rushed into the factory deriding and hooting workers.... women, leading the mob, called the men at work 'females' and offered their skirts to those who refused to quit." The actual term used by the women wildcatters was reported in Havana's *La Lucha* as "*afeminadas,*" suggesting that the men were feminine, or even effeminate, rather than that they were women.[1] Though Mayor D. B. McKay was probably unaware of the nuances of the insult, he assured Vega that police would be on hand the next day to secure the premises and protect the male rollers.[2]

Factory owners and city officials were not alone in opposing this strike. The male leaders of the local Cigar Makers' International Union (CMIU) derided the wildcat venture from the beginning and, even though some men joined the strike, accused the women of responding to "blind enthusiasm." The editor of *El Internacional* queried his readers, "May a man now say what he thinks without exposing himself to the dangers of being insulted by his female comrades who offer him their skirts?" The strike was soon settled, though the greatest benefits went to the cigar rollers (mostly men) rather than to the stemmers (all women) who had initiated the action.[3]

If the 1916 walkout had stood alone, it might be considered just a colorful anecdote, but it marked a turning point in women's public and political roles in the Latin community. In the 1901 and 1910 strikes, Cuban and Italian women had become politically active—petitioning the governor and the Anglo wives of vigilantes, marching on the mayor's office, attacking strikebreakers, and honoring heroic women through manifestos—but they had justified their actions largely in the language of class solidarity and maternal protection. By 1916, following Luisa Capetillo's visit, the proclamations of such socialist organizers as Adele Kossovsky and Elizabeth Gurley Flynn, the maturation of a generation of U.S.-born Latin women, and the expansion of women's employment in the cigar industry, women wildcatters chose sexual ridicule over labor solidarity and maternal rhetoric. Although the 1916 walkout failed to achieve its goals, over the next decade, the rising tide of women in the cigar labor force became increasingly critical to union success, and class and ethnic identities became increasingly infused with gender.

Latin women were not alone in their newfound sense of importance to public and political action. In the weeks before the wildcat strike, Anglo women launched a campaign on behalf of a woman school board candidate—Alice Snow—who ran in District 2, which included Ybor City.[4] A year earlier, the Florida legislature had passed the Municipal Reform Act, allowing municipalities to set their own rules on a number of electoral matters.[5] Neighboring cities, including St. Petersburg, instituted municipal suffrage for women; Tampa did not, so women remained dependent on male voters to make their case. Still, they insisted on running a woman candidate and learned a valuable lesson: Alice Snow lost to the Reverend Irwin Walden by only fifteen votes out of nearly four thousand cast, the margin of defeat provided by a set of contested ballots from Ybor City's Twenty-sixth Precinct.[6] Again, women acting independent of men failed to achieve their goal, but this failure, too, inspired women to demand additional rights based on sex.

The urge to organize around women's issues and concerns also intensified for African American women during this period, as their significance in community efforts expanded. The Tampa School of the Household Arts served as one base for such efforts, but even more important was a new array of women's clubs and women's institutions, including the Willing Workers, the Busy Merry Makers, the Mary Talbert

Club, and the Helping Hand Day Nursery. It was in the context of this profusion of single-sex organizing that women joined the effort to regain Black voting rights.

African American women, however, did not follow the lead of their Latin and Anglo counterparts in directly challenging the power and authority of men in their community. Rather, they continued to pursue common agendas in both mixed-sex and single-sex movements throughout the 1910s and 1920s. Now, however, women wielded skills honed in single-sex associations to ensure a critical place for themselves in wider efforts at community advancement. In fall 1920, for instance, they organized with men against a city charter "reform" that would further limit the electoral clout of African American and immigrant neighborhoods. Coming just after the federal woman suffrage amendment was ratified, Black women also used the occasion to launch a voter registration drive, insisting that the new law be implemented in racially inclusive ways.

These bursts of woman-centered activism in the late 1910s and early 1920s made many men take notice and made some, especially Anglo male civic leaders, wary of furthering women's formal political clout. The recognition of women's heightened influence occurred in a period when men were already anxious about female autonomy. On the very day of the wildcat walkout in November 1916, for instance, the *Tampa Morning Tribune* ran an article on women leading public prayers at a national woman suffrage convention, a practice the reporter considered "a rather new departure." That same week, Tampa's Wesleyan Baraca Club was debating the resolution, "That money has a greater influence on men than woman has," indicating that an organization once dedicated to prayer and missionary work had now turned its attention to more secular and gendered concerns. The *Ragged Princess*, showing at one local movie house that week, told the story of a poor orphan girl capturing the heart, and hand in marriage, of a wealthy man through her beauty and charm, while *Fifty-Fifty*, offered at another theater, presented a vampish Norma Talmadge in a tale of marriage, adultery, and intrigue. The *Tribune*, meanwhile, ran a feature story entitled "America a Market for Chinese Slave Women," which provided Sunday readers with lurid details about prostitution, slavery, and the sale of wives. A report in the same issue noted that the most fashionable evening clothes for women now featured "diaphanous hems" that only lightly veiled the ankles.[7]

Women's actions and the images conveyed in public debates, films, newspaper reports, and advertisements suggested the new opportunities available to women and the anxieties haunting men.[8] Despite the tendency of the national media and many historians to focus solely on the emergence of the "New Woman" in northeastern cities, Tampa residents knew that transformations in gender expectations and experiences also affected Black, Latin, and Anglo women in their hometown.

After 1915, Tampa women pursued public power in increasingly vocal ways and advocated agendas that took sex seriously. Collectively, they demonstrated a new sophistication regarding political action that drew on a range of resources—the Latin heritage of labor militancy, northern models of social housekeeping, the social gospel, racial pride, African American and Latin traditions of self-help and mutual aid, and ideals of the "New Woman." While the passage of the Nineteenth Amendment certainly reinforced this trajectory for some women in Tampa, the dynamics of sexual politics in Latin, African American, and Anglo communities were changing well before its ratification. The issues and timing varied, but in each case, a shift in the balance of public power between women and men occurred before women gained voting rights and proved significant even when the vote failed as an effective vehicle for implementing change.

Many Anglo and African American women eagerly embraced their newly won political rights in 1920. African American women in the South were soon disfranchised, however, which meant that once again they would follow paths traced out by earlier generations of Black women. Latin women, too, worked largely outside electoral politics. But they remained committed to workplace organizing as the most potent weapon in their arsenal, whereas African Americans pursued economic autonomy and community advancement through voluntary associations, church-based organizations, and schools.

Whether or not they wielded the power of the franchise, African American, Latin, and Anglo women each organized more frequently as women and around women's issues in the late 1910s and 1920s. At the same time, they joined mixed-sex associations in greater numbers than ever before, gaining leverage there through the benefits achieved by single-sex organizing. Despite women's increased participation in single-sex and mixed-sex organizations and in campaigns to advance the cause of women and various class, race, and ethnic communities, the fault lines of Tampa activism did not disappear. In some ways, the expansion of women's efforts and organizations actually highlighted differences among Latin, African American, and Anglo communities.

～ ～

National and international developments continued to shape women's activism in Tampa. The war that erupted in Europe in 1914, for example, justified women's entry into explicitly political arenas and reinforced the connections between family responsibilities and worldly affairs. By 1916, African American and Anglo women were actively demonstrating their administrative, professional, and domestic contributions to military success through local branches of the American Red Cross, the YWCA, canning clubs, hospital committees, and other organizations tied to the wartime emergency.

Debates over whether the war would encourage or hinder racial advancement reappeared, echoing the situation in 1898. This time Tampa's African American leaders supported the war effort, a position reflected in their 1916 invitation to W. E. B. Du Bois to serve as the featured speaker at the South Florida Fair's first "Negro Day." Du Bois argued that Blacks should "close ranks" to support the war despite continued discrimination at home. Before his speech at the fairgrounds, Du Bois visited the exhibits arranged by the Negro Fair Committee, composed of Emma Bryant, Christina Meacham, George Middleton, the Reverend Andrew J. Ferrell, Dr. J. A. White, Edwin J. Moore, and other local race leaders, and participated in the parade it had organized.[9] The carefully planned floats offered an ambiguous portrait of African American history and politics in an attempt to foster pride in Black participants without offending white spectators. One float, "The Negro's Fidelity in the 1860s," depicted a slave protecting a plantation mansion while his master fought for the Confederate cause. On another, "Tell Them We Are Rising," a boy stood on "a pedestal of agriculture, religion, and education" and unfurled an American flag. Student groups, marching bands, church and hospital organizations, men's and women's clubs and lodges, and autos and carriages carrying prominent Black citizens, including the guest speaker, rounded out the procession.[10]

The presence of Du Bois signaled local African Americans' sense of their place in the larger world. After Booker T. Washington's death in 1915, Du Bois filled the premiere place among "race men" in the United States. Although Washington's power to shape the dominant vision of racial advancement among African Americans had already begun to wane, many Black activists only embraced new approaches to race relations once they no longer had to fear Washington's disapproval. For white

Tampans, the replacement of Washington's vision with that of Du Bois may have generated some concern. As a founding member of the National Association for the Advancement of Colored People (NAACP), Du Bois embodied demands for race pride and racial equality that went far beyond his predecessor's accommodationist approach.[11] Yet the white press gave widespread coverage to the Black leader's visit and the events surrounding it and made only occasional disparaging remarks.[12]

On the day Du Bois appeared at the fair, his speech was nearly drowned out by the white crowd at a nearby racetrack. Despite the difficult conditions, Du Bois faced an eager audience. He declared that the war then raging in Europe "afforded the people of the colored race an opportunity to demonstrate their superiority," and he encouraged them to take full advantage of the situation to advance the interests of African American women and men. He received rousing applause and was honored that evening at a reception at the Odd Fellows Hall. He also met with leaders of the recently established West Tampa NAACP local, who had sought his advice the previous year.[13]

At the fair, the reception, and the NAACP meeting, Black women worked alongside men, making sure that their concerns were included in the larger community agenda. A year later, 107 African Americans formed the Tampa NAACP branch. Women, including the Afro-Bahamians Christina Meacham and Marion Rogers, were among the charter members. When the founding president, Daniel Perkins, enlisted in the army, Meacham and Dr. J. A. White carried on the work. Meacham sought to organize a silent protest march in Tampa, echoing the one sponsored by the national office to protest the anti-Black riot in East St. Louis in 1917. She also led a campaign to clean up a red light district located in one of the city's Black neighborhoods. Despite her efforts, the branch languished by the early 1920s.[14]

Like Perkins, many local African Americans threw themselves into war work to help the military effort abroad and to improve their standing at home. When the United States entered the war in 1917, women's clubs, churches, and schools joined Liberty Loan campaigns and supplied bandages, surgical dressings, clothing, and comfort bags for African American troops. Black women leaders also made certain that African American housewives had the knowledge and resources to contribute to wartime conservation efforts. Blanche Armwood, who relocated to New Orleans for most of 1917–19, promoted food conservation among southern Blacks throughout the war. As supervisor of home demonstration work in Louisiana, she gained state and federal sanction for her efforts. She also published a cookbook entitled *Food Conservation in the Home,* which, according to the National Association of Colored Women, was used by women of "both races" and was found in many Tampa homes.[15] The war fostered similar efforts in Tampa's Anglo community. Anglo women, too, rolled bandages, knit socks, sold war bonds, and contributed in a variety of ways to meet soldiers' needs. They also embraced government programs to conserve fuel, meat, and metal to increase the availability of items for military use.

The enlistment of hundreds of local men in 1917 intensified the activities of Tampa women. Even women's cultural clubs, such as the Students' Art Club, contributed by selling Liberty Bonds, advertising the federal Food Administration's potato campaign, publishing wheatless recipes in the local paper, promoting Red Cross Christmas seals, and contributing to the Women's War Relief fund. The Friday Morning Musicale offered similar support, buying as well as selling Liberty Bonds and contributing to the national Soldiers' Library and Women's War Relief. The members met daily in 1917 to roll bandages, knit socks and scarves, and prepare soldiers' comfort bags, which, unlike the WCTU version offered in 1898, contained tobacco and chewing gum as well as handkerchiefs, shoelaces, and writing tablets.[16]

The Tampa Civic Association joined the Friday Morning Musicale on food conservation and Liberty Loan drives, furnished speakers for Red Cross campaigns, donated funds to Near East relief and the children of Evian, France, and helped support recreation homes and medical dispensaries in France, a project directed by the General Federation of Women's Clubs. The Tampa Woman's Club also worked with the General Federation of Women's Clubs, filling a special request for jellies and marmalades for soldiers and hosting demonstration days to inspire local women to help the war effort by minimizing waste in their households.[17] Throughout the city, Red Cross auxiliaries brought clubwomen together in neighborhood groups, churches, and social clubs to produce the eight thousand surgical dressings the organization was committed to providing each month. By late 1917, meetings were scheduled on every afternoon and week night somewhere in the city.[18]

Anglo and African American women's solid support for the war was not replicated in the Latin enclaves. Although cigar unions did contribute to Liberty Loan campaigns, most working-class women and men focused their energies on labor organizing and other activities only tangentially related to the European conflict. For example, food cooperatives founded before the war increased their membership as inflation drove prices up, and Italian residents were much more generous with donations for re-building L'Unione Italiana's clubhouse, which burned down in 1917, than in supporting the U.S. war effort. Even the campaign to raise money for Italy's army floundered, gaining assistance from only a few wealthy immigrants, such as the cigar factory owner Val Antuono. Antuono's adamant support for the open shop guaranteed that few workers would follow his lead. Workers' antiwar sentiments were openly expressed in the Italian Socialist Federation and a variety of Italian- and Spanish-language newspapers as well as in anarchist and labor organizations. The Anglo press was convinced that Cuban men—"these husky young aliens"—were ignoring recruitment posters or returning to Havana to wait out the war free of pressures to enlist.[19] Latin women remained in Tampa, but they shared their countrymen's indifference or antagonism toward a war they viewed as fattening the pockets of capitalists instead of saving the world for democracy.

Whatever Tampa women's attitudes, World War I did not so much transform their activism as accentuate trends already evident. For in-stance, women's war work provided further justification for the establish-ment of single-sex associations among Black and Anglo women, quick-ened the movement of Latin women into the labor force, and fostered women's interest in national and international politics. The crises cre-ated by global conflict did not erase the divisions among women activ-ists, however. Instead, the wartime emergency intensified debates over women's proper place in their communities and in the larger society.

For African American women, the war crystallized efforts initiated ear-lier. In early 1917, graduates of the Tampa School of the Household Arts formed the first Black YWCA in Tampa, under the direction of Blanche Armwood. Its officers, all graduates of the school, dedicated themselves to the "interests of the working girls" and "mutual helpfulness." Since the leaders and members were working women—almost all were employed, and many were married—they met every other Sunday at the African American Odd Fellows Hall. The women who filled the positions of presi-dent, vice-president, corresponding and recording secretary, treasurer, and pianist in the new organization—Mrs. Lucy Hall, Mrs. Minnie Lorey, Mrs. Albertha Downing, Mrs. Anna Daniels, Mrs. Hattie Shingles, and Mrs. Bessie Johnson—had not been leaders in earlier organizations; but in January 1917, their names were published in the *Tampa Bulletin,* a local Black paper.[20] The African American YWCA survived for only two years, but it suggested the possibility for an expanded corps of leaders in the community.

Tampa's best-known Black woman activist was Blanche Armwood, who had organized and served as first president of the Colored Women's Clubs of Tampa in 1912. By the end of the decade, she had become a significant player in state, regional, and national organizations. Her very success, however, drew her away from Tampa and local concerns. She spent the war years in New Orleans, where she had been hired by municipal and gas company officials to establish a school for domestic servants and then to supervise home demonstration work. By 1920, she was traveling the country promoting candidates for the Republican party and woman suffrage for the National Association of Colored Women Clubs.[21]

As Armwood's absences from the city lengthened, the leadership of Black women's efforts shifted to teachers and businesswomen still rooted in the community. Mrs. Christina Meacham of the Harlem Academy; Mrs. Emma Mance from the West Tampa School; Mrs. Gertrude Chambers, Mrs. Lila B. Robinson, and Miss Annie House, all hairdressers; and Preston Murray, the wife of a prominent undertaker, were among the most active clubwomen in Tampa during the 1910s and 1920s. They eagerly embraced an African American version of the "New Woman" that emphasized cultural pride and civic activism, even as they remained concerned about the exploitation of southern Black women.[22]

The African American "New Woman," like her white counterpart, was encouraged to adopt new fashions in clothing, hair care, and cosmetics. Black beauticians in the city were especially active in combining innovative styles with racial advancement.[23] Rather than substitute fashion for activism, they used the profits offered by the former to fund the latter. By 1920, Chambers, Robinson, and House—all of whom worked in the same beauty shop—held leadership positions in several Black women's clubs. In the following years, they increased their involvement in these associations, joined in the establishment of the interracial and mixed-sex Urban League, and helped develop the first cooperative efforts with Afro-Cuban women in the city.

Latin women, too, combined work in mixed-sex associations focused on community advancement with activities in single-sex organizations that promoted women's interests. On the political front, Latin women and men raised funds to support the Russian Revolution, the Tom Mooney defense fund, the Joe Ettor and Arturo Giovannitti defense fund, and the

Nicola Sacco and Bartolomeo Vanzetti defense fund. They also joined efforts in some two dozen food and clothing cooperatives founded in the 1910s and held positions of leadership in some. Here, however, they often initiated their own projects. In 1915, Cuban and Italian housewives led the campaign against an ordinance that threatened to increase the price of bread; and in 1917, they sustained a potato, meat, and onion boycott.[24]

Despite cooperative community ventures, it became increasingly difficult for Latin working women to maintain their common ground with men on the factory floor. In March 1917, stemmers pleaded with their skilled male coworkers to join them in "improving the conditions of the stripping department." They conceded that this department was "a proper place for women of our people to earn their living," but they argued women would continue to compete with men for more skilled positions if their conditions and wages did not keep pace with those of the cigar makers. Claiming that "orphan girls, maids who fortunately or unfortunately have no male helper, widows with young children, the victims of divorce, the daughters of large families, the victims of vicious men or of sick or disabled men" constituted the bulk of this work force, the stemmers retreated from their earlier sexual innuendoes and called on Latin men to protect working women. At the same time, they implied that if men refused, competition between the sexes would be the consequence.[25]

Over the next two years, developments in the national industry further threatened labor solidarity among local Latins. First, the introduction of stemming machines lessened the need for hand workers and allowed "American girls"—that is native-born women with no experience—to enter the industry. Second, employers tried to substitute cans for boxes in cigarpacking, which again allowed unskilled workers, including women, to replace men in one of the industry's most highly coveted positions. When packed in boxes, owners demanded that the top row of cigars be of the same texture, leaf style, and color, which could be achieved only by highly skilled workers. When packed in cans, such aesthetic concerns and the skills they required were irrelevant. In 1919, in the midst of a national wave of postwar industrial strikes, cigar workers in Tampa walked out to protest both stemming machines and "girl" packers.[26]

What allowed Latin women and men to make common cause despite these structural changes was owners' interest in hiring "American girls" to pack cigar cans and operate stemming machines. In February 1919, stemmers and cigar makers walked out at the Samuel I. Davis, Argüelles,

López, and Celestino Vega factories in West Tampa after the owners installed stemming machines, which workers claimed would displace six to eight workers each. The issue, however, was not only mechanization but also the entrance of native-born white women as operators. Packers joined the struggle on behalf of their own issues, demanding that women packers serve the same apprenticeship as men and be paid the same wages, which would negate employers' interest in hiring them.[27]

The "American girls" who gained jobs in the cigar industry did not have a long history of labor activism behind them, but they did not accept their exclusion without a fight. They immediately sought the intervention of white civic leaders. A group of twenty-two machine tenders petitioned Tampa's mayor, D. B. McKay, noting that the "work is agreeable and we need the wages." "As residents of Tampa and American citizens," they claimed, "we are entitled to fair play." The native-born white women hired to operate the stemming machines shared much with their Latin counterparts; many were also orphaned, widowed, divorced, or daughters in large families. But the two groups rarely considered making common cause. Rather, "American girls" appealed to Anglo civic leaders and national values, while Latin women struck alongside union men.[28]

Women packers also called on Anglo civic leaders, including the American Legion and the city council as well as the mayor, but they turned to white working-class men as well, requesting a separate affiliation under the auspices of the American Federation of Labor (AFL) to counterbalance the power of the Latin-dominated CMIU packers. The men packers pointed out that their AFL charter eliminated the need and the possibility for a separate women's local. The men then struck those factories that allowed women to work without passing through the apprenticeship and the test of packing skills required by their charter. In this case, the factory owners backed down and accepted the terms of the Latin men, releasing the "American girls" they had once hoped would provide them leverage against the unions.[29]

Yet the story of Anglo women versus Latin workers was not quite as simple as it appeared in women's petitions and CMIU protests. The delegation of women packers that sought assistance from the American Legion and the group that petitioned the city council included a more diverse lot than suggested in either the English- or Spanish-language press. Several of the Anglo women had been employed in the cigar industry for some time but in jobs reserved for women. Myrtle Albritton, Rosa Hendrix, and Martha Gouch, for instance, worked as cigar banders before seeking employment as packers. Leila Barber, though new to the industry herself, shared a home with her sister, Fannie, who worked as a cigar trimmer. The conflict occurred, then, not because "American girls" sought work in a Latin industry but because they sought work as packers, a "man's" job. Similarly, Latin women protested native-born women working as machine operators not because they were native-born but because mechanization threatened to curtail work for women in general. Many Anglo civic leaders and factory owners, like Latin workers, assumed that native-born women sought these positions because they lacked any tradition of labor militancy. Yet the ethnic identities of several petitioners were more complicated than the term "American girls" suggests. Mary Alonzo, for example, was a native-born white woman, but she married an Italian cigar maker and lived on García Avenue in Ybor City. Similarly, Winona Cabrera married a Cuban cigar maker, Esteban; and the Anglo Cassie Fernández sought work as a packer alongside her husband, Adolphus, who had held that position for several years. Other petitioners, such as Carmen Bussetti, were born in the United States but had been reared in an immigrant family. Bussetti lived with her widowed mother and two sisters, both cigar banders, in Ybor City. These "American girls" thus included second-generation immigrants and the Anglo wives of Latin cigar workers.[30]

Despite the complexity of the petitioners' identities, the conflicts of 1919 revealed both the potential for Anglo working women to organize on their own behalf and their capacity to revitalize solidarity between Latin women and men. During the 1919 strike, male union leaders proclaimed the importance of Latin women's support and refused to accept a settlement that would have benefited the most skilled workers, mainly men, but would have left the "clerks, strippers, and banders, [mostly women] to 'paddle their own canoe.'" Forgetting the ridicule they heaped on women wildcatters three years earlier, union leaders now claimed that "labor will ever be subservient... so long as they stand divided." Latin men once again embraced their sisters as partners to stave off the entrance of women into men's jobs and the introduction of machinery into cigar factories.[31]

As Latin women and men collaborated to limit Anglo women's entry into the cigar industry, they also campaigned against illicit activities that threatened to turn Ybor City and West Tampa into havens for gambling and prostitution. They attacked both Anglos who invested large sums of money in such activities and Latins who were seduced into supporting them. *El Internacional* continually crusaded against organized crime in the ethnic enclaves, claiming that gambling and prostitution only served to impoverish workers. Mutual aid societies hosted social and cultural events at the various clubs on weekends to provide alternate forms of entertainment for the community, and the women's auxiliaries especially worked to attract young women and men to dances, concerts, and films.

Reform-minded Anglo women were equally concerned about the moral condition of Ybor City and West Tampa. After prohibition was finally mandated by the Eighteenth Amendment to the U.S. Constitution in 1918, bootlegging flourished in Tampa. Although there was plenty of evidence that Anglo men were in charge of operations, Ybor City was the primary site of their activities. The WCTU, now joined by members of the YWCA, the Tampa Civic Association, and other women's organizations, redoubled efforts to clean up the ethnic enclaves and to rescue women and children from the depredations of alcoholic husbands. At least some, however, may have realized that the root problem lay in the profits made by Anglo entrepreneurs, which fueled not only bootlegging in the ethnic enclaves but also political corruption in the city as a whole.

As early as 1912, the *Jacksonville Dixie*—a reform newspaper—had proclaimed, "Tampa is reeking in crime, and gamblers in the open operate in various parts of the city. . . ." The king of crime in the city, the report claimed, was Charlie Wall, descendant of the prominent pioneer family, cousin to Perry, John, and Joseph Wall, and related by marriage to D. B. McKay.[32] In 1916, the *Tribune* had accused McKay, who was the rival editor of the *Tampa Daily Times,* of being the beneficiary of Wall's gambling operations. McKay, married to the daughter of one of the largest cigar manufacturers, was then serving his second term as mayor and running for a third. Gambling and graft were linked to election fraud; and McKay received a large proportion of votes cast in Ybor City, the heart of Wall's machine.

The major form of profiteering in the ethnic enclaves was *bolita*—a numbers game.[33] In Cuba the numbers game functioned under the auspices of the state as the Cuban National Lottery, but in Tampa it flourished as part of a free enterprise system of gambling and graft. Manuel Suárez, a Spaniard, apparently introduced *bolita* to Ybor City in the late 1880s, and thereafter it was closely connected with the saloon trade. By 1900, there were more taverns in Ybor City than in all of the rest of Tampa. *Bolita* games were also being run from grocery stores and coffeehouses and in lavish gambling emporiums, such as El Dorado

Club, which also housed prostitutes. The clubs were generally owned and managed by Spaniards and "protected" by Anglo politicians and police. Convinced of the sexual desires and desirability of Caribbean women and confident that any illicit activities would be ignored, Anglo men haunted these clubs. After the ratification of prohibition, bootlegging joined *bolita* and brothels as a source of enormous profits and payoffs. Anglo sheriffs, county commissioners, mayors, and newspaper editors were linked into the system alongside their Latin collaborators.

Anglo women and Latin labor leaders were no match for the profits generated by gambling, prostitution, and rum-running. Any serious attempt to rein in corruption in Ybor City depended instead on a reconfiguration of local political power. When McKay won the mayoral election for a third time in 1916 based on disputed ballots from Ybor City, his opponents finally had sufficient moral authority to push for charter reform. Their plan, following municipal reform in other American cities, was to replace corrupt ward-based politics with a city commission form of government. Success was still a few years away, but the issue of good government had finally gained center stage.

In the face of these heated debates over political corruption, Anglo women began to question their exclusion from voting and officeholding. Throughout the South, the suffrage cause gained new adherents in the 1910s. In Florida, the first statewide suffrage meeting held in more than two decades opened in Tampa in 1917. Just a year after Alice Snow's defeat in the school board election, the gathering inspired twenty-one local women to organize the Tampa Equal Suffrage League. The war had directed attention to other issues, but members of the league felt certain that women's patriotic activities would reinforce arguments for their enfranchisement. Though claiming to support "equal suffrage," the organization was composed entirely of native-born white women.[34]

At the founding meeting, held in the council chamber at city hall, Snow signed on as a charter member and the organization's first secretary. The other officers, most of whom were residents of Hyde Park, were less well known. The president, Ada Price, and vice-presidents, Mabel Bean and Elizabeth Hurn, had not been leaders in local clubs or voluntary organizations. But like Alice Snow, whose son, Fred, worked as a postal clerk, these women had connections to local civic affairs through male relatives. Ada's husband, Ivil O. Price, was active in the Republican party and would run for sheriff on that ticket in 1920; Bean's father had served as postmaster in the 1890s; and Hurn's husband also worked for the post office. The other officers—Sarah Chapman and Jane Davis—had fewer visible ties to political appointments or partisan contests; Chapman was a teacher, and Davis was the wife of a salesman and the mother of a teacher and a stenographer.[35]

The Tampa Equal Suffrage League officers may have had personal experiences that inspired their entrance into an arena of activism long ignored by the city's better-known Anglo voluntarists. For instance, in 1898, Mabel Williams, then a young woman, had served as a courier and interpreter for General William Shafter when the U.S. military sought inside information by intercepting mail from Spanish residents in Tampa. The following year, she married George Bean, and on their spring honeymoon in Cuba, she attended the first Memorial Day exercise held in Havana and watched the last Spanish soldiers leave the island. She was clearly proud of her wartime activities, which she described in detail to an interviewer in the 1930s, and may have been eager, once again, to play a role in weighty affairs.[36]

Whatever their individual motives, league members agreed to circulate petitions to Florida's congressional delegation urging passage of the Nineteenth Amendment. Their petition drive gained attention in the *Tribune,* which published an article that also announced a January 1918 meeting at city hall. That winter, Mabel Bean hosted an Equal Suffrage League tea at her Hyde Park home that included entertainment by Miss Carmen Fernández, a neighbor of Sarah Chapman. There is no indication, however, that the Latin woman's participation suggested any wider ties to the Cuban community.[37]

Over the next two years, support for a state woman suffrage bill grew exponentially among Anglo Tampans, partly because those who insisted that voting rights should be regulated only by the states feared passage of a federal suffrage amendment. In March 1919, for instance, the *Tribune* editor declared, "Give them the ballot," but demanded that it be granted by amending the state constitution, not by ratifying the federal amendment. Women advocates appear to have been less concerned about the *means* of obtaining the vote than about the end. Some supported state legislation granting women the right to vote in primaries (the most important elections in Florida's one-party system); others advocated a state constitutional amendment; and still others favored ratification of the Nineteenth Amendment.[38] Whatever position they took, a growing number of women were now demanding electoral rights.

In spring 1919, a "suffrage conference" was held in conjunction with the annual meeting of the white women's clubs in the city. It attracted representatives from a wide array of local organizations and from state and regional groups whose leaders would have shunned the cause just a few years earlier. The president of the Florida Federation of Women's Clubs and a Virginia leader of the United Daughters of the Confederacy offered rousing pro-suffrage speeches. The UDC spokeswoman advocated primary suffrage as the surest and quickest means of obtaining votes for southern women—which also virtually eliminated the possibility that Black women would benefit from an expanded electorate—and both argued for electoral rights on the basis of women's responsibilities to children, home, and community. A *Tribune* reporter in attendance assured readers that had a straw vote been taken at the conclusion of the meeting, "the women present were unanimously agreed" in favor, as were half the reporters.[39]

On Halloween weekend that year, the Tampa Equal Suffrage League hosted a second suffrage convention, attracting participants from the Tampa Civic Association, the Tampa Woman's Club, and other Anglo voluntary associations as well as attention from Doyle Carlton, a state senator; Dr. Louis Bize, a bank president; William Brorien, the president of the Peninsular Telephone Company; and Fred Turner, the secretary of the YMCA. Speeches by male civic leaders as well as Ada Price, Kate Jackson, and other league officers reflected the now widespread support for female suffrage in the city. The women speakers in particular emphasized the need to educate Florida women for their new responsibilities.[40]

Although racist diatribes against woman suffrage were popular among many southern legislators, Tampa Anglo civic leaders instead emphasized nativist claims for the vote's power to quash immigrant radicalism. Louis Bize declared that the "men of the South must push aside the old idea that the negro women will ever interfere by the voting privilege. It is nothing but a bugaboo." Instead, he claimed, "If there was ever a time when the women should have it [the vote], it is the present when the institutions that our fathers fought for are menaced by this propaganda of bolshevism." Claiming that Bolsheviks have "no religion and no God" and pointing out the links between bolshevism and labor unrest in Tampa, Bize concluded that "if the women had the ballot now, there would be fewer strikes."[41] Once again, the multicultural character of the Cigar City subverted racial orthodoxy, this time in the service of white women's rights.

In the following months, both the Tampa Civic Association and the Tampa Woman's Club sponsored Suffrage Days to keep their members informed on the issue of enfranchisement. Yet the most important weapon Anglo women wielded remained their collective strength as lobbyists. It appears that even as leading clubwomen were drawn to suffrage, leading suffragists were drawn to clubwork. In 1920, both Ada Price and Jane Davis were elected for the first time to offices in the Tampa Civic Association—Price as president—and they carried on their suffrage activities increasingly in the context of larger voluntarist efforts.[42]

Tampa clubwomen also expanded their work within statewide and national organizations, including the Florida Federation of Women's Clubs, the General Federation of Women's Clubs, the WCTU, and the YWCA, all of which now endorsed suffrage. At the October 1917 meeting of the state federation, held in Tampa, president May Mann Jennings, the wife of the former governor and an active suffragist, announced a campaign to double the membership of the organization, urging affiliated clubs to recruit additional members and encouraging them to form new associations. Caroline Hawkins of Tampa was elected vice-president of the state organization and was placed in charge of Americanization and child welfare programs. Kate Jackson was active in raising an endowment fund for the federation and expanding the organization's work on civic development. Local members campaigned for laws regulating child labor, juvenile crime, gambling, prostitution, public health, the environment, and civil service while lobbying for fire escapes at schools, teacher certification guidelines, traveling libraries, women school board appointees, state reformatories for boys and girls, and the abolition of convict leases.[43] All of these efforts would be enhanced if women gained the vote.

Local Anglo women were also involved with international concerns. In 1919, clubwomen sponsored a tag day to raise funds for Armenian relief. Meeting at the YWCA on the morning of January 26, they fanned out through the city, seeking contributions from businesses and individuals to add to the national campaign in support of war refugees.[44] The Tampa branch of the Southern Association of College Women, which had been founded by three young graduates of Columbia University—two Anglo and one Latin—in 1916, wrote to President Calvin Coolidge regarding the World Court and sponsored a public lecture on the League of Nations.[45] These efforts, too, intensified interest in women's access to electoral politics.

In August 1920, when Tennessee became the thirty-sixth state to ratify the Nineteenth Amendment granting woman suffrage, Florida legislators still refused to approve the measure. Nonetheless, Tampa women would soon have the opportunity to test their electoral capacities as a result of the continuing feud over charter reform among local politicians. Supporters of a commission system of municipal government wanted to reduce electoral graft, but their plan would also limit the power of immigrant and African American voters, who, under the existing ward system, could influence the choice of representatives from racially and ethnically homogeneous districts.[46] Charges of corruption in the 1916 mayoral election gave commission supporters their first serious chance at success, but it took until June 1920 for a charter committee to be elected. Just a month later, the committee proposed the replacement of the ward-based city council with a commission, all five members of which would be elected at large. In September, the state's attorney informed Tampa officials that the charter issue could not be resolved through the white Democratic primary but must be introduced to the general electorate, including newly enfranchised women. A binding referendum on the issue was scheduled for October.[47]

Politicians on both sides of the charter issue were suddenly confronted with an unexpected and unfamiliar constituency. A number of Tampa civic leaders voiced anxiety about "what the women voter [will] do with her newly acquired rights and privileges." Some envisioned African Americans flocking to the polls, while others imagined their Anglo counterparts forming "a party run and managed by women only."[48] Local men reassured one another, however, that women *would* "affiliate with one of the two old parties in this country" and that the new type of woman in politics "is not afraid to be charming. She works with, not against, men."[49] To ensure such solidarity, at least among whites, city officials traded in their earlier ambivalence about women's political capacities for paeans to "intelligent" womanhood. The state Democratic party chairman also began urging white women to register in order to counterbalance the feared influx of their African American counterparts. City officials aided the effort by assuring white residents that any Black registrants would be assigned to separate lines at polling places, thereby forestalling fears of racial mingling.

Throughout the fall, accusations that each side was courting Black ballots appeared alongside pleas for white female participation. On September 21, 1920, Wallace Stovall, editor of the *Tribune*, decried the "unexpected and uncouth treatment of the white women of Tampa" by opponents of the proposed city charter. The attack was aimed most directly at the *Tribune*'s journalistic rival, the *Tampa Daily Times,* which supported the existing system of electing the council by ward. Stovall granted that the registration of women to vote was newsworthy, but he cried foul when the *Times* "embarrassed" socially prominent and "home-loving" women by making fun of their anxiety at the registration office, ridiculing them as "potential candidates for the office of commission," and, worst of all, printing "the age of those offering to register." Such actions are "certainly indicative," argued Stovall, "that among a certain class the old-time chivalry, deference and honor, reverence and protection, which the Southern gentlemen throw about woman has decayed most lamentably."[50]

In explaining the ill treatment of white women registrants, Stovall pointed to the opposition's deference to potential Black voters. He noted as evidence that "[n]ot one negro woman of Tampa has been embarrassed or humiliated by having cheap fun poked at her" in the *Times.* "Can it be that the opposition knows it can count on Negro women's vote to help defeat the charter... adoption of which means a cleaner Tampa, a better governed Tampa, a Tampa such as we have dreamed of?"[51] While concerned primarily with the *Times*'s alleged racial perfidy, the *Tribune* also acknowledged the likelihood that African American women would manage to register and vote. When state officials waived poll taxes for women in 1920 and ruled that the charter referendum had to be decided by the general electorate rather than through the white primary system, they opened the door for Black women's participation, and local officials, caught off guard, had not succeeded in closing it.

Although the *Tribune* suggested that only African American women would oppose the charter, white women were not simply pawns of pro-charter forces. Anglo women leapt into the fray on both sides. Members of the Equal Suffrage League and the Tampa Woman's Club met immediately after ratification to discuss their responsibilities and practically overnight published a pamphlet entitled "An Open Forum on Our Government for Women Voters." They then organized a series of meetings designed to prepare women to cast their first ballots.[52] Ada Price, presiding over one of these gatherings, noted that both Democrats and Republicans now claimed the honor of having produced suffrage for women. "Neither party has us roped and branded," she warned, "and they will never get us gagged."[53] White women thus declared their political independence.

The newly formed Commission Government Club, created to promote passage of the proposed charter, attracted several leading clubwomen, including Julia Norris and Minnie Albury. Equally prominent activists, including Tampa Civic Association founder Kate Jackson and Tampa Woman's Club president Annie Givens, joined the Home Rule Club, which opposed the change.[54] Other women organized nonpartisan efforts. A local chapter of the Business and Professional Women, established by ten women in spring 1920, promoted educational campaigns to prepare women for their first election.[55]

Anglo women were suddenly organizing, attending, and speaking at dozens of political meetings and rallies throughout the city. In early October, Julia Norris, past president of the Florida United Daughters of the Confederacy, spoke "eloquently" on behalf of the proposed charter. But her primary concern, like that of white male civic leaders, was "the heavy registration of Negro women," and she "emphasized the necessity of white women to accept it as their duty to register and vote since equal suffrage is now the policy of the country."[56] And 2,462 white women did register in 1920, constituting 32 percent of all whites on the voter rolls that year.[57]

The concern whites voiced about the potential political power of Black women was not simply a convenient trope for inspiring racial fears and inducing white women to vote. Such fears were certainly at work among charter advocates, but Black women and men were eager to participate for their own reasons. African American registration soared in 1920 when nearly 32 percent of local Blacks signed up to vote, including 1,298 women, who formed over 60 percent of the total Black registrants.[58] African American women claimed the right to vote both to redress men's disfranchisement and to further ongoing efforts at community advancement.[59] They not only registered and voted but also participated in the public debates preceding the referendum. Mrs. Inez Alston, for instance, who had gained community respect and experience in public speaking as a teacher and clubwoman, presided over a series of meetings on charter reform held at Black churches.

Much to the consternation of editor Stovall, several pro-charter advocates, including Julia Norris, Minnie Albury, and Judge Ernest Drumright, agreed to participate in these meetings. The *Tribune* refused to cover the discussion at the Bowman African Methodist Episcopal Church, until its anticharter rival, the *Tampa Daily Times,* pointed out the irony of "Judge Drumright, one of the founders of the White Municipal party and a staunch Democrat, addressing a Negro Republican meeting." Although the *Times* ignored the role of Black women in organizing the event, the *Tribune* noted that it was "earnest negro men and women" who had extended the invitation to Judge Drumright and three white women. Claiming that these "worthwhile negro residents" were seeking "advice and guidance" from the white speakers, Stovall insisted that it was only proper to comply. The danger to the racial status quo lay, he claimed, with the anticharter group, which sought "the support of the motley crowd of black people who were herded to the registration places by the negro policemen" or those registering at the Sunshine Club, a local gambling den that had been recently raided by federal prohibition agents.[60]

Awareness of activism in African American neighborhoods and fear that such efforts would disrupt fragile racial hierarchies help explain why so many Anglos, already in control of elections through the white primary, felt it necessary to further dilute minority voting power through at-large elections. These fears of Black political power, which drove the establishment of the White Municipal party a decade earlier, motivated white civic leaders to enlist the electoral aid of their female counterparts even if they could not entirely control their political opinions.

When the referendum was completed, white women had fulfilled the hopes of charter advocates. On October 20, the *Tribune* headline blared, "Charter Wins by 770, Commission Plan Triumphant Despite a High Vote Cast against in the Town's Black Belt." The story credited the victory to white women. According to the report, they recognized "that it was largely a contest between their votes and those of negroes" and that the new charter would provide "a weapon by means of which they could protect their homes and children." The *Tribune* concluded, "Tampa women have shown they are able to rock the cradle and the politicians at the same time."[61]

For several days, the *Tribune* and the *Times* devoted column after column to analyses of the charter vote and women's role in the outcome. The *Tribune* claimed that "out of 2,999 votes cast against the charter, 1,976 were cast by Negroes and Latins leaving but 1,023 white Americans in Tampa who voted against the adoption of the charter. In other words, out of a white American vote of approximately 3,100, only 1,023 voted against the adoption of the charter. A three to *one* majority."[62] Miscounting the Anglo vote—2,077 for and 1,023 against provided a two-to-one majority—and discounting the substantial turnout of African Americans, city officials reassured themselves of their continued control.

Ignoring the anticharter sentiments of some white women and the presence of Black women, the *Tribune* cheered "the advent of women into politics." White women, a reporter claimed, were so eager to participate on election day that they "brought their babies with them in many instances to the polls." Even among Latins and African Americans, the article declared, "the better and more intelligent... the higher class, better informed, honest set,... helped to win the election by counterbalancing the votes" of the "idle and worthless."[63]

Of course, the *Tribune* reporters could only guess at how any group of city residents had actually voted. They based such speculations on a combination of wishful thinking—wanting to believe that most white women had followed the path to the polls carved out for them by white pro-charter men—and the analysis of precinct totals. The largest number of Black registrants, for instance, lived in the Second Precinct and the Third Precinct, which were among the three areas with the highest anticharter vote margins. (The third was the Twelfth Precinct in Ybor City.) The highest pro-charter margins came from precincts three, five, and eighteen, where white women had registered in particularly large numbers. In the Fifth Precinct, including sections of Tampa's affluent Hyde Park, white women constituted nearly half of the registrants and reportedly turned out in larger numbers than did men on election day.[64] Thus, civic leaders had some basis for applauding the "efficiency and intelligence" of white women who cast their first ballots. Hafford Jones, an inspector in the predominantly white Seventeenth Precinct, declared that "the women had voted 99 percent strong in that precinct and that he believed the women of the city deserved great credit for the way they had taken hold of things. He thought that at least one member of the city commission should be a woman."[65]

The reactions to African American voters, especially women, were more vituperative. Amos Norris, husband of the pro-charter advocate Julia Norris and an inspector in the heavily Black Ninth Precinct, claimed that the "worst class of negroes imaginable were present." Norris rejected the ballot of a Black man who purportedly gave the wrong address and several African American women who he thought "were under age." He also swore out a warrant against "Julia Sacio, negress," claiming that she was "paying off" voters at the polling station. Throughout the city, it was reported, "a large number of negroes had been systematically herded into the registration and poll tax offices by a negro policeman, and it is presumed that all of these voted against the charter." In addition, the members of the "old political ring" were accused of "forgetting their color and standing in life sufficiently as to engage in taking negro men and women to the polling places."[66]

Even though Black Tampans had been organizing for political rights, economic justice, and social services for more than a decade, Anglo civic leaders rejected the possibility that African American women and men might justifiably pursue political power on their own terms. Yet the very presence of a Black policeman and hundreds of Black voters reveals their ongoing desire for political power. Unfortunately, even effective organization among local African Americans could be defeated by a combination of racism and political corruption. The advent of woman suffrage did little to change that.

Suffrage actually proved a relatively weak weapon in the activist arsenal of Tampa women from any racial or ethnic group in the 1920s. Most continued to rely on voluntarism rather than voting as the best vehicle for promoting social reform in the city. Anglo women continued to vote, but widespread corruption made voting in local elections practically meaningless for men or women until the 1950s. Moreover, all but a handful of the African American women registered to vote in 1920 were knocked off the rolls by 1924 as white officials imposed racist literacy and poll tax requirements. When they were excluded, so were most of the Black men, who had used woman suffrage as a counterweight against their earlier disfranchisement. Blacks were thus forced, once again, to join Latins, who continued to voice their concerns through community-based organizations rather than electoral politics.

The most severe problems that confronted Latins—declining opportunities in the cigar industry, mechanization, and lack of union recognition—defied electoral solutions. Thus, when Cuban and Italian workers sought change, few viewed the vote as a likely weapon, despite the importance of Ybor City ballot boxes to the careers of Anglo civic leaders. In addition, Florida's poll tax and residency requirements discouraged immigrants from registering. In 1910, fewer than 10 percent of the city's adult Cubans and Spaniards and fewer than 3 percent of adult Italians had even become citizens. By 1930, Tampa ranked at the bottom of American cities with over 100,000 population with respect to the percentage of foreign-born adults who had acquired citizenship and voting privileges; and Latin women were less likely than their male kin to gain the benefits of citizenship, even after the passage of woman suffrage.[67] Woman suffrage, then, like so many other avenues of activism in Tampa, quickly became race-specific.

Latin women, however, made abundantly clear the importance of alternative political strategies and tactics. The industrywide cigar strike of

1920–21 proved the limits of both electoral and economic pressure. Despite growing tensions over changes in the sexual division of labor within the industry, the unity among the nearly 8,700 striking cigar workers was astounding. The union did not even bother to post pickets around the factories: "the committee says they don't need any as they have no fear that strikers will desert the ranks."[68]

Such unity had inspired white reactions from the first days of the strike in July 1920. Just as the charter committee was completing its work, Mayor D. B. McKay, at the behest of Anglo women leaders, offered the Children's Home as a refuge for the children of strikers. The Children's Home, however, which had been gutted by fire in June, had relocated to a refurbished cigar factory; and one of the new vice-presidents of the Children's Home, Mrs. Carolina Vega, was married to the man whose factory had been raided by unruly women four years earlier. He had been among the first to install stemming machines. Moreover, several board members had petitioned the state the previous year for a compulsory education statute that would require stricter enforcement of child labor laws in Ybor City, depriving some families of much needed wages.[69] Recognizing the links between Anglo women reformers and Latin factory owners, the workers rejected the offer, refusing to "leave [their] children to the tender mercy of men [or women] who will try to squeeze the lifeblood out of [us] while living."[70]

Latin families that needed assistance had an array of more palatable alternatives, which had been created by their own collective efforts. The CMIU, as in previous strikes, offered monetary benefits, soup kitchens, and moral support; and the local Labor Temple and mutual aid societies provided places where strikers could meet to exchange not only information but also food, clothing, and other necessities of life. During the 1920 battle over the closed shop, CMIU affiliates also formed the Committee of Public Health to coordinate relief efforts. The committee received donations not only from Latin shopkeepers and community leaders but also from union locals across the country.[71] Individual strikers could seek help as well from the clubs of which they were members. El Centro Asturiano, for instance, offered meeting rooms, medical services, emergency relief, and recreational activities for children throughout the strike. Church-sponsored missions and settlement houses, located in the heart of the Latin enclaves, provided another source of support.[72]

Throughout the summer of 1920, local business and political leaders, who still hoped that woman suffrage would be defeated, expressed far more concern with strikers' solidarity than with woman's rights.[73] Once again, the strategy for disrupting working-class unity involved offering "American girls" opportunities to replace Latin women and men in well-paying factory jobs. On the very day that Tennessee legislators ensured the ratification of the suffrage amendment, a manufacturers' journal, *Tobacco Leaf,* declared a new day for women, but their focus was economic rather than electoral. Noting that the Tampa strike had already lasted for two months, the *Tobacco Leaf* assured its readers that "girl packers" from across the country were pouring into the Cigar City and were finding "working conditions superior to their expectations." These young women, "earning twice as much as they have been accustomed" to, were declared the wave of the future by both leading manufacturers and local politicians.[74]

There were signs, however, that the owners' version of events might be more propaganda than reality. The vice-president of the Committee on Public Health was Mrs. Elizabeth Law, who was then head of the tobacco stemmers' union. She was native-born but native-born Black rather than Anglo.[75] A reporter for the *Tampa Citizen,* a labor paper, claimed that in general it was African American not Anglo women who entered stemmers' and packers' ranks during the 1920 strike. Manufacturers' hopes of filling the cigar benches with white women was "swiftly fleeting," declared the *Citizen,* since "American girls cannot be secured as long as they are forced to work at the same benches with negro girls."[76] Given cigar workers' earlier opposition to the hiring of Anglos and the contemporary attacks on Black women voters, Latin women's acceptance of African American coworkers is even more notable. Instead of walking out to protest Law's hiring, the stemmers elected her head of their union. This decision may have been intended more to challenge Anglo civic leaders than to embrace African American rights, or it may have reflected Law's acceptance by Afro-Cuban women, who now dominated the stemming rooms.

Latin cigar workers vied for attention with the charter fight during September and October 1920. When the referendum threatened to overtake union demands in the minds of Anglo residents, Latin women and children regained center stage by leading the "Biggest Labor Parade Ever Seen in Tampa," as one of the newspapers described it. While politicians sought support from local voters, strikers sought assistance from workers nationwide. As the charter battle neared its climax, workers called a mass meeting to reconfirm their commitment to continuing the strike.[77] On October 14, five days before the charter vote, more than twenty-five hundred strikers, "about 50 per cent of them women, crowded the Centro

Asturiano Clubhouse to the doors" for a mass meeting called by the Committee of Public Health. Latin missionaries joined the ranks of those listening to the remarks of José Rojo, secretary of the Havana branch of the Federation of Labor. He assured strikers of the "hearty support" of their Cuban compatriots and then turned the platform over to a stream of speakers. One of these was Mrs. Cándida Bustamente, a widow who roomed with Miss María Cosa, a cigar bander. Bustamente was active in the Methodist Home Missionary Society in both Ybor City and West Tampa and was preparing to present the local groups' report to the Latin district conference of the Methodist church the following week. Perhaps she was the "old lady" described by an *El Internacional* reporter who "electrified" the audience. Combining traditional paeans to women's familial roles with an anticapitalist jeremiad, she declared, "We, the wives and mothers, must choose to die, together with our children and our husbands, rather than submit to the unparalleled condition of servitude which the manufacturers impose upon us."[78]

Though "no vote was taken," the *Tribune* reported that the participants demonstrated their support for the leaders of the strike and their confidence in achieving victory.[79] Anglo leaders who focused only on the charter fight concluded that "very few Latin women voted, apparently taking little interest in government." Yet most recognized that this group was in fact the most effective among Tampa women in pursuing power by other means.[80]

On November 2, as Tampans in other sections of the city cast ballots in the national presidential election, the union's Committee of Public Health launched a publicity campaign to offset the lurid stories appearing in the local press, which union leaders believed were intended "to stir up mob spirit among the people of Tampa."[81] On November 6, AFL unions around the country participated in a "National Donation Day" in support of Tampa cigar workers. The *Tribune* ignored the effort, focusing instead on the activities of the White Municipal party as it prepared for the election of city commissioners necessitated by the passage of charter reform. The paper was sure, moreover, that the strike would soon be broken, allowing the city to return to normal after months of political and economic turmoil.

The strike, however, lasted another three months, and before it ended, Latin women did turn out to vote. On February 5, 1921, they cast their ballots on a resolution to end the strike.[82] We do not know how women voted, though the resolution passed. We do know that the following fall, women stemmers initiated a general strike. They walked out in protest over "short pay," suggesting that owners had not lived up to their part of the earlier agreement. When the union called a strike vote a few days later, the stemmers proclaimed that they "would stay out on strike regardless of the outcome of the vote."[83] Even within the union, Latin women viewed the ballot as only one instrument for wielding power; another was their control over the first step in the production process.

In the context of labor unrest and the entrance of women into electoral politics, activist identities and alliances were reconfigured. Sex-specific issues and organizations became more central to the activities of Latin, African American, and Anglo women even as women from each group continued to collaborate with men to achieve shared goals. But tensions over women's roles and gender priorities were more evident by 1920, particularly in the contest over charter reform among Anglos and in reaction to changing labor conditions among Latins. Even for African American men, women's prominence in the debates and the vote on charter reform must have caused some consternation.

The heightened focus on gender issues and women's organizations illuminated fault lines within African American, Latin, and Anglo communities, but it also provided the basis for strengthening and creating coalitions among women across these communities. For example, the circle of Latin women participating in Anglo women's voluntary associations widened. The changes were visible in 1921, when Anglo women followed the lead of their African American counterparts and formed a citywide federation, the Tampa League of Women's Clubs. Of course, Black women were excluded from this venture, and no Latin women were elected to a major office. Yet five Latin women served on the twenty-five-member board of directors, representing both older organizations, such as the Friday Morning Musicale and the Children's Home, and newer ones, including the American Association of University Women and the Business and Professional Women. Of course, those Latins who found their way into the offices of Anglo-dominated organizations did not represent the experiences of the masses of first- and second-generation immigrant workers. Mrs. Josefina Díaz, who achieved the loftiest position in Anglo voluntary ranks, served for a year as acting president of the Children's Home. She was married to a cigar factory owner, as was Mrs. Celestino Vega, who joined her on the board of the Tampa League of Women's Clubs. Their younger counterparts were college-educated professional women, mainly teachers, nurses, and the daughters of bankers, insurance agents, and ministers rather than cigar makers.[84]

Although there was some fear that female voluntarism would lose its significance once women gained the right to vote, such was not the case in Tampa.[85] Rather, when charter reform failed to resolve the problems of corruption and cronyism in Tampa politics, well-to-do women expanded their social reform efforts, ensuring that participation in electoral politics would supplement rather than substitute for voluntarism. In this context, Latin women's failure to embrace suffrage in significant numbers had little impact on interethnic cooperation.

African American women were far more committed to suffrage than were their Latin neighbors, but ultimately they were no more effective in using the vote to their advantage. In the context of Black women's disfranchisement, economic strategies reemerged as the lifeblood of racial advancement. It was on this ground that African American and Latin working women built their coalition. Although some Afro-Cuban women had attended classes at the Tampa School of the Household Arts, there was no sense then that they were coworkers with Blanche Armwood and other African American middle-class leaders of the program. Only with Elizabeth Law's election as head of the stemmer's local did Afro-Cuban and African American women forge their first truly collaborative efforts. By the mid-1920s, these connections would be extended by more affluent African American and Afro-Cuban women working on behalf of child care and community improvement.

The increasing salience of gender identity to social activism in the late 1910s and early 1920s helped bridge differences of nationality among Black (African American and Afro-Cuban) and white (Latin and Anglo) women, at least those of the same class. Formidable barriers to communitywide efforts by women remained, however. Anglo, Black, and Latin activists might declare themselves "New Women," but differences of race and class would continue to obscure commonalities of sex as Tampa activists forged interracial and interethnic coalitions over the following decade.

## Notes

1. *La Lucha,* November 25, 1916. All articles were originally in Spanish, translated by Jane Mangan.

2. On the 1916 incident, see *Tampa Morning Tribune,* November 11, 17, and 25, 1916; and *El Internacional,* December 1, 1916.

3. On the male strikers' response and the quote, see *El Internacional,* December 1, 1916. Original printed in Spanish and English, suggesting that union leaders and the paper's editors wanted to be sure that Anglo as well as Latin

residents would take note of their concerns. On the outcome of the strike, see *Tampa Morning Tribune,* November 17 and 25, 1916.

4. Alice Snow is often touted as the first woman in Tampa to run for elected office, but Adele Kossovsky apparently preceded her as a candidate, running in 1910. Kossovsky, campaigning as a Socialist would not have received widespread support from Anglo women or much attention from the mainstream press. See Richard Deutsch, "Donna Tampa: The Letters of Adele Kossovsky during the Cartabón Strike," 1999 (unpublished paper in author's possession).

5. Gardner and Lawson, "At-Large Elections and Black Voting Rights in Tampa/Hillsborough County, 1910–1984," 3.

6. *Tampa Morning Tribune,* September 19, 1916.

7. Ibid., November 10, 11, and 12, 1916. The fashion and cosmetic ads, as well as the images accompanying theater ads and the help wanted listings for stenographers and hairdressers, suggest that the "New Woman" had arrived in Tampa at least by that fall.

8. The "New Woman" has been widely studied by historians, who in recent years have illuminated its working-class manifestations. The work still focuses, however, on northern cities. See, for example, June Sochen, *The New Woman in Greenwich Village, 1910–1920* (New York: Quadrangle Books, 1972); Carroll Smith-Rosenberg, *Disorderly Conduct: Visions of Gender in Victorian America* (New York: Oxford University Press, 1985), 245–96; Kathy Peiss, *Cheap Amusements: Working Women and Leisure in Turn-of-the-Century New York* (Philadelphia: Temple University Press, 1986); Joanne Meyerowitz, *Women Adrift: Independent Wage-Earning Women in Chicago, 1880–1930* (Chicago: University of Chicago Press, 1988); John D'Emilio and Estelle Freedman, *Intimate Matters: A History of Sexuality in America* (New York: Harper and Row, 1988), chap. 8; and Nan Enstad, *Ladies of Labor, Girls of Adventure: Working Women, Popular Culture, and Labor Politics at the Turn of the Twentieth Century* (New York: Columbia University Press, 1999).

9. Leland Hawes, "A Special Day for Blacks," *Tampa Tribune-Times,* February 4, 1996; *Tampa Morning Tribune,* February 15, 1916. On Du Bois's position on World War I, see Gaines, *Uplifting the Race,* 223 and passim.

10. Hawes, "A Special Day for Blacks"; *Tampa Morning Tribune,* February 15, 1916 (quote).

11. On Du Bois's life and politics, see David Levering Lewis, *W. E. B. Du Bois* (New York: Henry Holt, 1993); on debates among African American intellectuals in the early twentieth century, see Gaines, *Uplifting the Race,* esp. chap. 4.

12. Hawes, "A Special Day for Blacks."

13. Ibid. See also *Tampa Morning Tribune,* February 15, 1916; and Brady, *Things Remembered,* 187. Du Bois returned to Tampa in the 1920s to speak at St. Paul's AME Church, which became the favorite site for speeches by national leaders, from Du Bois, Oscar De Priest, and Mary McLeod Bethune in the 1920s

and 1930s to Jackie Robinson, Thurgood Marshall, and Rosa Parks in the civil rights era.

14. Saunders, *Bridging the Gap,* 8–10; Walter T. Howard and Virginia M. Howard, "The Early Years of the NAACP in Tampa, 1915–1930," *Tampa Bay History* 16 (Fall-Winter 1994): 41–56.

15. On Armwood's war work, see Davis, *Lifting as They Climb,* 264–65, 287; and boxes 2 and 3, Armwood Family Papers.

16. Crake, "'In Unity There Is Strength,'" 53–56. On Tampa men's wartime service, see Mormino and Pizzo, *Tampa,* 150–51.

17. Crake, "'In Unity There Is Strength,'" 53–56.

18. Weatherford, *A History of Women in Tampa,* 106–8. At the end of the war, many of these same circles of women continued their efforts, this time in the face of the devastating influenza epidemic. The flu hit Tampa in October and November 1918, taking 283 lives in just two months. The Girl Scouts joined older clubwomen in delivering kettles of soup to needy families, caring for the sick, and assisting families in which mothers and daughters had taken ill.

19. Mormino and Pozzetta, *The Immigrant World of Ybor City,* 127, 128, 145, 154–56, 193.

20. *Tampa Bulletin,* January 20, 1917, clipping, Miscellaneous file, box 3, Armwood Family Papers.

21. On Armwood's political career in the late 1910s and early 1920s, see boxes 2–4, Armwood Family Papers; and Davis, *Lifting as They Climb,* 264–65, 287.

22. Annie House married Emma Mance's son in the early 1920s and continued her work as a club leader. In 1915, "Womanhood," an article in the *Afro-American Monthly,* published by the Afro-American Civic League, expressed concerns about the exploitation of Black womanhood. Cited in Anthony and Wade, *A Collection of Historical Facts about Black Tampa.* On the development of a Black "New Woman" in the same period, see Kathy Peiss, "Making Faces: The Cosmetics Industry and the Cultural Construction of Gender, 1890–1930," in *Unequal Sisters,* ed. Ruiz and DuBois, 324–45; Gwendolyn Robinson, "Class, Race and Gender: A Transcultural, Theoretical, and Sociohistorical Analysis of Cosmetic Institutions and Practices to 1920" (Ph.D. diss., University of Illinois at Chicago, 1984); and Tiffany Gill, "Civic Beauty: Beauty Salons, Beauty Culturists, and the Politics of African American Female Entrepreneurship, 1900–1965" (Ph.D. diss., Rutgers University, 2003). I thank Rhonda Lee for introducing me to Black beauty culture in Durham, North Carolina.

23. Black beauty culture associations were founded nationally in this period with the express purpose of encouraging beauty culturists "to take the full responsibilities as good citizens by participating in civic and community work" as well as promoting their occupation and improving their techniques. The National Beauty Culturists' League was formed in 1919 with this mandate. In the 1940s, it would meet in Tampa at the Martí-Maceo Hall. On African American beauty

culturists, see Tiffany Gill, "'Never Wanted to Do Anything but Hair': Beauty Salons, Hairdressers, and the Formation of African American Female Entrepreneurship" (paper presented at the Black Atlantic Seminar, Rutgers University, Spring 1999), 11 (quote).

24. On communitywide organizing, see Mormino and Pozzetta, *The Immigrant World of Ybor City*, 151, 152, 157–59; and *El Internacional*, September 5 and 12 and November 7 and 14, 1919.

25. "The Strippers' Problem," *El Internacional*, March 2, 1917 (original in English). *Tobacco stripper* and *stemmer* were synonymous terms.

26. *Tampa Morning Tribune*, August 17, 1918, January 16, February 6 and 8, and November 16, 1919; *Tampa Times*, January 7, 1919; *Tobacco Leaf*, March 13, 1919. The events of 1919 were also covered extensively in Havana's *La Lucha*.

27. Ibid.

28. The American stemmers' petition is covered in *Tampa Morning Tribune*, February 8, 1919, along with the strike of Latin stemmers, which is also covered in *Tampa Morning Tribune*, February 6, 1919; and *Tobacco Leaf*, March 13, 1919.

29. On women packers, see *Tampa Morning Tribune*, November 16 and December 5 and 12, 1919.

30. The names of petitioners listed in the *Tampa Morning Tribune*, December 5, 1919, were linked with information in the Tampa City Directory, 1919, 1920, to determine residence, previous occupation, and husband's or sister's occupation. The only name that appeared twice in the directory was Mary Alonzo, but the second listing was for an African American helper at the Eagle Cafe, and it is unlikely that a predominantly white group of petitioners to the American Legion would have welcomed an African American ally.

31. *El Internacional*, December 1919 (date illegible).

32. Charles E. Jones, "Sodom or Gomorrah—or Both," *Jacksonville Dixie*, June 27, 1912, quoted in Gary Mormino and George Pozzetta, "The Political Economy of Organized Crime, Bolita and Bootlegging in Tampa," n.d. (unpublished paper in author's possession), 417.

33. The discussion of *bolita* and political corruption is based on Mormino and Pozzetta, "The Political Economy of Organized Crime," 416–20.

34. On suffrage campaigns in the South generally, see Marjorie Spruill Wheeler, *New Women of the New South: The Leaders of the Woman Suffrage Movement in the Southern States* (New York: Oxford University Press, 1993); and Elna C. Green, *Southern Strategies: Southern Women and the Suffrage Question* (Chapel Hill: University of North Carolina Press, 1997). On the Equal Suffrage League, see Weatherford, *A History of Women in Tampa*, 92–93; and "Florida," in *History of Woman Suffrage*, ed. Harper, 6:113–20.

35. On the backgrounds of Equal Suffrage League officers, see Tampa City Directory, 1918; and the *Tampa Daily Times*, October 8, 1920. It is possible that

Mrs. Davis was related to the Lizzie F. Davis who circulated petitions on behalf of Alice Snow for the 1916 school board election.

36. Mabel Williams Bean, "My Service in the Spanish American War," Florida State Archives Survey, 1937, cited in Weatherford, *A History of Women in Tampa,* 69–70.

37. Ibid. Latin women may have seemed an unlikely group to recruit for the suffrage movement because of their low naturalization rate, but there is no indication that it was this logic rather than anti-immigrant sentiment that led to their exclusion.

38. *Tampa Morning Tribune,* March 22, 1919, includes an editorial and discussion of a range of women's positions on woman suffrage.

39. See coverage in ibid., March 22 (first quote) and April 1 and 3 (second quote), 1919.

40. Ibid., November 1, 1919.

41. On the activities of the Equal Suffrage League, see ibid., October 28 and 31 and November 1, 1919; Weatherford, *A History of Women in Tampa,* 92–93; Crake, "'In Unity There Is Strength,'" 56–58; and Tampa Civic Association, Minute Book, 1916–23, HCFWC Papers. On the more typical racial politics of the southern suffrage campaign, see Lebsock, "Woman Suffrage and White Supremacy."

42. Tampa Civic Association, Minute Book, 1916–23.

43. Blackman, *The Florida Federation of Women's Clubs, 1895–1939,* 30–35; *Florida Times-Union,* October 4, 1917.

44. *Tampa Morning Tribune,* January 25, 1919.

45. American Association of University Women, Tampa Branch, Scrapbooks, in personal possession of Dr. Gladys Kashdin, Tampa. See also Ruthmary Tyre, "The Tampa Branch of the American Association of University Women, 1916–1946," 1992 (unpublished paper in author's possession). The Tampa affiliate of the Southern Association of College Women soon joined the American Association of University Women. This was the first organization of university women in the state, and its members were more concerned with academic achievement than with ethnic identity.

46. Although the institution of the white primary minimized African American voting after 1910, white civic leaders continued to voice concern about Black ballots and sought additional ways to ensure African American disfranchisement.

47. On the charter battle, see Gardner and Lawson, "At-Large Elections and Black Voting Rights in Tampa/Hillsborough County, 1910–1984"; and *Tampa Morning Tribune* and *Tampa Daily Times,* for July through October 1920, esp. July 24, August 25, and October 2, 6, 14, 20, and 21.

48. *Tampa Morning Tribune,* August 25, 1920; *Tampa Daily Times,* October 2, 1920. Many articles between August 25 and October 20, 1920, discussed the "problem" of African American women voters. On debates and concerns over

women's partisanship, see Melanie Gustafson, *Women and the Republican Party, 1854–1924* (Urbana: University of Illinois Press, 2001).

49. *Tampa Daily Times,* October 2, 1920. The final quote was reprinted in the *Times* from an article in *Good Housekeeping* magazine.

50. Editorial, *Tampa Morning Tribune,* September 21, 1920.

51. Ibid.

52. Crake, "'In Unity There Is Strength,'" 67.

53. *Tampa Morning Tribune,* October 8, 1920. Ivil Price was a Republican party candidate for sheriff in 1920. Ada Price apparently shared her husband's party affiliation, which made her an interesting choice for president of the Equal Suffrage League in this heavily Democratic community. It did, however, place her on common ground with the majority of national suffrage leaders, who were Republicans.

54. Despite taking opposing positions on the benefits of commission government, Annie Givens and Julia Norris shared the stage at a Cox-Roosevelt presidential rally just days before the charter vote.

55. On the founding of the Tampa Business and Professional Women, see *Tampa Morning Tribune,* May 25, 1987; on educational programs for women, see *Tampa Daily Times,* October 2 and 6, 1920.

56. *Tampa Daily Times,* October 6, 1920.

57. For registration figures, see *Tampa Morning Tribune,* October 18, 1920. For population figures, see U.S. Bureau of the Census, *Abstract of the Fourteenth Census of the United States, 1920* (Washington, D.C., Government Printing Office, 1923), 114–15, 130–31. If you exclude the Latin precincts, where the meaning of "white" and "colored" voters in the *Tribune* tally is unclear, women form just over 37 percent of white registrants.

58. Registration and population figures are taken from the sources listed in note 57. The percentages are approximate because the size of the African American population of voting age is not completely clear from the 1920 census data and was not provided by the *Tribune* report. This estimate also does not include the 153 "colored" women that the *Tribune* reported registered in Ybor City in 1920 because it is impossible to know whether any of these were African Americans.

59. For an analysis of Black women's importance in electoral politics nationally, see Evelyn Brooks Higginbotham, "In Politics to Stay: Black Women Leaders and Party Politics in the 1920s," in *Women, Politics, and Change,* ed. Louise Tilly and Patricia Gurin (New York: Russell Sage Foundation, 1990), 199–220.

60. The editorial in the *Tampa Morning Tribune,* October 11, 1920, quoting the *Tampa Daily Times* article published earlier that week.

61. *Tampa Morning Tribune,* October 20, 1920.

62. Ibid., October 31, 1920. It is not clear how the editors determined who cast which votes, other than by assuming that all those voting against the charter in certain precincts must have been African American or Latin.

63. Ibid., October 20, 1920.

64. For registration totals, see *Tampa Daily Times,* October 18, 1920; on pro-charter and anticharter vote margins by precinct, see *Tampa Daily Times,* October 21, 1920. Since the *Times* was opposed to the charter, it would have little reason to report favorably on the heavy pro-charter vote from predominantly white precincts and the heavy anticharter vote in Black precincts. For coverage of voter turnout, see also *Tampa Morning Tribune,* October 20, 1920.

65. *Tampa Morning Tribune,* October 20, 1920. Julia Norris did run for a council seat, though she was opposed by most Anglo clubwomen, who thought it was too soon for such a move. She received only 997 votes out of more than 20,000 cast in the November election.

66. Norris, quoted in *Tampa Morning Tribune,* October 20, 1920.

67. For figures on citizenship, see Mormino and Pozzetta, "The Political Economy of Organized Crime," 426, and on corruption more generally, passim. On issues of disfranchisement, see Lawson and Gardner, "At-Large Elections and Black Voting Rights in Tampa/Hillsborough County, 1910–1984."

68. R. S. Sexton to Samuel Gompers, July 31, 1920, reel 36, American Federation of Labor Papers. Sexton was the CMIU organizer on the scene.

69. Even though the union refused the offer, it did donate ten dollars toward the rebuilding fund, a gesture no doubt made in recognition that the Children's Home had cared for Cuban orphans for many years.

70. Letters column, *Tampa Citizen,* July 20, 1920.

71. The *Cigar Makers' Official Journal* of September 15, 1920, included a list of locals donating to the A.F. of L. Fund in Aid of the Tampa Strikers between August 10 and September 10, 1920. The donors ranged from the Garment Workers Local 26 of St. Louis, through the Cracker Packers and the Laundry Workers of San Francisco, to the Tobacco Strippers of Bayamon, Puerto Rico. Other contributors included locals of bricklayers, mine workers, switchmen, and bookbinders from all over the United States and the Caribbean.

72. On missions, see report on Methodist conference in *Tampa Morning Tribune,* October 20, 1920.

73. Until August 25, the *Tribune* and the *Times* ran far more articles and editorials on the cigar strike than on woman suffrage or women's emancipation. Between then and October 20, the day of the charter vote, they featured woman suffrage and the charter contest far more prominently. After October 20, they returned to a focus on the strike.

74. *Tobacco Leaf,* August 26 (first quote) and September 23 (second quote), 1920.

75. On Committee of Public Health, see *Tampa Morning Tribune,* October 15 and November 2, 1920. The editors of *El Internacional,* in disputing the mainstream press's characterizations of cigar workers' locals, claimed that 30 percent of the city's 8,125 cigar workers were American-born, many of American-born

parents, and that the president of the stemmers' union was an American woman. Elizabeth Law was African American but lived on Garcia Street in Ybor City with her husband, William, a fireman. Manufacturers and Anglo civic leaders always used the term *American girls* to mean white women only; union leaders, when they used the term at all, meant native-born women, white or Black.

76. *Tampa Citizen,* August 13, 1920, responding to claims in *Tobacco Leaf* that "American girls," meaning native-born white women, were pouring into Tampa to take jobs as packers that striking Latin men had left vacant.

77. On workers' activities between August and October 1920, see, for example, *Tampa Morning Tribune,* September 7 and October 15 (quote), 1920; *Tampa Citizen,* September 12 and November 12, 1920; *El Internacional,* September 10, 1920; and *Cigar Makers International Journal,* September 15, 1920.

78. The presence of Cándida Bustamente as a speaker is recorded in the *Tampa Morning Tribune,* October 15, 1920. The description of the electrifying speech appeared in *El Internacional,* October 22, 1920. The coverage of Bustamente's missionary work is in *Tampa Morning Tribune,* October 20, 1920.

79. *Tampa Morning Tribune,* October 15, 1920. The *Tampa Daily Times,* October 14, 1920, claimed that a vote was taken and that women strikers voted with the majority to continue the strike.

80. *Tampa Morning Tribune,* October 20, 1920.

81. Letter from Committee of Public Health, ibid., November 2, 1920.

82. Ibid., February 6, 1921. The vote was 2,514 for ending the strike and 1,054 against, but there was no report on differences in women's and men's positions on the issue.

83. Ibid., November 27, 1921 (quote); *Tampa Daily Times,* November 26, 1921. The outcome of this episode is unclear, though the cigar factories were operating at nearly full capacity by the end of 1921.

84. Tampa League of Women's Clubs, Scrapbook, vol. 1, and Handbook, 1921–22, Tampa League of Women's Clubs Papers, Special Collections, University of South Florida Library; Tampa City Directory, 1922.

85. On the relation of suffrage to women's voluntarism nationally, see Nancy Cott, "Across the Great Divide: Women in Politics before and after 1920," in *Women, Politics, and Change,* ed. Tilly and Gurin, 153–76. Cott argues that historians have too easily assumed that women's enfranchisement curtailed their nonelectoral activities. She claims that female voluntarism expanded alongside voting after 1920.

# 9

# WE JUST KEPT GOING

## CAROLYN DANIELS

From *Hands on the Freedom Plow:
Personal Accounts by Women in SNCC,*
edited by Faith S. Holsaert et al. (2010)

*In spite of almost losing her life, a local beautician and
movement host refuses to stop her civil rights activities.*

### Getting Involved in the Movement

I got involved in the Movement and SNCC because of my son, Roy. At the time, I owned my own beauty shop in Dawson, Georgia. Dawson is the county seat of Terrell County and is located twenty-five miles from Albany. I had made a little money and bought the land. Then I made a little more money and built the shop, made a little more and built my house. This was very important, because black people who did not have their own businesses and homes had to work for white people who were in business. Since I owned my own home and business, I was free to do what I chose. Roy, who was in high school, and I were the only people in my house, so I really did answer only to myself.

I can't really explain why Roy became active. Roy is just Roy. Even to this day, he can't fit into a "Do as I say do, punch a time clock" kind of thing. Early in the 1960s, when Roy was president of the student body at Carver High School, he gave a speech about civil rights that the principal didn't like. The principal called in the police and Roy was expelled. Shortly after this, Roy brought Charles Sherrod to stay with us, saying, "Sherrod wants to spend a night or two." Sherrod would go out and Roy would be with him. At first I didn't know what Sherrod was really there for, but after a while Roy started telling me a little bit about the civil rights work they were doing.

Next they wanted to have meetings at my church, Atoc A.M.E. Church. It was our right as members to ask to hold meetings there, but when I asked, none of the other church members agreed, because we were about voting and civil rights. They said, "You know these white people will burn our church down" (which turned out to be true later on for the churches that did hold voting classes), and they refused to let us use the church.

Still Sherrod kept going. Roy kept going. One day in the fall of 1961, Roy—who was not old enough to vote or drive, really—drove one of their recruits, Mrs. Inez Calloway, up to the courthouse to register. While Roy was waiting outside, the sheriff, Z. T. Mathews, slapped and kicked Roy. When Roy came home and told me what had happened, the hair rose on the back of my head. I knew I couldn't stand by and let things like this happen. The thing I couldn't get over was that Roy was just a youngster who didn't bother anybody, yet he couldn't go into the courthouse, a public building, without the sheriff slapping and kicking him. And I was a taxpayer. That just made me mad. I had no other choice. I started working and really got involved in the Movement. Through anger I became active.

I got out there with Sherrod and Roy. This was the way to make a change, to get people to register. That way the white people would have to hear what we had to say. We knew that if we had gone in and gotten angry, there would have been a bloody battle. So a night or two turned into a week or two. A week or two turned into a month or two, and a month or two turned into years. We held meetings at the churches to teach people to register to vote. We started studying the Constitution and all these long words that we didn't know. I was the teacher, with a blackboard, some crayons, and other materials, which I bought with the thirty dollars Andy Young at SCLC sent me every month for this purpose. After people went through the training sessions, they went down to the courthouse.

Fearing that Roy would be killed if he remained in Dawson, I sent him to his father's in Jacksonville, Florida, to finish high school, which he did, with honors, and then on to Paine College for a year. Finally Andy Young arranged a scholarship for Roy at UCLA. In the summer of 1962 the white segregationists burned down the three churches we did use in Terrell and Lee counties. That didn't stop us. Sherrod put up tents instead, and we kept going and met in those tents. I taught my voter education classes in those tents. The harassment was always there. At one point they suspended my driver's license. I had done not one thing, yet still I had to go three months without a driver's license. They really tried to make it hard for us. Teachers would call me and say they couldn't come to me to have their hair done or they'd lose their jobs, but somehow I kept going.

At that time there were only five registered black voters in Terrell County. The test was so hard that it was difficult for people with limited education to pass it, but even teachers had not been able to pass the test, because the white registrar arbitrarily determined who passed and who didn't. We started going up to the courthouse by ones and twos. I took about four people up with me, and we all passed the test and got on the voters' roster. Even though some people were discouraged by that long, drawn-out test or when they were not passed, enough black people did get registered as a result of our campaign to elect quite a few black officials in Terrell County.

Things changed after people started to register and vote. When the next election came, the students and teachers would call me late at night and whisper, "We have to get this superintendent out." I laughed at all their tiptoeing around. I knew they had to keep their jobs, but I still laughed at their caution. When the superintendent lost, he said, "It was on account of that Carolyn Daniels."

## Terrorism in Terrible Terrell

What made Terrell County so terrible before we got the vote was that the white people felt, "This is my county; this is the way things are going to be. And I don't want it to change." They would actually kill black people by lynching and other methods. From the time I was growing up in the 1930s, I would hear stories about beatings and lynchings of people I knew. When a black man who owned the dry cleaners became involved with a white woman, they took him out, beat him, and castrated him. Another man, arrested for a domestic situation, was beaten so badly in jail that when they brought him to court, they had to drag and carry him in. They had to sit him up, because he couldn't sit up by himself. He died shortly afterward. Of course, these incidents were intimidating.

During the Movement, Terrell County white folks shot into my home because I housed young civil rights workers, both white and black, and, of course, this was unacceptable in that area then. From time to time I would have as many as nine SNCC workers staying with me. My house was shot into at least twice when they were there. Once was late in the summer of 1962 when I was over in Albany; two civil rights workers were hit. Prathia Hall was shot in the finger, Jack Chatfield in the arm. Ralph Allen was at the house also. When the shooting started, they all tried to hide: Sherrod under a bed and Roy behind the refrigerator. But we kept going, kept in the streets, kept taking people to register, kept getting people to vote.

One Saturday night in December 1963, about eleven at night, after all the volunteers and my son, Roy, had gone back to school, I had closed my beauty shop and was lying on my bed in my house alone. I heard footsteps and car doors slamming. I thought, *What is going on this late at night?* My bed was right next to the window. Just as I started to peep out of the window, the shooting began. As I rolled over onto the floor and got under the bed, all the windows were shot out. Then a bomb was thrown in and rolled right under the bed with me. All I could think was, *Oh, Lord, what is Roy going to do without me?* I knew this was the end. But somehow the bomb did not go off.

Finally the shooting stopped, and I could hear the cars drive away. I crawled out from under the bed, went into my son's room at the back, turned on the light, and saw that blood was just pouring from my foot. I ran outside to the neighbor's and she took me to the hospital.

When I came back, my house was gone. The bomb had gone off after I left. There was a big hole in the floor where my bed had been. Slats from the roof were everywhere. They never found who bombed my house or who shot into it. Different organizations sent money to repair my house. After it was fixed, Sherrod and the SNCC workers continued to use my house, and we just kept going, we just kept going.

# 10

# RACE, CLASS, AND GENDER

## Prospects for an All-Inclusive Sisterhood

### BONNIE THORNTON DILL

From *U.S. Women in Struggle: A* Feminist Studies
*Anthology*, edited by Claire Goldberg Moses
and Heidi Hartmann (1995)

The concept of sisterhood has been an important unifying force in the contemporary women's movement. By stressing the similarities of women's secondary social and economic positions in all societies and in the family, this concept has been a binding force in the struggle against male chauvinism and patriarchy. However, as we review the recent past, it becomes apparent that the cry "Sisterhood is powerful!" has engaged only a few segments of the female population in the United States. Black, Hispanic, Native American, and Asian American women of all classes, as well as many working-class women, have not readily identified themselves as sisters of the white middle-class women who have been in the forefront of the movement.

This essay examines the applications of the concept of sisterhood and some of the reasons for the limited participation of racially and ethnically distinct women in the women's movement, with particular reference to the experience and consciousness of African-American women. The first section presents a critique of sisterhood as a binding force for all women and examines the limitations of the concept for both theory and practice when applied to women who are neither white nor middle class. In the second section, the importance of women's perception of themselves and their place in society is explored as a way of understanding the differences and similarities between Black and white women. Data from two studies, one of college-educated Black women and the other of Black female household workers, are presented to illuminate both the ways in which the structures of race, gender, and class intersect in the lives of Black women and the women's perceptions of the impact of these structures on their lives. This essay concludes with a discussion of the prospects for sisterhood and suggests political strategies that may provide a first step toward a more inclusive women's movement.

## The Limitations of Sisterhood

In a political critique of the concept of sisterhood, historian Elizabeth Fox-Genovese identifies some of the current limitations of this concept as a rallying point for women across the boundaries of race and class.[1] Sisterhood is generally understood as a nurturant, supportive feeling of attachment and loyalty to other women which grows out of a shared experience of oppression. A term reminiscent of familial relationships, it tends to focus upon the particular nurturant and reproductive roles of women and, more recently, upon commonalities of personal experience. Fox-Genovese suggests that sisterhood has taken two different political directions. In one, women have been treated as unique, and sisterhood was used as a basis for seeking to maintain a separation between the competitive values of the world of men (the public-political sphere) and the nurturant values of the world of women (the private-domestic sphere). A second, more recent and progressive expression of the concept views sisterhood as an element of the feminist movement which serves as a means for political and economic action based upon the shared needs and experiences of women. Both conceptualizations of sisterhood have limitations in encompassing the racial and class differences among women. These limitations have important implications for the prospects of an all-inclusive sisterhood.

Fox-Genovese argues that the former conceptualization, which she labels "bourgeois individualism," resulted in "the passage of a few middle class women into the public sphere" but sharpened the class and racial divisions between them and lower-class minority women. In the latter conceptualization, called the "politics of personal experience," sisterhood is restricted by the experiential differences that result from the racial and class divisions of society.

> Sisterhood has helped us, as it helped so many of our predecessors, to forge ourselves as political beings. Sisterhood has mobilized our loyalty to each other and hence to ourselves. It has given form to a dream of genuine

equality for women. But without a broader politics directed toward the kind of social transformation that will provide social justice for all human beings, it will, in a poignant irony, result in our dropping each other by the wayside as we compete with rising desperation for crumbs.[2]

These two notions of sisterhood, as expressed in the current women's movement, offer some insights into the alienation many Black women have expressed about the movement itself.

The bourgeois individualistic theme present in the contemporary women's movement led many Black women to express the belief that the movement existed merely to satisfy needs for personal self-fulfillment on the part of white middle-class women.[3] The emphasis on participation in the paid labor force and escape from the confines of the home seemed foreign to many Black women. After all, as a group they had had higher rates of paid labor force participation than their white counterparts for centuries, and many would have readily accepted what they saw as the "luxury" of being a housewife. At the same time, they expressed concern that white women's gains would be made at the expense of Blacks and/or that having achieved their personal goals, these so-called sisters would ignore or abandon the cause of racial discrimination. Finally, and perhaps most importantly, the experiences of racial oppression made Black women strongly aware of their group identity and consequently more suspicious of women who, initially at least, defined much of their feminism in personal and individualistic terms.

Angela Davis, in "Reflections on the Black Woman's Role in the Community of Slaves," stresses the importance of group identity for Black women. "Under the impact of racism the black woman has been continually constrained to inject herself into the desperate struggle for existence. . . . As a result, black women have made significant contributions to struggles against racism and the dehumanizing exploitation of a wrongly organized society. In fact, it would appear that the intense levels of resistance historically maintained by black people and thus the historical function of the Black liberation struggle as harbinger of change throughout the society are due in part to the greater objective equality between the black man and the black woman."[4] The sense of being part of a collective movement toward liberation has been a continuing theme in the autobiographies of contemporary Black women.

Ideas and experiences vary, but Shirley Chisholm, Gwendolyn Brooks, Angela Davis and other Black women who wrote autobiographies during the seventies offer similar . . . visions of the black woman's role in the struggle for Black liberation. The idea of collective liberation . . . says that society is not a protective arena in which an individual black can work out her own destiny and gain a share of America's benefits by her own efforts. . . . Accordingly, survival, not to mention freedom, is dependent on the values and actions of the groups as a whole, and if indeed one succeeds or triumphs it is due less to individual talent than to the group's belief in and adherence to the idea that freedom from oppression must be acted out and shared by all.[5]

Sisterhood is not new to Black women. It has been institutionalized in churches. In many Black churches, for example, membership in the church entitles one to address the women as "sisters" and the men as "brothers." Becoming a sister is an important rite of passage which permits young women full participation in certain church rituals and women's clubs where these nurturant relationships among women are reinforced.[6] Sisterhood was also a basis for organization in the club movements that began in the late 1800s.[7] Finally, it is clearly exemplified in Black extended family groupings that frequently place great importance on female kinship ties. Research on kinship patterns among urban Blacks identifies the nurturant and supportive feelings existing among female kin as a key element in family stability and survival.[8]

Although Black women have fostered and encouraged sisterhood, we have not used it as the anvil to forge our political identities. This contrasts sharply with the experiences of many middle-class white women who have participated in the current women's movement. The political identities of African-American women have largely been formed around issues of race. National organizations of Black women, many of which were first organized on the heels of the nineteenth-century movement for women's rights, "were (and still are) decidedly feminist in the values expressed in their literature and in many of the concerns which they addressed, yet they also always focused upon issues which resulted from the racial oppression affecting *all* black people."[9] This commitment to the improvement of the race has often led Black women to see feminist issues quite differently from their white sisters. And racial animosity and mistrust have too often undermined the potential for coalition between Black and white women since the women's suffrage campaigns.

Many contemporary white feminists would like to believe that relations between Black and white women in the early stages of the women's movement were characterized by the beliefs and actions of Susan B. Anthony, Angelina Grimké, and some others. The historical record suggests, however, that these women were more exceptional than normative. Rosalyn Terborg-Penn argues that "discrimination against Afro-American women reformers was the rule rather than the exception within the woman's rights movement from the 1830's to 1920."[10] Although it is beyond the scope of this article to provide a detailed discussion of the incidents that created mistrust and ill-feeling between Black and white women, the historical record provides an important legacy that still haunts us.

The movement's early emphasis upon the oppression of women within the institution of marriage and the family, and upon educational and professional discrimination, reflected the concerns of middle-class white women. During that period, Black women were engaged in a struggle for survival and a fight for freedom. Among their immediate concerns were lynching and economic viability. Working-class white women were concerned about labor conditions, the length of the working day, wages, and so forth. The statements of early women's rights groups do not reflect these concerns, and, "as a rigorous consummation of the consciousness of white middle-class women's dilemma, the (Seneca Falls) Declaration all but ignored the predicament of white working-class women, as it ignored the condition of Black women in the South and North alike."[11]

Political expediency drove white feminists to accept principles that were directly opposed to the survival and well-being of Blacks in order to seek to achieve more limited advances for women. "Besides the color bar which existed in many white women's organizations, black women were infuriated by white women's accommodation to the principle of lynch law in order to gain support in the South . . . and the attacks of well-known feminists against anti-lynching crusader, Ida Wells Barnett."[12] The failure of the suffrage movement to sustain its commitment to the democratic ideal of enfranchisement for all citizens is one of the most frequently cited instances of white women's fragile commitment to racial equality. "After the Civil War, the suffrage movement was deeply impaired by the split over the issue of whether black males should receive the vote before white and black women . . . in the heated pressures over whether black men or white and black women should be enfranchised first, a classist, racist, and even xenophobic rhetoric crept in."[13] The historical and continued abandonment of universalistic principles in order to benefit a privileged few, on the part of white women, is, I think, one of the reasons why Black women today have been reluctant to see themselves as part of a sisterhood that does not extend beyond racial boundaries. Even for those Black women who are unaware of the specific history, there is the recognition that under pressure from the white men with whom they live and upon whom they are economically dependent, many white women will abandon their "sisters of color" in favor of self-preservation. The feeling that the movement would benefit white women and abandon Blacks or benefit whites at the expense of Blacks is a recurrent theme. Terborg-Penn concludes: "The black feminist movement in the United States during the mid 1970's is a continuation of a trend that began over 150 years ago. Institutionalized discrimination against black women by white women has traditionally led to the development of racially separate groups that address themselves to race-determined problems as well as the common plight of women in America."[14]

Historically, as well as currently, Black women have felt called upon to choose between their commitments to feminism and to the struggle against racial injustice. Clearly, they are victims of both forms of oppression and are most in need of encouragement and support in waging battles on both fronts. However, insistence on such a choice continues largely as a result of the tendency of groups of Blacks and groups of women to battle over the dubious distinction of being the "most" oppressed. The insistence of radical feminists upon the historical priority, universality, and overriding importance of patriarchy in effect necessitates acceptance of a concept of sisterhood that places one's womanhood over and above one's race. At the same time, Blacks are accustomed to labeling discriminatory treatment as racism and therefore may tend to view sexism only within the bounds of the Black community rather than see it as a systemic pattern.[15] On the one hand, the choice between identifying as Black or female is a product of the "patriarchal strategy of divide-and-conquer"[16] and, therefore, a false choice. Yet the historical success of this strategy and the continued importance of class, patriarchal, and racial divisions perpetuate such choices both within our consciousness and within the concrete realities of our daily lives.

Race, of course, is only one of the factors that differentiate women. It is the most salient in discussions of Black and white women, but it is perhaps no more important, even in discussions of race and gender, than is the factor of class. Inclusion of the concept of class permits a broader perspective on the similarities and differences between Black and white women than does a purely racial analysis. Marxist feminism has focused primarily upon the relationship between class exploitation and patriarchy. Although this literature has yielded several useful frameworks for beginning to examine the dialectics of gender and class, the role of race, though acknowledged, is not explicated.

Just as the gender-class literature tends to omit race, the race-class literature gives little attention to women. Recently, this area of inquiry has been dominated by a debate over the relative importance of race or class in explaining the historical and contemporary status of Blacks in this country. A number of scholars writing on this issue have argued that the racial division of labor in the United States began as a form of class exploitation which was shrouded in an ideology of racial inferiority. Through the course of U.S. history, racial structures began to take on a life of their own and cannot now be considered merely reflections of class structure.[17] A theoretical understanding of the current conditions of Blacks in this country must therefore take account of both race and class factors. It is not my intention to enter into this debate but instead to point out that any serious study of Black women must be informed by this growing theoretical discussion. Analyses of the interaction of race, gender, and class fall squarely between these two developing bodies of theoretical literature.

Black women experience class, race, and sex exploitation simultaneously, yet these structures must be separated analytically so that we may better understand the ways in which they shape and differentiate women's lives. Davis, in her previously cited article, provides one of the best analyses to date of the intersection of gender, race, and class under a plantation economy.[18] One of the reasons this analysis is so important is because she presents a model that can be expanded to other historical periods. However, we must be careful not to take the particular historical reality which she illuminated and read it into the present as if the experiences of Black women followed some sort of linear progression out of slavery. Instead, we must look carefully at the lives of Black women throughout history in order to define the peculiar interactions of race, class, and gender at particular historical moments.

In answer to the question: Where do Black women fit into the current analytical frameworks for race and class and gender and class? I would ask: How might these frameworks be revised if they took full account of Black women's position in the home, family, and marketplace at various historical moments? In other words, the analysis of the interaction of race, gender, and class must not be stretched to fit the procrustean bed of any other burgeoning set of theories. It is my contention that it must begin with an analysis of the ways in which Black people have been used in the process of capital accumulation in the United States. Within the contexts of class exploitation and racial oppression, women's lives and work are most clearly illuminated. Davis's article illustrates this. Increasingly, new research is being presented which grapples with the complex interconnectedness of these three issues in the lives of Black women and other women of color.[19]

## Perceptions of Self in Society

For Black women and other women of color an examination of the ways in which racial oppression, class exploitation, and patriarchy intersect in their lives must be studied in relation to their perceptions of the impact these structures have upon them. Through studying the lives of particular women and searching for patterns in the ways in which they describe themselves and their relationship to society, we will gain important insights into the differences and similarities between Black and white women.

The structures of race and class generate important economic, ideological, and experiential cleavages among women. These lead to differences in perception of self and their place in society. At the same time, commonalities of class or gender may cut across racial lines, providing the conditions for shared understanding. Studying these interactions through an examination of women's self-perceptions is complicated by the fact that most people view their lives as a whole and do not explain their daily experiences or worldview in terms of the differential effects of their racial group, class position, or gender. Thus, we must examine on an analytical level the ways in which the structures of class, race, and gender intersect in any woman's or group of women's lives in order to grasp the concrete set of social relations that influence their behavior. At the same time, we must study individual and group perceptions, descriptions, and conceptualizations of their lives so that we may understand the ways in which different women perceive the same and different sets of social structural constraints.

Concretely, and from a research perspective, this suggests the importance of looking at both the structures which shape women's lives and their self-presentations. This would provide us not only with a means of gaining insight into the ways in which racial, class, and gender oppression are viewed but also with a means of generating conceptual categories that will aid us in extending our knowledge of their situation. At the same time, this new knowledge will broaden and even reform our conceptualization of women's situations.

For example, how would our notions of mothering, and particularly mother-daughter relationships, be revised if we considered the particular experiences and perceptions of Black women on this topic? Gloria I. Joseph argues for and presents a distinctive approach to the study of Black mother-daughter relationships, asserting that

> to engage in a discussion of Black mothers and daughters which focused on specific psychological mechanisms operating between the two, the dynamics of the crucial bond, and explanations for the explicit role of patriarchy, without also including the important relevancy of racial oppression ... would necessitate forcing Black mother/daughter relationships into pigeonholes designed for understanding white models.
>
> In discussing Black mothers and daughters, it is more realistic, useful, and intellectually astute to speak in terms of their roles, positions, and functions within the Black society and that society's relationship to the broader (White) society in America.[20]

Unfortunately, there have been very few attempts in the social sciences to systematically investigate the relationship between social structure and self-perceptions of Black women. The profiles of Black women that have been appearing in magazines like *Essence,* the historical studies of Black women, fiction and poetry by and about Black women, and some recent sociological and anthropological studies provide important data for beginning such an analysis. However, the question of how Black women perceive themselves with regard to the structures of race, gender, and class is still open for systematic investigation.

Elizabeth Higginbotham, in a study of Black women who graduated from college between 1968 and 1970, explored the impact of class origins upon strategies for educational attainment. She found that class differences within the Black community led not only to different sets of educational experiences but also to different personal priorities and views of the Black experience.[21] According to Higginbotham, the Black women from middle-class backgrounds who participated in her study had access to better schools and more positive schooling experiences than did their working-class sisters. Because their parents did not have the economic resources to purchase the better educational opportunities offered in an integrated suburb or a private school, the working-class women credited their parents' willingness to struggle within the public school system as a key component in their own educational achievement. Social class also affected college selections and experience. Working-class women were primarily concerned with finances in selecting a college and spent most of their time adjusting to the work load and the new middle-class environment once they had arrived. Middle-class women, on the other hand, were freer to select a college that would meet their personal, as well as their academic, needs and abilities. Once there, they were better able to balance their work and social lives and to think about integrating future careers and family lives.

Among her sample, Higginbotham found that a larger proportion of women from working-class backgrounds were single. She explained this finding in terms of class differences in socialization and mobility strategies. She found that the parents of women from working-class backgrounds stressed educational achievement over and above other personal goals.[22] These women never viewed marriage as a means of mobility and focused primarily upon education, postponing interest in, and decisions about, marriage. In contrast, women from middle-class backgrounds were expected to marry and were encouraged to integrate family and educational goals throughout their schooling.

My own research on household workers demonstrates the ways in which class origins, racial discrimination, and social conceptions of women and women's work came together during the first half of the twentieth century to limit work options and affect family roles and the self-perceptions of one group of African-American women born between 1896 and 1915.[23] Most of them were born in the South and migrated North between 1922 and 1955. Like the majority of Black working women of this period, they worked as household workers in private homes. (During the first half of the twentieth century, labor force participation rates of Black women ranged from about 37 percent to 50 percent. Approximately 60 percent of Black women workers were employed in private household work up until 1960.)[24]

The women who participated in this study came from working-class families. Their fathers were laborers and farmers; their mothers were housewives or did paid domestic work of some kind (cooking, cleaning, taking in washing, and so forth). As a result, the women not only had limited opportunities for education but also often began working when they were quite young to help support their families. Jewell Prieleau (names are pseudonyms used to protect the identity of the subjects), one of eight children, described her entrance into work as follows:

> When I was eight years old, I decided I wanted a job and I just got up early in the morning and I would go from house to house and ring doorbells and ask for jobs and I would get it. I think I really wanted to work because in a big family like that, they was able to feed you, but you had to earn your shoes. They couldn't buy shoes although shoes was very cheap at that time. I would rather my mother give it to the younger children and I would earn my way.

Queenie Watkins lived with her mother, aunt, and five cousins and began working in grammar school. She described her childhood jobs in detail.

> When I went to grammar school, the white ladies used to come down and say "Do you have a girl who can wash dishes?" That was how I got the job with the doctor and his wife. I would go up there at six o'clock in the morning and wash the breakfast dishes and bring in scuttles of coal to burn on the fireplace. I would go back in the afternoon and take the little girl down on the sidewalk and if there were any leaves to be raked on the yard, I'd rake the leaves up and burn them and sweep the sidewalk. I swept off the front porch and washed it off with the hose and washed dishes again—for one dollar a week.

Although class position limited the economic resources and educational opportunities of most of these women, racial discrimination constricted work options for Black women in such a way as to seriously undercut the benefits of education. The comments of the following women are reflective of the feelings expressed by many of those in this sample:

> When I came out of school, the black man naturally had very few chances of doing certain things and even persons that I know myself who had finished four years of college were doing the same type of work because they couldn't get any other kind of work in New York.

> In my home in Virginia, education, I don't think was stressed. The best you could do was be a schoolteacher. It wasn't something people impressed upon you you could get. I had an aunt and cousin who were trained nurses and the best they could do was nursing somebody at home or something. They couldn't get a job in a hospital. I didn't pay education any mind really until I came to New York. I'd gotten to a certain stage in domestic work in the country and I didn't see the need for it.

> Years ago there was no such thing as a black typist. I remember girls who were taking typing when I was going to school. They were never able to get a job at it. In my day and time you could have been the greatest typist in the world but you would never have gotten a job. There was no such thing as getting a job as a bank teller. The blacks weren't even sweeping the banks.

For Black women in the United States, their high concentration in household work was a result of racial discrimination and a direct carryover from slavery. Black women were in essence "a permanent service caste in nineteenth and twentieth century America."[25] Arnold Anderson and Mary Jean Bowman argue that the distinguishing feature of domestic service in the United States is that "the frequency of servants is correlated with the availability of Negroes in local populations." By the time most of the women in this sample entered the occupation, a racial caste pattern was firmly established. The occupation was dominated by foreign-born white women in the North and Black freedwomen in the South, a pattern which was modified somewhat as southern Blacks migrated north. Nevertheless, most research indicates that Black women fared far worse than their white immigrant sisters, even in the North. "It is commonly asserted that the immigrant woman has been the northern substitute for the Negro servant. In 1930, when one can separate white servants by nativity, about twice as large a percentage of foreign as of native women were domestics. . . . As against this 2:1 ratio between immigrants and natives, the ratio of Negro to white servants ranged upward from 10:1 to 50:1. The immigrant was not the northerner's Negro."[26]

Two major differences distinguished the experiences of Black domestics from that of their immigrant sisters. First, Black women had few other employment options. Second, Black household workers were older and more likely to be married. Thus, although private household work cross-culturally, and for white women in the United States, was often used as a stepping-stone to other working-class occupations, or as a way station before marriage, for Black American women it was neither. This pattern did not begin to change substantially until World War II.

Table 10.1 indicates that between 1900 and 1940 the percentage of Black women in domestic service actually increased, relative to the percentage of immigrant women which decreased. The data support the contention that Black women were even more confined to the occupation than their immigrant sisters. At the turn of the century, large numbers of immigrants entered domestic service. Their children, however, were

Table 10.1: Percentage of Females of Each Nativity in U.S. Labor Force Who Were Servants, by Decades, 1900–1940

|  | 1900 | 1910 | 1920 | 1930 | 1940 |
|---|---|---|---|---|---|
| Native white | 22.3 | 15.0 | 9.6 | 10.4 | 11.0 |
| Foreign-born white | 42.5 | 34.0 | 23.8 | 26.8 | |
| Negro | 41.9 | 39.5 | 44.4 | 54.9 | 54.4 |
| Other | 24.8 | 22.9 | 22.9 | 19.4 | 16.0 |
| Total | 30.5 | 24.0 | 17.9 | 19.8 | 17.2 |
| (N, in thousands) | (1,439) | (1,761) | (1,386) | (1,906) | (1,931) |
| (Percent of all domestic servants) | (95.4) | (94.4) | (93.3) | (94.1) | (92.0) |

Source: George J. Stigler, *Domestic Servants in the United States: 1900–1940*, Occasional Paper no. 24 (New York: National Bureau of Economic Research, 1946), 7.

much less likely to become household workers. Similarly, many Black women entered domestic service at that time, but their children tended to remain in the occupation. It was the daughters and granddaughters of the women who participated in this study that were among the first generation of Black women to benefit from the relaxation of racial restrictions which began to occur after World War II.

Finally, Black women were household workers because they were women. Private household work is women's work. It is a working-class occupation, has low social status, low pay, and few guaranteed fringe benefits. Like the housewife who employs her, the private household worker's low social status and pay is tied to the work itself, to her class, gender, and the complex interaction of the three within the family. In other words, housework, both paid and unpaid, is structured around the particular place of women in the family. It is considered unskilled labor because it requires no training, degrees, or licenses, and because it has traditionally been assumed that any woman could or should be able to do housework.

The women themselves had a very clear sense that the social inequities which relegated them and many of their peers to household service labor were based upon their race, class, and gender. Yet different women, depending upon their jobs, family situations, and overall outlooks on life, handled this knowledge in different ways. One woman described the relationship between her family and her employer's as follows:

> Well for *their* children, I imagine they wanted them to become like they were, educators or something that-like [*sic*]. But what they had in for my children, they saw in me that I wasn't able to make all of that mark but raised my children in the best method I could. Because I wouldn't have the means to put *my* children through like they could for their children.

When asked what she liked most about her work, she answered, "Well, what I like most about it, the things that I weren't able to go to school to do for my children. I could kinda pattern from the families that I worked for, so that I could give my children the best of my abilities."

A second woman expressed much more anger and bitterness about the social differences which distinguished her life from that of her female employer.

> They don't know nothing about a hard life. The only hard life will come if they getting a divorce or going through a problem with their children. But their husband has to provide for them because they're not soft. And

> if they leave and they separate for any reason or [are] divorced, they have
> to put the money down. But we have no luck like that. We have to leave
> our children; sometime leave the children alone. There's times when I
> have asked winos to look after my children. It was just a terrible life and
> I really thank God that the children grow up to be nice.

Yet while she acknowledged her position as an oppressed person, she
used her knowledge of the anomalies in her employers' lives—particularly
the woman and her female friends—to aid her in maintaining her sense
of self-respect and determination and to overcome feelings of despair
and immobilization.

When asked if she would like to switch places with her employers, she
replied,

> I don't think I would want to change, but I would like to live differently.
> I would like to have my own nice little apartment with my husband and
> have my grandchildren for dinner and my daughter and just live comfort-
> able. But I would always want to work. . . . But, if I was to change life with
> them, I would like to have just a little bit of they money, that's all.

Although the women who participated in this study adopted different
personal styles of coping with these inequities, they were all clearly aware
that being Black, poor, and female placed them at the bottom of the social
structure, and they used the resources at their disposal to make the best
of what they recognized as a bad situation.

Contemporary scholarship on women of color suggests that the barriers to an all-inclusive sisterhood are deeply rooted in the histories of
oppression and exploitation that Blacks and other groups encountered
upon incorporation into the American political economy.[27] These histories affect the social positions of these groups today, and racial ethnic
women[28] in every social class express anger and distress about the forms
of discrimination and insensitivity which they encounter in their interactions with white feminists. Audre Lorde has argued that the inability of
women to confront anger is one of the important forces dividing women
of color from white women in the feminist movement. She cites several
examples from her own experience which resonate loudly with the experiences of most women of color who have been engaged in the women's
movement.

> After fifteen years of a women's movement which professes to address the
> life concerns and possible futures of all women, I still hear, on campus
> after campus, "How can we address the issues of racism? No women of

color attended." Or, the other side of that statement, "We have no one in our department equipped to teach their work." In other words, racism is a Black women's problem, a problem of women of color, and only we can discuss it.

White women are beginning to examine their relationships to Black women, yet often I hear you wanting only to deal with the little colored children across the roads of childhood, the beloved nursemaid, the occasional second-grade classmate. . . . You avoid the childhood assumptions formed by the raucous laughter at Rastus and Oatmeal . . . the indelible and dehumanizing portraits of Amos and Andy and your daddy's humorous bedtime stories.[29]

Bell hooks points to both the racial and class myopia of white feminists as a major barrier to sisterhood.

When white women's liberationists emphasized work as a path to liberation, they did not concentrate their attention on those women who are most exploited in the American labor force. Had they emphasized the plight of working class women, attention would have shifted away from the college-educated suburban housewife who wanted entrance into the middle and upper class work force. Had attention been focused on women who were already working and who were exploited as cheap surplus labor in American society, it would have de-romanticized the middle class white woman's quest for "meaningful" employment. While it does not in any way diminish the importance of women resisting sexist oppression by entering the labor force, work has not been a liberating force for masses of American women.[30]

As a beginning point for understanding the potential linkages and barriers to an all-inclusive sisterhood, Lorde concludes that "the strength of women lies in recognizing differences between us as creative, and in standing to those distortions which we inherited without blame but which are now ours to alter. The angers of women can transform differences through insight into power. For anger between peers births change, not destruction, and the discomfort and sense of loss it often causes is not fatal, but a sign of growth."[31]

## Prospects for an All-Inclusive Sisterhood

Given the differences in experiences among Black women, the differences between Black and white women, between working-class and middle-class women, between all of us, what then are the prospects for sisterhood? Although this essay has sought to emphasize the need to study and explicate these differences, it is based upon the assumption that the knowledge we gain in this process will also help enlighten us as to our similarities. Thus, I would argue for the abandonment of the concept of sisterhood as a global construct based on unexamined assumptions about our similarities, and I would substitute a more pluralistic approach that recognizes and accepts the objective differences between women. Such an approach requires that we concentrate our political energies on building coalitions around particular issues of shared interest. Through joint work on specific issues, we may come to a better understanding of one another's needs and perceptions and begin to overcome some of the suspicions and mistrust that continue to haunt us. The limitations of a sisterhood based on bourgeois individualism or on the politics of personal experience presently pose a very real threat to combined political action.

For example, in the field of household employment, interest in the needs of a growing number of middle-class women to participate in the work force and thus find adequate assistance with their domestic duties (a form of bourgeois individualism) could all too easily become support for a proposal such as the one made by writer Anne Colamosca in a 1980 article in the *New Republic*.[32] She proposed solving the problems of a limited supply of household help with a government training program for unemployed immigrant women to help them become "good household workers." Although this may help middle-class women pursue their careers, it will do so while continuing to maintain and exploit a poorly paid, unprotected, lower class and will leave the problem of domestic responsibility virtually unaddressed for the majority of mothers in the work force who cannot afford to hire personal household help. A socialist feminist perspective requires an examination of the exploitation inherent in household labor as it is currently organized for both the paid and unpaid worker. The question is, what can we do to upgrade the status of domestic labor for ALL women, to facilitate the adjustment and productivity of immigrant women, and to insure that those who choose to engage in paid private household work do so because it represents a potentially interesting, viable, and economically rewarding option for them?

At the same time, the women's movement may need to move beyond a limited focus on "women's issues" to ally with groups of women and men who are addressing other aspects of race and class oppression. One example is school desegregation, an issue which is engaging the time and energies of many urban Black women today. The struggles over school desegregation are rapidly moving beyond the issues of busing and racial balance. In many large cities, where school districts are between 60 and 85 percent Black, Hispanic, or Third World, racial balance is becoming less of a concern. Instead, questions are being raised about the overall quality of the educational experiences low-income children of all racial and ethnic groups are receiving in the public schools. This is an issue of vital concern to many racially and ethnically distinct women, because they see their children's future ability to survive in this society as largely dependent upon the current direction of public education. In what ways should feminists involve themselves in this issue? First, by recognizing that feminist questions are only one group of questions among many others that are being raised about public education. To the extent that Blacks, Hispanics, Native Americans, and Asian Americans are miseducated, so are women. Feminist activists must work to expand their conceptualization of the problem beyond the narrow confines of sexism. For example, efforts to develop and include nonsexist literature in the school curriculum are important. Yet this work cannot exist in a vacuum, ignoring the fact that schoolchildren *observe* a gender-based division of labor in which authority and responsibility are held primarily by men while women are concentrated in nurturant roles or that schools with middle-class students have more funds, better facilities, and better teachers than schools serving working-class populations. The problems of education must be addressed as structural ones. We must examine not only the kinds of discrimination that occur within institutions but also the ways in which discrimination becomes a fundamental part of the institution's organization and implementation of its overall purpose. Such an analysis would make the linkages between different forms of structural inequality, like sexism and racism, more readily apparent.

While analytically we must carefully examine the structures that differentiate us, politically we must fight the segmentation of oppression into categories such as "racial issues," "feminist issues," and "class issues." This is, of course, a task of almost overwhelming magnitude, and yet it seems to me the only viable way to avoid the errors of the past and to move forward to make sisterhood a meaningful feminist concept for all women, across the boundaries of race and class. For it is through first seeking to understand struggles that are not particularly shaped by one's own immediate personal priorities that we will begin to experience and understand the needs and priorities of our sisters—be they Black, brown, white, poor, or rich. When we have reached a point where the differences between us ENRICH our political and social action, rather than divide it, we will have gone beyond the personal and will, in fact, be "political enough."

## Notes

The author wishes to acknowledge the comments of Lynn Weber Cannon and Elizabeth Higginbotham on an earlier version of this essay.

1. Elizabeth Fox-Genovese, "The Personal Is Not Political Enough," *Marxist Perspectives* (Winter 1979–80): 94–113.

2. Ibid., 97–98, 112.

3. For discussions of Black women's attitudes toward the women's movement, see Linda LaRue, "The Black Movement and Women's Liberation," *Black Scholar* 1 (May 1970): 36–42; Renee Ferguson, "Women's Liberation Has a Different Meaning for Blacks," in *Black Women in White America: A Documentary History,* ed. Gerda Lerner (New York: Pantheon, 1972); Inez Smith Reid, *"Together" Black Women* (New York: Emerson-Hall, 1972); Cheryl Townsend Gilkes, "Black Women's Work As Deviance: Social Sources of Racial Antagonism within Contemporary Feminism" (Paper presented at the Seventy-fourth Annual Meeting of the American Sociological Association, Boston, August 1979).

4. Angela Davis, "Reflections on the Black Woman's Role in the Community of Slaves," *Black Scholar* 2 (December 1971): 15.

5. Mary Burgher, "Images of Self and Race," in *Sturdy Black Bridges,* ed. Roseann P. Bell, Bettye J. Parker, and Beverly Guy-Sheftall (Garden City, N.Y.: Anchor Books, 1979), 118.

6. For a related discussion of Black women's roles in the church, see Cheryl Townsend Gilkes's paper "Institutional Motherhood in Black Churches and Communities: Ambivalent Sexism or Fragmented Familyhood."

7. For a discussion of the club movement among black women, see, in addition to Lerner's book, Alfreda Duster, ed., *Ida Barnett, Crusade for Justice: The Autobiography of Ida B. Wells* (Chicago: University of Chicago Press, 1970); Rackham Holt, *Mary McLeod Bethune: A Biography* (Garden City, N.Y.: Doubleday & Co., 1964); Jeanne L. Noble, *Beautiful, Also, Are the Souls of My Black Sisters: A History of the Black Woman in America* (Englewood Cliffs, N.J.: Prentice-Hall, 1978); Mary Church Terrell, *A Colored Woman in a White World* (Washington, D.C.: Ransdell Publishing Co., 1940).

8. Carol Stack, *All Our Kin* (New York: Harper & Row, 1970); and Elmer P. Martin and Joan Martin, *The Black Extended Family* (Chicago: University of Chicago Press, 1977).

9. Gilkes, "Black Women's Work as Deviance," 21.

10. Rosalyn Terborg-Penn, "Discrimination against Afro-American Women in the Woman's Movement, 1830–1920," in *The Afro-American Woman: Struggles and Images,* ed. Sharon Harley and Rosalyn Terborg-Penn (Port Washington, N.Y.: Kennikat Press, 1978), 17.

11. Angela Davis, *Women, Race, and Class* (New York: Random House, 1981), 54.

12. Gilkes, "Black Women's Work As Deviance," 19. In this quotation Gilkes cites Jay S. Walker, "Frederick Douglass and Woman Suffrage," *Black Scholar* 4 (7 June 1973).

13. Adrienne Rich, "'Disloyal to Civilization': Feminism, Racism, and Gynephobia," *Chrysalis*, no. 7 (1978): 14.

14. Terborg-Penn, 27.

15. Elizabeth Higginbotham, "Issues in Contemporary Sociological Work on Black Women," *Humanity and Society* 4 (November 1980): 226–42.

16. Rich, 15.

17. This argument has been suggested by Robert Blauner in *Racial Oppression in America* (New York: Harper & Row, 1972); and William J. Wilson in *The Declining Significance of Race: Blacks and Changing American Institutions* (Chicago: University of Chicago Press, 1978).

18. Davis, "Reflections on the Black Woman's Role."

19. See Cheryl Townsend Gilkes, "Living and Working in a World of Trouble: The Emergent Career of the Black Woman Community Worker" (Ph.D. diss., Northeastern University, 1979); and Elizabeth Higginbotham, "Educated Black Women: An Exploration in Life Chances and Choices" (Ph.D. diss., Brandeis University, 1980).

20. Gloria I. Joseph and Jill Lewis, *Common Differences: Conflicts in Black and White Feminist Perspectives* (Garden City, N.Y.: Anchor Books, 1981), 75–76.

21. Higginbotham, "Educated Black Women."

22. Elizabeth Higginbotham, "Is Marriage a Priority? Class Differences in Marital Options of Educated Black Women," in *Single Life*, ed. Peter Stein (New York: St. Martin's Press, 1981), 262.

23. Bonnie Thornton Dill, "Across the Boundaries of Race and Class: An Exploration of the Relationship between Work and Family among Black Female Domestic Servants" (Ph.D. diss., New York University, 1979).

24. For detailed data on the occupational distribution of Black women during the twentieth century, see U.S. Bureau of the Census, *Historical Statistics of the United States: Colonial Times to 1970*, H. Doc. 83–78 (Washington, D.C.: GPO, 1973).

25. David Katzman, *Seven Days a Week: Women and Domestic Service in Industrializing America* (New York: Oxford University Press, 1978), 85.

26. Arnold Anderson and Mary Jean Bowman, "The Vanishing Servant and the Contemporary Status System of the American South," *American Journal of Sociology* 59 (November 1953): 216, 220.

27. Elizabeth Higginbotham, "Laid Bare by the System: Work and Survival for Black and Hispanic Women," in Amy Swerdlow and Hannah Lessinger, *Race, Class, and Gender: The Dynamics of Control* (Boston: G.K. Hall, 1983); and Bonnie Thornton Dill, "Survival as a Form of Resistance: Minority Women and the Maintenance of Families" (Working Paper no. 7, Inter University Group on Gender and Race, Memphis State University, 1982).

28. The term "racial ethnic women" is meant as an alternative to either "minority," which is disparaging; "Third World," which has an international connotation; or "women of color," which lacks any sense of cultural identity. In contrast to "ethnic," which usually refers to groups that are culturally distinct but members of the dominant white society, "racial ethnic" refers to groups that are both culturally and racially distinct and in the United States have historically shared certain common conditions as oppressed and internally colonized peoples.

29. Audre Lorde, "The Uses of Anger," *Women's Studies Quarterly* 9 (Fall 1981): 7.

30. bell hooks, *Ain't I a Woman? Black Women and Feminism* (Boston: South End Press, 1981), 146.

31. Lorde, 9.

32. Ann Colamosca, "Capitalism and Housework," *New Republic,* 29 Mar. 1980, 18–20.

---

Reprinted, with changes, from *Feminist Studies* 9, no. 1 (Spring 1983): 131–50.

# 11

# SOURCES OF POLITICAL UNITY AND DISUNITY AMONG WOMEN

Placing the Gender Gap in Perspective

LEONIE HUDDY, ERIN CASSESE,

AND MARY-KATE LIZOTTE

From *Voting the Gender Gap*,
edited by Lois Duke Whitaker (2008)

The gender gap has become a staple feature of the political landscape during the past several decades. Women have consistently voted in greater numbers than men for Democratic presidential and congressional candidates since the early 1980s.[1] They have also expressed greater identification with the Democratic Party over the same time period.[2] In the 1980s, Ronald Reagan polarized the genders more than other recent presidents had, which carried over into gender polarization on party identification, resulting in the widely broadcast notion of a "gender gap."[3]

But women's political commonality is far from pervasive. Although women are more inclined than men to support Democratic candidates, they do not act as a cohesive political force. Political group unity is typically marked by homogeneity of vote choice among group members and a sharp divergence from nongroup members. Such unity is highly visible among blacks, among whom 80 to 90 percent have supported Democratic presidential candidates in recent elections and have done so to a far greater degree than whites, whose support for Democratic candidates is closer to 40 percent.[4] Women do not form a cohesive, unified political force in this way. The gender gap in vote choice between men and women has hovered around ten percentage points over the last several decades, resulting, for example, in 54 percent of women supporting Bill Clinton in 1996 as compared to 43 percent of men, according to exit poll data.[5] This is very far from the unanimity exhibited by black voters in recent elections.[6]

Group-based political solidarity or cohesion is also typically marked by the degree to which a group's common interests motivate political commonality. But women's political cohesion also appears weak when examined from this perspective.[7] There is no evidence that the electoral "gender gap" reflected political unity among women by originating in a distinctive response to women's shared interests. In the 1930s and 1940s, women were substantially more supportive than men of liberalized roles for women, particularly their suitability for paid work and political office. However, such gender differences diminished through the 1960s, so that contemporary research typically turns up almost no major gender differences in support for such women's issues. The gender difference in support for the Equal Rights Amendment, which most explicitly promoted women's collective interests, was negligible during the late 1970s and early 1980s, when it was receiving the most publicity and its fate was largely determined. Similarly, much research has shown that men and women have not differed significantly in recent years on other women's issues, such as whether "a woman's place" is properly in the home, whether women should be drafted, how much discrimination there is against women, favorability toward women's organizations, and support for legalized abortion, issues on which both women and men are divided.[8]

Group members may also evince political cohesion through a greater political emphasis on group-linked issues. But women fail to pass the cohesion test in this respect. Ronald Reagan and the Republican Party took unsympathetic stances on women's issues in the 1980s, and leaders of the women's movement were outspokenly opposed to the Reagan administration. So women might well have been more inclined than men to vote for candidates who support women's issues. But here, too, the evidence suggests disunity rather than solidarity. Klein found large gender differences in the impact of women's issues on the presidential vote in 1980.[9] But others have not found such gender differences. Indeed, Mansbridge refutes the notion that the ERA had greater impact on women's than men's vote choice in the 1980 presidential election; the impact of the ERA was minimal among both genders.[10] Frankovic reported that support for women's issues such as the ERA and abortion had about the same small influence on women's job approval ratings of Reagan as it did on men's in the 1980–82 era.[11] And both Klein and Mueller report no gender differences in 1972 and 1976 surveys.[12] The weight of this and recent evidence is against strong gender differences on women's issues or in their political impact.[13]

Thus, when taken as a whole, there is little evidence that women are very unified politically. There are political differences between men and women. But these differences are modest and seem unrelated to gender-linked issues such as legalized abortion, the ERA, or other women's issues.[14] Our goal in this article is to look more closely at different kinds of women across diverse employment, marital, economic, and religious backgrounds to account for women's shared political commonality and scrutinize further the sources of their political disunity.[15] We favor a sociological approach in which we focus on demographic and religious factors rather than attitudes or subjective beliefs in order to assess the origins of the gender gap in women's real-life circumstances. We do not want to suggest, however, that attitudes are unimportant. Indeed, they are critical to the existence of the gender gap.

We also ask the following questions about women's admittedly limited political unity: Is it exhibited across the board, regardless of women's circumstances? Or is the gender gap confined to specific subgroups of women? We examine these issues across a broad time frame—from 1980 to 2004—in order to uncover general trends across a number of different presidential elections. This article serves to update an earlier analysis of the 1984 ANES data in which we found considerable disunity among women, revolving around their general political beliefs.[16]

## Women's Political Unity

The electoral and partisan gender gap is fueled by women's somewhat different positions than men on several political issues.[17] Women's stronger (or men's weaker) support of government social welfare spending is the most consistent explanation for the gender gap over time.[18] The centrality of social welfare issues to the gender gap raises questions about whether women's political unity is observed among all women or is confined to specific subgroups. One obvious possibility is that the gender gap is isolated among economically vulnerable women. In the aftermath of welfare reform in 1996, low-income women have had to rely on government assistance with child care to obtain employment and undertake job retraining. Prior to 1996, they were also more dependent on direct government assistance through Aid to Families with Dependent Children (AFDC). They may also have been more invested in programs directed at low-income children such as Head Start.[19] Box-Steffensmeier and colleagues find that in the aggregate, the gender gap in Democratic Party identification increases over time with an increase in the number of single women in American society, a potentially vulnerable group economically.[20] The gender gap and political unity may thus be especially pronounced among low-income women. We refer to this as the "economic vulnerability" hypothesis.

Alternatively, the gender gap might be driven by those who are economically autonomous from men (not economically vulnerable women) as Carroll has suggested.[21] From this perspective, the gender gap is confined to single women or well-educated women who are in professional employment because, in part, women are especially likely to be employed in the public sector (education, health care, etc.), and so have more to gain from the success of the Democratic Party.[22] This argument can be extended to working women more generally who may have more to gain than nonemployed women from Democratic administrations that are inclined to actively support assistance to working parents and promote affirmative action programs that help women's advancement in the workforce. And, finally, women employed in higher-status, male-dominated occupations may benefit the most from specific legislation concerning job discrimination and affirmative action and court decisions mandating redress of pay inequities. These considerations suggest that professional or well-educated working women may have the most to gain from the Democratic Party and Democratic candidates. We refer to this as the "economic autonomy" hypothesis.

## Women's Political Disunity

Overall, women and men alike show considerable political disunity when it comes to partisanship and electoral choice; these political differences are sizeable and largely independent of gender. We thus turn from women's common interests, or interests shared by specific subgroups of women (but not men), to focus more squarely on gender-neutral life situations and interests that divide men and women equally. We consider a number of demographic factors that have served as important lines of cleavage in American electoral politics, including race and ethnicity, religiosity and religion, and economic factors. When taken together, these characteristics account for a good deal of diversity in electoral choice and partisanship.

## Race

One of the most visible sources of division in American politics revolves around race. African Americans vote overwhelmingly for Democratic candidates and identify largely with the Democratic Party. Among whites, support for the Democratic Party is far more tepid. Voting studies conducted in the 1940s and 1950s demonstrated that blacks were more likely than whites to support Democratic candidates and identify as Democrats.[23] And blacks continue to display tremendous political unity in an era characterized by a marked decline in the political cohesion of many other sociodemographic groups.[24] Blacks' continued identification as Democrats goes hand in hand with widespread racial differences across a broad range of racial and social issues.[25] Overall, there are sizeable racial differences in support of government economic policy, social welfare spending, and explicit racial issues that are associated, in turn, with large racial differences in vote choice and partisanship.[26]

## Religion and Religiosity

From Ronald Reagan's 1980 election victory onward, there has been much discussion of the role of religiosity and the religious Right as a source of support for Republican candidates. In fact, it was not Ronald Reagan but rather Bill Clinton who triggered the most powerful religious cleavage in recent electoral history, resulting in strong support for Republican candidates among highly religious individuals that has persisted over time.[27] The political role of religion came to a head in the 2004 presidential election when pundits were quick to conclude that Christian fundamentalists had handed President Bush his reelection victory, leading in turn to demands by fundamentalist leaders for political payback.[28] Pew researchers conclude that religious voters, especially white fundamentalists, formed a powerful base of support for Bush in both 2000 and 2004 (http://people-press.org/commentary/display.php3?AnalysisID=103). This trend began earlier, with a steady increase in the percentage of white Protestant fundamentalists who identified with the Republican Party through the 1980s and early 1990s.[29]

Christian fundamentalists' strong support for the Republican Party stands in marked contrast to the political inclinations of Jews, who have typically supported the Democratic Party, a tendency that was apparent in the very first electoral studies and that has continued through the 1990s.[30] However, it is insufficient to look only at gross differences between major religious denominations to assess the political effects of religion. The frequency and nature of religious practice and belief are also politically consequential. The effect of religion or religious identity on partisanship and electoral behavior is likely most pronounced among individuals who frequently attend religious service—particularly those who attend weekly as opposed to attendance solely on religious holidays.

But one can expect diversity in political attitudes and behavior, even among individuals who report frequent religious practice. Several scholars have argued that the primary religious cleavages have shifted from those dividing major religious denominations to more cross-cutting cleavages that pit orthodox subdenominations against progressive or liberal subdenominations.[31] For example, we expect smaller differences in partisanship and electoral choice between mainline Protestants and respondents reporting no religious affiliation than between mainline Protestants and fundamentalist Protestants—and this seems to be borne out in the examples offered above. Overall, religion—denominational affiliation, religious practice, and religious beliefs—forms an important source of cleavage in both partisanship and vote choice among men and women, and has done so from the early 1980s. Religion and religiosity thus form a potentially powerful source of political division among women.

## Economic Factors

Economic factors also influence vote choice and partisanship independently of gender, and must be considered as a further gender-neutral source of disunity among women. The traditional Democratic New Deal coalition included members of the working class and union households. There has been some decline over time in support for the Democratic Party among members of union households, although they are still more likely to identify as Democrats than Republicans.[32] And there is a continued link between household income, with wealthier households supporting Republican candidates and identifying as Republicans, and low-income households supporting Democratic candidates and identifying as Democrats.[33] We note above the possibility that economic factors may unite women and exacerbate differences with men of the same economic background, but they are also likely to divide women and men equally. We examine both possibilities empirically in this study.

## Region

Finally, geographic region and urbanism also influence vote choice and partisanship. The South, once a Democratic stronghold, has slowly drifted toward the Republican Party. In the past, Southerners were distinctive politically in their strong identification as Democrats. But they may now look very similar to other regions of the country.[34] In recent years, another political divide has emerged between urban and nonurban voters, with increasingly strong support for Democrats in urban areas.[35]

We examine several key propositions concerning political unity and disunity among women. First, we examine whether the gender gap in support of Democratic presidential candidates and identification with the Democratic Party is pervasive among all women and men regardless of their demographic characteristics or whether it is confined to specific subgroups. We examine two distinct sources of unity: (1) economic vulnerability and (2) affluence and economic autonomy. Second, we evaluate the size of the gender gap in relation to several broader sources of disunity among women and men, including race, religious preference, level of religiosity, income, region, and other demographic characteristics. Overall, our expectation is that the sources of disunity among women outweigh their commonalities.

## Data and Analytic Approach

### Sample

Our data come from the pooled ANES data set for the seven presidential elections between 1980 and 2004 ($N$ = 23,290; ranging from $N$ = 1,212 in 2004 to $N$ = 2,485 in 1992).[36] Each election year is analyzed separately to identify trends that are stable across elections. Analyses focus on two key dependent variables: (1) Democratic versus Republican vote choice and (2) partisanship split three ways in which leaning independents are collapsed with partisans (Democrat, Republican, independent).[37] The sample is confined to individuals who voted for one of the two major party candidates in analyses predicting vote choice. The percentage voting for a Republican or Democratic candidate ranges from a low of 54 percent of the sample in 1980 when John Anderson ran as an independent presidential candidate ($N$ = 877) to a high of 67 percent in 2004 ($N$ = 811).

## Key Variables

We examine the impact of various demographic factors on presidential vote choice and partisanship to uncover sources of political unity and disunity among women. Multivariate analyses are conducted with a series of dummy variables derived from standard demographic factors in the data including respondent gender, respondent race (white, black, and other race),[38] respondent religion (Protestant, Catholic, Jewish, and other),[39] frequency of church attendance (almost weekly and more than weekly attendance, monthly attendance, or less-frequent religious service attendance), whether the respondent endorses a fundamentalist interpretation of the Bible, and respondent education (high school degree or less, some college or an associate's degree, a bachelor's degree, or an advanced degree).[40]

A variety of economic factors are also considered. Multivariate models include respondent's current employment status, whether the respondent holds a professional position, household union membership, and whether the respondent reported a high, medium, or low household income.[41] In addition to these economic considerations, marital status, the presence of children in the household,[42] and birth cohort—whether respondents reached their late teens/early adulthood during WWII (born between 1895 and 1944), the postwar period (baby boomers; born between 1943–58), or after the baby boom (born after 1958)—are included.[43] In addition, we consider the political effect of region (residence in the Northeast, West, South, or Midwest), and urbanism (rural, suburban, or urban residence). These variables were assessed in all presidential elections between 1980 and 2004 with a few exceptions, making it possible to run exactly the same analytic model in all years.[44]

## Analytic Strategy

We first examine the size of the gender gap in Democratic candidate support and identification, then delve into sources of unity and disunity among women by employing a multivariate technique—logistic regression. We use a multivariate approach to examine the gender gap because some of the factors thought to influence vote choice and partisanship are linked to gender. Women tend to be more religious than men, for example, which might incline them toward the Republican Party. But they also tend to reside in lower income households, which should steer them toward the Democratic Party. An analysis of the gender gap based solely on cross-tabulations of exit poll results does not allow researchers to demonstrate decisively that the gender gap is a result of gender and not other demographic factors, such as religion or income, with which it may be confounded.

The ANES studies included between one and two thousand respondents in each survey (fewer actually voted), but even that sample is insufficient to assess the effects of gender while still controlling for a number of other demographic factors. A table that depicted vote choice by all possible combinations of gender, race, education, age, religion, and religiosity would quickly exceed the sample size of ANES studies. A multivariate technique such as logistic regression gets around this problem by controlling simultaneously for many factors that influence vote choice in order to isolate the electoral effect of gender independently of the other factors with which it is related.

Logistic regression has one other important feature: It allows for the construction of predicted probabilities—that is, predictions as to how particular groups of people with one characteristic in common (such as gender) would vote, controlling for a number of other characteristics (such as religiosity, race, or income). Calculated on the basis of a logistic regression equation, predicted probabilities allow for the isolation of the "pure" effect of gender among specific groups of people, such as highly religious white Protestants, and permit us to estimate the electoral effects of one single factor (such as gender) within the same demographic group. They also allow for a careful comparison of the effects of gender among specific subgroups of women and men across all presidential elections between 1980 and 2004.

## Gender Gap, 1980–2004

There is a consistent gender gap in support of presidential Democratic candidates between 1980 and 2004, as depicted in Table 11.1. In all years, women demonstrate greater support than men for the Democratic candidate. As noted elsewhere, this does not always translate into majority female support. For example, a majority of women in the ANES sample preferred Ronald Reagan to his Democratic opponents in 1980 and 1984 (out of the two major party candidates), although by a smaller majority than found among men. In all other presidential elections, however, a majority of women in the ANES sample voted for the Democratic over the Republican candidate. In contrast, a majority of men supported only one Democratic presidential candidate—Bill Clinton in 1992 and 1996—expressing a preference for the Republican candidate in all other elections. And even this support for Clinton among men is inflated because of the omission of voters who supported third-party candidate Ross Perot. In exit poll data, somewhat more men than women voted for Perot in both 1992 and 1996.[45] The gender gap in Democratic support is smallest in 1988 and 1992 and largest in 1996. It is also slightly larger in 2004 than in 2000, a finding that is at odds with evidence of a smaller gender gap in 2004 than in 2002 in exit poll data.[46]

The gender gap in Democratic partisanship (examined with and without partisan leaners) is presented in Table 11.1 and is similar in magnitude to the gender gap in support of Democratic presidential candidates.

Table 11.1: Gender Gap in Democratic Vote Choice and Partisanship

|  | 1980 | 1984 | 1988 | 1992 | 1996 | 2000 | 2004 |
|---|---|---|---|---|---|---|---|
| Vote Choice (N) | (877) | (1,376) | (1,195) | (1,357) | (1,034) | (1,120) | (811) |
| Women | 47 | 45 | 50 | 61 | 64 | 57 | 57 |
| Men | 39 | 38 | 44 | 55 | 51 | 47 | 45 |
| *Democratic Gap (Women–Men)* | *8* | *7* | *6* | *6* | *13* | *10* | *12* |
| Party Identification (*N*) | | | | | | | |
| Democratic party ID (no leaners) | | | | | | | |
| Women | 45 | 41 | 40 | 39 | 43 | 39 | 38 |
| Men | 38 | 34 | 30 | 32 | 34 | 30 | 26 |
| *Democratic Gap (Women–Men)* | *7* | *7* | *10* | *7* | *9* | *9* | *12* |
| Democratic party ID (plus leaners) | | | | | | | |
| Women | 56 | 51 | 51 | 55 | 58 | 54 | 54 |
| Men | 50 | 46 | 43 | 45 | 46 | 46 | 45 |
| *Democratic Gap (Women–Men)* | *4* | *5* | *8* | *10* | *12* | *8* | *9* |
| Republican party ID (no leaners) | | | | | | | |
| Women | 24 | 28 | 28 | 23 | 25 | 23 | 28 |
| Men | 22 | 28 | 29 | 28 | 32 | 29 | 30 |
| *Republican Gap (Women–Men)* | *2* | *0* | *−1* | *−5* | *−7* | *−6* | *−2* |
| Republican party ID (plus leaners) | | | | | | | |
| Women | 32 | 39 | 39 | 34 | 33 | 34 | 37 |
| Men | 35 | 42 | 46 | 43 | 46 | 44 | 44 |
| *Republican Gap (Women–Men)* | *−3* | *−3* | *−7* | *−9* | *−13* | *−10* | *−7* |

*Source:* ANES pooled data set.

*Note:* Data are unweighted. Entries are percentage who supported the Democratic candidate or identified with the Democratic Party in each year. Cross-tabulations for vote choice are confined to respondents who reported voting for one of the two major party candidates. Leaners are independents who identify with either the Democratic or Republican Party. Missing values are excluded in the calculation of percentages.

Excluding partisan leaners (independents who lean toward one of the parties), women were more likely than men to identify as Democrats in all presidential election years between 1980 and 2004. This gender partisan gap was modest in size, ranging from twelve percentage points in 2004 to seven points in 1980, 1983, and 1992. A comparable gender gap in support of Democratic candidates emerges when leaners are added to partisans. Once again, women are more inclined than men to identify as Democrats, with the gender gap ranging from a low of seven to a high of twelve points. Overall, Table 11.1 demonstrates a decline over time in the strength of Democratic identification among both men and women (when leaners are excluded), but no decline in the simple percentage who identify as Democrats (including leaners).

The decline in Democratic identification is coupled with an increase in Republican identification among men but not women, fueling a symmetrical gender gap in Republican identification. This difference is most pronounced when leaners are included in the analyses, replicating the findings reported by Barbara Norrander.[47] The number of women Republicans did not increase dramatically between 1980 and 2004 (with or without leaners). But the number of Republican men did increase (although the biggest increase occurs between 1980 and 1984). By 2004, similar percentages of men (including leaners) identified with the Democratic and Republican parties, whereas substantially more women identified as Democrats. This resulted in a sizeable gender gap in Republican partisanship, ranging from a low of three points in 1980 to a high of thirteen points in 1996.

Overall, the gender gap in vote choice and partisanship is relatively modest, with somewhere between 6 and 12 percent more women than men voting for the Democratic than Republican presidential candidate in the past seven elections, and between 7 and 12 percent more women than men identifying with the Democratic Party. Although modest in size, women's greater support of Democratic candidates remains important. Even a gap of eight to ten points matters in a tight electoral contest, and is further amplified by higher levels of voter turnout among women than men in recent elections.[48]

## Isolating the Gender Gap within Specific Subgroups

The gender gap is thus robust across vote choice and partisanship—but does the gap extend to all women? Or is it concentrated among a subset of women and men, indicating the existence of specific economic or life circumstances that especially incline women to support the Democratic Party or vote for Democratic candidates?

Initial analyses suggest that the gender gap is relatively uniform among women and men of different economic, racial, and social backgrounds. Simple bivariate cross-tabulations are presented in Table 11.2 for vote choice and Table 11.3 for partisanship. In these analyses, the gender gap is examined among subgroups of women sharing similar interests in government policy (based on income, work status, occupation, education,

Table 11.2: Support for Democratic Presidential Candidate within Specific Subgroups

|  | 1980 | 1984 | 1988 | 1992 | 1996 | 2000 | 2004 |
|---|---|---|---|---|---|---|---|
| All |  |  |  |  |  |  |  |
| Women | 47 | 45 | 50 | 61 | 64 | 57 | 52 |
| Men | 39 | 38 | 44 | 55 | 51 | 47 | 45 |
| *Democratic Gap* | *8** | *7*** | *6** | *6** | *13*** | *10*** | *7** |
| Professional occupation |  |  |  |  |  |  |  |
| Women | 48 | 45 | 50 | 64 | 61 | 59 | 60 |
| Men | 33 | 32 | 40 | 50 | 46 | 44 | 52 |
| *Democratic Gap* | *15** | *13*** | *10** | *14*** | *15*** | *15*** | *8* |
| High income |  |  |  |  |  |  |  |
| Women | 38 | 35 | 43 | 54 | 51 | 51 | 47 |
| Men | 34 | 27 | 34 | 47 | 44 | 44 | 39 |
| *Democratic Gap* | *4* | *8** | *9+* | *7* | *7* | *7* | *8* |
| Low income |  |  |  |  |  |  |  |
| Women | 58 | 54 | 59 | 66 | 76 | 65 | 63 |
| Men | 51 | 63 | 54 | 75 | 71 | 54 | 51 |
| *Democratic Gap* | *7* | *−9* | *5* | *−9* | *5* | *11** | *12** |
| Not married |  |  |  |  |  |  |  |
| Women | 54 | 51 | 54 | 67 | 69 | 65 | 63 |
| Men | 46 | 46 | 50 | 72 | 61 | 54 | 52 |
| *Democratic Gap* | *8** | *5* | *4* | *−5* | *8* | *11** | *11** |
| At least one child in household |  |  |  |  |  |  |  |
| Women | 45 | 46 | 47 | 57 | 71 | 54 | 54 |
| Men | 30 | 31 | 41 | 46 | 60 | 43 | 48 |
| *Democratic Gap* | *15*** | *15*** | *6* | *11* | *11* | *11** | *6* |
| Baby boomer cohort |  |  |  |  |  |  |  |
| Women | 47 | 46 | 50 | 63 | 65 | 59 | 47 |
| Men | 33 | 35 | 44 | 54 | 53 | 51 | 40 |
| *Democratic Gap* | *14** | *11*** | *6* | *9* | *12** | *8* | *7* |

* $p < .05$.

** $p < .01$.

*Source:* ANES pooled data set.

*Note:* Data are unweighted. Entries are the percentage of respondents who supported the Democratic candidate in each year. Cross-tabulations for vote choice are confined to respondents who reported voting for one of the two major party candidates, and subject to a chi-square test of association.

marital status, and children) to test the economic vulnerability and economic autonomy hypotheses. We also added generation (baby boom, pre-baby boom, and post-baby boom) to control for any possible greater support of the Democratic Party among women who came of age during the women's movement of the 1960s and 1970s (baby boomers).

Consider vote choice first. As a baseline, the overall gender gap is presented in the top section of Table 11.2 and is significant in all years (as indicated by a chi-square test of association). Looking further down the table, there are only minor variations in the size of this gap in a given year. There is a slightly greater preference for the Democratic Party between

Table 11.3: Democratic Partisan Identification within Specific Subgroups

|  | 1980 | 1984 | 1988 | 1992 | 1996 | 2000 | 2004 |
|---|---|---|---|---|---|---|---|
| Women | 56 | 51 | 51 | 55 | 58 | 54 | 54 |
| Men | 50 | 46 | 43 | 45 | 46 | 46 | 45 |
| *Total Democratic Gap* | 6* | 5 | 8** | 10** | 12** | 8** | 9** |
| Professional occupation |  |  |  |  |  |  |  |
| Women | 53 | 50 | 49 | 54 | 59 | 51 | 63 |
| Men | 42 | 42 | 37 | 41 | 38 | 40 | 47 |
| *Democratic Gap* | 11* | 8 | 12** | 13** | 21** | 11** | 16** |
| High income |  |  |  |  |  |  |  |
| Women | 51 | 45 | 43 | 48 | 46 | 50 | 56 |
| Men | 41 | 37 | 39 | 37 | 36 | 42 | 39 |
| *Democratic Gap* | 10* | 8* | 4 | 11** | 10* | 8 | 17** |
| Low income |  |  |  |  |  |  |  |
| Women | 62 | 58 | 58 | 57 | 65 | 59 | 59 |
| Men | 65 | 56 | 50 | 57 | 61 | 54 | 50 |
| *Democratic Gap* | -3 | 2 | 8 | 0 | 4 | 5 | 9 |
| Not married |  |  |  |  |  |  |  |
| Women | 60 | 55 | 55 | 59 | 63 | 59 | 61 |
| Men | 57 | 51 | 46 | 51 | 54 | 51 | 53 |
| *Democratic Gap* | 3 | 4 | 9* | 8* | 9* | 8* | 8 |
| At least one child in household |  |  |  |  |  |  |  |
| Women | 60 | 52 | 49 | 49 | 64 | 51 | 51 |
| Men | 42 | 40 | 42 | 39 | 51 | 42 | 50 |
| *Democratic Gap* | 8** | 12** | 7* | 10* | 13 | 9* | 1 |
| Baby boomer cohort |  |  |  |  |  |  |  |
| Women | 57 | 49 | 49 | 56 | 57 | 56 | 48 |
| Men | 45 | 41 | 42 | 45 | 48 | 46 | 42 |
| *Democratic Gap* | 12** | 8* | 7* | 11** | 9* | 10* | 6 |

* $p < .05$.
** $p < .01$.

*Source:* ANES pooled data set.

*Note:* Data are unweighted. Entries are the percentage of respondents who identified with the Democratic Party in each year (including independent leaners). All cross-tabulations are subject to a chi-square test of association.

professional men and women than among men and women in general, consistent with the economic autonomy hypothesis. But the gap is largely driven by professional men's weaker support of Democratic candidates, not women's stronger support (2004 is the exceptional year in which male professionals were more supportive of Kerry than men overall).

In other groupings the gap is a little larger in some years, smaller in others, but generally tracks the overall gender gap. At odds with the economic vulnerability hypothesis, the gender gap is no greater among low-income than high-income individuals. Low-income women, single women, and mothers are somewhat more supportive of Democratic candidates than their male counterparts, but a comparable gap is also found among high-income women and men.

Generational explanations for the gap are also unsupported by the data; female baby boomers are more likely than males of their generation to identify as Democrats, but not more so than women in general. In a similar vein, there are few demographic differences in the magnitude of the gender gap in partisanship, as seen in Table 11.3. Professional men and women are the most politically divergent (although the gap among them is not significantly larger than the overall gap in subsequent multivariate analyses). And professional women are actually slightly less, not more, supportive of Democratic candidates than women overall in most years (with the exception of 1996 and 2004). There is thus little support here for the autonomy hypothesis. The economic vulnerability hypothesis also fares poorly. The gender gap is of comparable size regardless of men and women's income level. Low-income women are more likely than low-income men to identify as Democrats in five of the seven elections, but no more so than women in general. If anything, the gender gap is a little more consistent among high-income Americans. Overall, the gender gap in both partisanship and vote choice is widespread and cannot be isolated among specific subgroups of women and men.

## Multivariate Analyses

Does the gender gap in vote choice and partisanship persist with controls for various other factors linked to gender, such as low income or single marital status, which might actually account for the observed gender gap? To answer this question, we ran a series of multivariate analyses (logistic regression models) in which we assessed the extent to which vote choice varied by gender and a number of other sociodemographic and religious factors for each election between 1980 and 2004. Similar analyses were

conducted to examine the origins of Democratic and Republican identification (using ordered probit analyses). In these analyses, individuals who
describe themselves as politically independent but lean toward one of the
two parties were included as partisans. The analyses for electoral choice
are presented in Table 11.4, and the findings for partisanship in Table 11.5.

The gender gap in party identification in vote choice holds even when
we control for possible differences among men and women based on the
demographic and religious characteristics listed in Tables 11.3 and 11.4.
The effects of gender are positive in each election except 1992, the only
year in which the gender gap (of roughly six points) disappears (and this
is because of other factors). The gender gap in partisanship persists in
multivariate analyses in all years from 1988 onward, but it is not statistically significant in either 1980 or 1984. In sum, the gender gap is
not simply an artifact of related factors such as economic vulnerability,
work status, professional occupation, or educational level that promote
support for the Democratic Party regardless of gender. The gender gap
exists independently of a slew of demographic and religious factors.

We also expanded the multivariate models in Tables 11.3 and 11.4 by
adding a series of interaction terms between gender and other factors. In
essence, this approach provides a rigorous test of the economic vulnerability and autonomy hypotheses to determine whether the gender gap is
bigger in some groups than others. In these analyses, gender is interacted
with variables that tap economic factors and women's life circumstances:
professional occupation, income, marital status, the presence of children,
and generation. Analyses were run for vote choice and partisanship in
each election year. We do not show the analyses here because very few
of the interactions were significant, indicating that the gender gap was
of roughly the same size in all of these subgroups.

In confirmation of findings reported earlier in Tables 11.2 and 11.3, the
gender gap did not vary consistently in size across specific subgroups of
men and women. There was no year in which the gender gap in partisanship varied significantly in size within specific religious, occupational,
union, income, marital status, birth cohort, or regional subgroups in
the expanded multivariate analyses. None of the interaction terms with
gender reached significance (at the .05 level in a two-way test) out of a
total of eighty-one coefficients (thirteen coefficients in seven elections).

There were a few instances in which the gender gap in vote choice
varied significantly among demographic and religious groupings. For
instance, women baby boomers and pre-boomers were substantially
more inclined than men in the same birth cohorts to support Jimmy

Table 11.4: The Determinants of Democratic Presidential Vote Choice

| | 1980 | 1984 | 1988 | 1992 | 1996 | 2000 | 2004 |
|---|---|---|---|---|---|---|---|
| Female | .40* | .34* | .39** | .21 | .67** | .47** | .42* |
| | (.18) | (.14) | (.14) | (.14) | (.16) | (.14) | (.17) |
| White | -1.84** | -1.54** | -1.87** | -1.52** | -1.75** | -1.38** | -1.61** |
| | (.28) | (.20) | (.22) | (.21) | (.24) | (.20) | (.23) |
| Protestant | -.35 | -.83** | -1.25** | -.86** | -1.01** | -.71** | -.07 |
| | (.29) | (.23) | (.28) | (.25) | (.26) | (.24) | (.26) |
| Catholic | -.09 | -.46 | -.87** | -.47 | -.63* | -.74** | .22 |
| | (.32) | (.25) | (.30) | (.27) | (.29) | (.25) | (.28) |
| Weekly Church | -.18 | -.14 | .00 | -.66** | -.80** | -.48** | -.50* |
| Attendance | (.18) | (.16) | (.16) | (.16) | (.18) | (.17) | (.21) |
| Monthly Church | .42 | .28 | .13 | -.47* | -.03 | .09 | -.64* |
| Attendance | (.28) | (.21) | (.23) | (.23) | (.24) | (.21) | (.25) |
| Fundamentalist | -.19 | -.23 | -.32* | -.79** | -.43* | -.44** | -.69** |
| | (.18) | (.15) | (.16) | (.16) | (.18) | (.17) | (.21) |
| Some College | -.38+ | -.18 | -.50** | -.26 | -.54** | .31 | -.29 |
| | (.22) | (.17) | (.18) | (.18) | (.21) | (.25) | (.21) |
| College Degree | -.75** | -.07 | -.80** | -.84 | -.59* | .22 | -.19 |
| | (.28) | (.22) | (.23) | (.21) | (.24) | (.19) | (.25) |
| Post Graduate Degree | .28 | .60* | -.05 | -.19 | -.43 | .10 | n.a. |
| | (.37) | (.30) | (.30) | (.27) | (.29) | (.25) | |
| Professional | .17 | .07 | .30 | -.01 | .05 | .00 | .72** |
| | (.21) | (.18) | (.18) | (.17) | (.19) | (.16) | (.20) |
| Currently Working | .08 | -.12 | .15 | .12 | .29 | -.33 | .07 |
| | (.19) | (.17) | (.17) | (.17) | (.20) | (.18) | (.23) |
| Union Member | .86** | 1.14** | .78** | .56** | 1.31** | .74** | .95** |
| | (.20) | (.16) | (.18) | (.19) | (.20) | (.20) | (.22) |
| High Income | -.12 | -.66** | -.45** | -.37* | -.36* | -.32 | -.44* |
| | (.21) | (.17) | (.17) | (.17) | (.19) | (.19) | (.21) |
| Low Income | .51* | .53** | .15 | .06 | .68** | .24 | .29 |
| | (.23) | (.18) | (.20) | (.21) | (.23) | (.20) | (.24) |
| Missing Income | -.05 | .02 | .09 | -.27 | -.03 | -.24 | -.42 |
| | (.31) | (.26) | (.26) | (.31) | (.29) | (.23) | (.32) |
| Married | .14 | -.06 | .10 | -.43** | -.14 | -.39* | -.47** |
| | (.20) | (.15) | (.16) | (.16) | (.18) | (.16) | (.18) |
| Children | -.32 | -.14 | -.38* | -.17 | .45 | -.14 | .24 |
| | (.18) | (.17) | (.18) | (.18) | (.33) | (.17) | (.21) |
| Baby Boomer | -.42 | .26 | .15 | .30 | .24 | .36* | -.12 |
| | (.42) | (.24) | (.22) | (.18) | (.20) | (.17) | (.20) |
| Pre–Baby Boomer | -.44 | .36 | .04 | .33 | .18 | .12 | .39 |
| | (.41) | (.24) | (.23) | (.20) | (.22) | (.22) | (.25) |
| Northeast | -.13 | -.16 | -.36 | .32 | .47* | -.16 | -.15 |
| | (.25) | (.20) | (.21) | (.20) | (.24) | (.21) | (.26) |
| West | -.07 | .32 | -.09 | -.31 | -.08 | -.08 | -.11 |
| | (.26) | (.19) | (.19) | (.20) | (.23) | (.21) | (.24) |
| South | .35 | .07 | -.01 | .29 | .26 | -.41* | -.06 |
| | (.21) | (.18) | (.18) | (.18) | (.20) | (.18) | (.22) |
| Urban | .72** | .58** | .36* | .43* | .21 | n.a. | n.a. |
| | (.21) | (.18) | (.19) | (.17) | (.20) | | |
| Rural | .00 | .12 | .10 | .08 | .06 | n.a. | n.a. |
| | (.19) | (.15) | (.17) | (.16) | (.18) | | |
| Constant | 1.37* | .99* | 2.36** | 2.83** | 2.33 | 2.29** | 1.47** |
| | (.60) | (.45) | (.49) | (.45) | (.50) | (.18) | (.48) |
| N | 818 | 1233 | 1097 | 1165 | 989 | 1027 | 766 |
| Pseudo R² | .15 | .15 | .15 | .16 | .20 | .11 | .14 |

Source: ANES pooled data set. * p < .05, ** p < .0.
Note: Entries are logit coefficients with robust standard errors in parentheses. All variables are coded on a 0 to 1 scale.

Carter in 1980. White women were significantly more likely than white men to support Michael Dukakis in 1988. Married women were much more likely than married men to support Bill Clinton in 1992. And employed women were especially likely to vote for Clinton in 1996 when compared to employed men. But none of these instances of a heightened gender gap in vote choice represent a consistent trend across elections, and overall there were only four elections in which there was a statistically significant heightened gender gap in one of these subgroups (out of a total of eighty-one possible instances). This is no greater than what might be observed by chance. Efforts to examine more complex combinations of background factors (such as single professional women or single mothers) also fail to uncover any consistent trends in vote choice.[49]

## Sources of Women's (and Men's) Disunity

Our analysis of the gender gap demonstrates its persistence across specific demographic groups; it also clearly illuminates factors that divide women (and men) politically. A closer examination of Tables 11.4 and 11.5 highlights the powerfully divisive influence of race, religion, and economics on men and women's political preferences.

### Race

Whites have been significantly more likely than nonwhites to support Republican presidential candidates in every election between 1980 and 2004. When blacks are broken out from other nonwhites in Table 11.5, it is clear that they are much more likely to identify as Democrats than any other racial group. Whites are also somewhat more likely to identify with the Republican Party than individuals in the "other" racial grouping (the omitted category). To flesh out these findings for vote choice, we calculated the predicted probability of Democratic support for the "average" voter (with modal characteristics) who is Protestant, nonfundamentalist, has a high school degree or less, is nonprofessional, is employed, lives in a medium-income household, is married with at least one child at home, is a baby boomer, and is living in a suburb in the Northeast. We varied race and gender in the calculation of predicted probabilities to see how these factors shape support for the Democratic presidential candidate in a given election. These predicted probabilities better illustrate the impact of race on vote choice than coefficients in the logistic regressions (which are difficult to interpret).

## Table 11.5: The Determinants of Democratic Party Identification

| | 1980 | 1984 | 1988 | 1992 | 1996 | 2000 | 2004 |
|---|---|---|---|---|---|---|---|
| Female | .10 | .10 | .19** | .25** | .35** | .22** | .30** |
| | (.08) | (.06) | (.07) | (.06) | (.07) | (.06) | (.08) |
| White | −.21 | −.35** | −.44** | −.24* | −.27** | −.14 | −.16 |
| | (.17) | (.11) | (.11) | (.10) | (.10) | (.10) | (.11) |
| Black | .76** | .52** | .65** | .75** | .79** | 1.18** | 1.41** |
| | (.21) | (.15) | (.16) | (.13) | (.15) | (.15) | (.17) |
| Protestant | −.05 | −.32** | −.38** | −.29** | −.40** | −.19* | −.27* |
| | (.13) | (.11) | (.12) | (.09) | (.10) | (.10) | (.13) |
| Catholic | .33* | .03 | −.09 | .15 | −.02 | −.03 | .05 |
| | (.14) | (.12) | (.13) | (.10) | (.12) | (.11) | (.13) |
| Jewish | 1.22** | .65** | .37 | .94** | .60* | .96** | .64* |
| | (.31) | (.24) | (.24) | (.27) | (.29) | (.25) | (.28) |
| Weekly Church | −.22** | −.07 | −.13 | −.33** | −.29** | −.27** | −.19* |
| Attendance | (.08) | (.07) | (.08) | (.07) | (.08) | (.08) | (.10) |
| Monthly Church | −.14 | .02 | −.05 | −.12 | −.02 | −.09 | −.31** |
| Attendance | (.13) | (.09) | (.10) | (.06) | (.10) | (.10) | (.12) |
| Fundamentalist | .04 | −.13 | .00 | −.07 | −.17* | −.14 | −.26** |
| | (.08) | (.07) | (.07) | (.06) | (.08) | (.07) | (.10) |
| Some College | −.11 | −.11 | −.14 | −.18* | −.16* | −.11 | −.17+ |
| | (.09) | (.08) | (.08) | (.07) | (.08) | (.11) | (.10) |
| College Degree | −.16 | −.21 | −.37** | −.34** | −.22* | −.19* | −.16 |
| | (.13) | (.11) | (.11) | (.09) | (.11) | (.09) | (.12) |
| Post Graduate Degree | .15 | .07 | −.02 | −.10 | −.05 | −.18 | n.a. |
| | (.18) | (.16) | (.16) | (.12) | (.14) | (.13) | |
| Professional | −.09 | .09 | .04 | .04 | .06 | −.06 | .32** |
| | (.10) | (.09) | (.09) | (.07) | (.08) | (.08) | (.10) |
| Currently Working | .00 | .06 | .07 | .07 | .11 | −.04 | .09 |
| | (.09) | (.08) | (.08) | (.07) | (.09) | (.08) | (.11) |
| Union Membership | .36** | .47** | .39** | .46** | .41** | .43** | .38** |
| | (.08) | (.08) | (.08) | (.08) | (.09) | (.10) | (.11) |
| High Income | −.16 | −.28** | −.08 | −.31** | −.36** | −.01 | −.15 |
| | (.09) | (.08) | (.08) | (.07) | (.09) | (.09) | (.11) |
| Low Income | .23* | .21* | .16 | .01 | .10 | .13 | .12 |
| | (.10) | (.08) | (.09) | (.08) | (.09) | (.09) | (.11) |
| Missing Income | .02 | −.06 | .17 | −.11 | −.13 | −.15 | −.17 |
| | (.13) | (.11) | (.12) | (.11) | (.12) | (.10) | (.14) |
| Married | −.02 | −.04 | −.02 | −.08 | −.05 | −.14* | −.26** |
| | (.08) | (.07) | (.07) | (.06) | (.07) | (.07) | (.09) |
| Children | .03 | .01 | −.04 | −.13 | .15 | −.11 | .03 |
| | (.08) | (.07) | (.08) | (.08) | (.12) | (.08) | (.10) |
| Baby Boomer | −.13 | .09 | .24** | .24** | .16* | .10 | −.09 |
| | (.15) | (.09) | (.09) | (.07) | (.08) | (.08) | (.09) |
| Pre–Baby Boomer | −.10 | .22* | .35** | .27** | .17 | .10 | .12 |
| | (.15) | (.10) | (.10) | (.08) | (.09) | (.10) | (.12) |
| Northeast | −.16 | −.09 | −.04 | .13 | −.01 | −.03 | −.03 |
| | (.10) | (.09) | (.09) | (.08) | (.10) | (.10) | (.12) |
| West | .18 | .14 | .03 | −.04 | .09 | −.01 | .06 |
| | (.11) | (.09) | (.10) | (.09) | (.10) | (.09) | (.11) |
| South | .27** | .30** | .36** | .22** | .03 | −.10 | −.02 |
| | (.09) | (.08) | (.08) | (.07) | (.08) | (.08) | (.11) |
| Urban | .24** | .17* | .17 | .39** | .24** | n.a. | n.a. |
| | (.10) | (.08) | (.09) | (.07) | (.09) | | |
| Rural | .00 | −.01 | −.05 | .05 | .18* | n.a. | n.a. |
| | (.08) | (.07) | (.08) | (.06) | (.08) | | |
| Cut point 1 | −.37 | −.33 | −.29 | −.40 | −.42 | −.58 | −.35 |
| | (.27) | (.20) | (.20) | (.18) | (.19) | (.17) | (.22) |
| Cut point 2 | −.01 | −.04 | .01 | −.05 | −.17 | −.26 | −.08 |
| | (.27) | (.21) | (.20) | (.18) | (.19) | (.17) | (.22) |
| N | 1264 | 1718 | 1600 | 2089 | 1607 | 1598 | 1116 |
| Pseudo R² | .08 | .08 | .09 | .10 | .10 | .09 | .12 |

*Source:* ANES pooled data set. \*$p < .05$, \*\*$p < .01$.

*Note:* Entries are ordered logit coefficients with robust standard errors in parentheses. All variables are coded on a 0 to 1 scale.

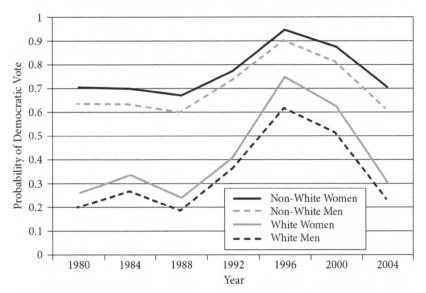

Figure 11.1: Predicted support for Democratic candidates by race and gender. *Note:* Predicted values are based on logit equations in Table 11.4 and are calculated for respondents with modal sample characteristics (Protestant, nonfundamentalist, monthly church attendance, high school educated, nonprofessional, employed, medium household income, married with at least one child at home, baby boomer, living in a suburb in the Northeast), who vary in terms of their race and gender.

Figure 11.1 depicts the gender gap in vote choice for the "average" voter who is either black or white and male or female across all election years. The divergence between black and white females is made plain by this graph. The largest racial difference among women occurs in 1980 when 70 percent of black and only 25 percent of "average" white women voters supported Jimmy Carter, the Democratic candidate. Among the same group of women, racial differences reach their lowest value, just under twenty points, in 1996 (although once again it is worth remembering that Clinton support is inflated because of the exclusion of Perot voters). The difference between "average" black and white women voters is enormous, but so is the difference between comparable black and white men. There is simply a large racial divide in support of Democratic candidates that swamps the gender gap in every presidential election studied in this data set.

Figure 11.1 also makes clear the persistence of a small gender gap among whites and blacks, respectively. Across all election years, the mean gender gap between "average" white men and white women voters is roughly eight percentage points. The comparable gap among black men and women is six percentage points. In other words, even with very large racial differences in vote choice, both black and white women are somewhat more likely to support Democratic candidates than their male counterparts.

## Religion

Race produces the greatest divide in American politics among women and men. But religion is close behind and has had a growing influence on both vote choice and partisanship in recent elections. Protestants have consistently supported Republican candidates when compared to individuals who describe their religion as "other" (the omitted category), as can be seen in the multivariate analyses presented in Table 11.4 (with the exception of 1980 and 2004). Catholics were once part of the Democratic coalition, but they too have been more inclined to support Republican candidates in these data than those with an "other" religion, although these effects are less consistent. The effects of religion also emerge in analyses of partisanship in Table 11.5. It is possible to further separate Jews from Christians and other religions in this larger sample, which includes nonvoters. And analyses in Table 11.5 make clear that Protestants identify less as Democrats, Jews identify more, and Catholics about the same as individuals in the "other" religion category, although once again effects vary in strength across elections.[50] These findings are consistent with the expected impact of religion on partisan leanings.

Religiosity (independent of specific religion) has more fully consistent political effects than religion, especially on vote choice. As seen in Table 11.4, individuals who attend religious services at least weekly have been substantially less likely than those who attend services infrequently to support Democratic candidates since the 1992 presidential election. They have also been less likely to identify as Democrats over the same time period, a trend that emerged initially in 1980 (Table 11.5). Individuals who believe in a fundamentalist or literal interpretation of the Bible have been consistently more supportive of Republican candidates since the 1988 election, although they are not consistently less Democratic in identification.[51]

When considered together, religion and religiosity produce a second large divide among American women and men. To illustrate this divide, we calculated the predicted probability of support for the Democratic presidential candidate among "average" Protestant men and women who

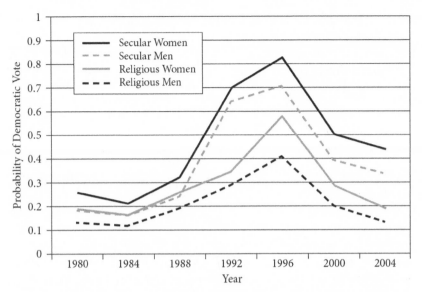

Figure 11.2: Predicted support for Democratic candidates among Protestants by religiosity and gender. *Note:* Predicted values are based on logit equations in Table 11.4 and are calculated for respondents with modal sample characteristics (white, Protestant, high school educated, nonprofessional, employed, medium household income, married with at least one child at home, baby boomer, living in a suburb in the Northeast), who vary in terms of their religiosity and gender. Secular respondents do not hold a literal interpretation of the Bible and attend religious services rarely or never. Religious respondents attend services weekly or more often and believe in the literal interpretation of the Bible.

are either secular (nonfundamentalists who attend religious services infrequently) or very religious (fundamentalists who attend services at least weekly). We calculate these probabilities for Protestants although we expect similar findings for other religions based on the analyses presented in Tables 11.4 and 11.5. The magnitude of both the gender and religiosity gap over time is evident in Figure 11.2. Prior to 1988, there was almost no "religiosity" gap in support of Democratic candidates. But it emerged quite visibly in 1992, resulting in a gap of roughly thirty-five percentage points between secular and religious women, a gap that has persisted over time at somewhere between twenty-two and twenty-five points. A comparable religiosity gap is observed among men.

In contrast, the gender gap is present among religious and nonreligious individuals, but is much smaller. There has been a persistent gender gap among religious men and women that was smallest in 1984 (four points) and largest in 1996 (seventeen points). A gender gap of similar magnitude emerges among secular women, as can be seen in Figure 11.2. Our findings reveal that, despite their differences, religious and secular women have something in common: they are more likely to support Democratic candidates than their male counterparts.

## Social Class

Conventional political wisdom tends to minimize the importance of class in contemporary American politics. However, evidence presented in both Tables 11.4 and 11.5 contradicts this conclusion. Union membership, household income, and, to a lesser extent, education all influence electoral choice and partisanship. The political effects of living in a union household may have subsided over time but they still remain a strong source of Democratic identification and support for Democratic candidates. Members of union households have been more likely than others to support Democratic candidates and identify as Democrats in every presidential election between 1980 and 2004. These effects are large and statistically significant.

Income and education also influence electoral choices, although less consistently. Individuals in high-income households (the top third) were more supportive than those in mid-income households of Republican presidential candidates in all years except 1980 and 2000, and were more likely to identify as Republicans in 1984, 1992, and 1996. In contrast, low income increased support for Democratic candidates and Democratic partisanship in some but not all years. Having at least some college education or a college degree inclines Americans toward greater support of Republican candidates and the Republican Party when compared to those with no more than a high school degree. But once again these effects are sporadic, as can be seen in Tables 11.4 and 11.5. Those with at least a college education or a college degree evince some greater support of Republican candidates or the party in 1980, 1988, 1992, 1996, and 2000, but only eleven out of a total of twenty-eight coefficients (for some college or a college degree) reach statistical significance.[52] This is clearly better than chance but is not a consistent trend. It is important to note that these effects do not extend to Americans with postgraduate degrees, who are no different in their support for Democratic candidates or the party than those with a high school education (except in 1984, when they supported Mondale).

Both women and men are therefore also divided by class-related factors, especially residence in a union household. The magnitude of class differences becomes clearer in examination of the predicted probabilities of support for a Democratic presidential candidate. Predicted probabilities were calculated for the "average" voter who varied in gender, household income, and union membership. These probabilities are depicted in Figure 11.3 and illustrate the large class gap among women (and men). The gap among women ranges from a low of eighteen points in 1996 to a sizeable thirty-four points in 2004. In all instances, medium-income women in a union household are more likely to support Democratic candidates than wealthier nonunion women. The "class" gap is equally pronounced among men, ranging from a low of eighteen points to a high of thirty-two. For the years under examination, the percentage of respondents living in a union household ranged from a high of 26 percent (in 1980) to a low of 15 percent (in 2000). An even smaller percentage of respondents live in medium-income union households (7 percent on average). Thus, some of the differences depicted in Figure 11.3 do not reach statistical significance

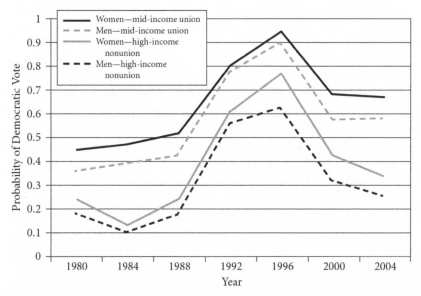

Figure 11.3: Predicted support for Democratic candidates by income, union household, and gender. Note: Predicted values are based on logit equations in Table 11.4 and are calculated for respondents with modal sample characteristics (white, Protestant, nonfundamentalist, high school educated, nonprofessional, employed, married with at least one child at home, baby boomer, living in a suburb in the Northeast), who vary in terms of their income, residence in a union household, religiosity, and gender. High income is the top third of the distribution of household income in each year, and low is the bottom third.

because of small sample sizes and large standard errors. Nonetheless, the trend is consistent over time and in the expected direction for all years.

In comparison, the gender gap is relatively small within both class groupings. When averaged across all years, the gender gap is eight points among both low-income individuals living in a union household and among individuals in high-income, nonunion households. Overall, women are more supportive of Democratic candidates than their male counterparts.

Finally, there are a few other sources of disunity among women and men in Tables 11.4 and 11.5 that deserve mention. Living in an urban area is fairly consistently linked to support of Democratic candidates and the Democratic Party, although we lack data on this for the most recent election years. In contrast, the effects of geographic region are very weak. Southerners were still more likely to identify as Democrats up until 1992 but have not differed in partisanship since, and there are no consistent effects of region on vote choice over time. Thus, urban women (and men) are likely to differ from nonurban women (and men) in their stronger support of Democratic candidates and the Democratic Party. But there are no obvious regional differences that currently divide women politically.

## Conclusion

Race, religion, and economics form powerful sources of cleavage among women (and men) that vastly outweigh women's commonality, a finding observed in our research and elsewhere.[53] These differences emerge, in part, from the persistence of the traditional Democratic coalition. Black women are more supportive than white women of the Democratic Party; both black and Jewish women are more likely to identify as Democrats than other women; and women in union households are more supportive than others of Democratic candidates and more inclined to identify with the Democratic Party. A more recent Republican coalition of high-income and religious individuals is also apparent in our data, producing further cleavages among women. Women in wealthier households support Republican candidates and identify with the Republican Party. Women who believe in the Bible as the literal word of God and frequently attend religious services, regardless of denomination, are more supportive than secular women of Republican candidates. And women who frequently attend religious services are also more inclined to identify as Republicans.

Women's political differences based on race, religion, and economics are larger, on average, than the gender gap and place it in needed perspective.

Nonetheless, there is a small, stable gender gap in vote choice and partisanship of roughly eight to ten percentage points that exists even after controlling for a variety of sociodemographic and religious characteristics, and cannot be isolated among one or more subgroups of women and men in these analyses. A robust difference of this magnitude has obvious electoral importance and its origins deserve careful scrutiny. It is not a product of women's shared material interests in the ANES pooled data because it is observed among men and women across a very broad array of sociodemographic and religious groupings. This raises an obvious question. What are the origins of the gender gap if not in women's shared economic interests?

Attitudinal factors that transcend material circumstances, such as political beliefs or specific policy positions, are an obvious alternative source of the gender gap. We noted earlier that the gap is often traced empirically to women's greater support of social welfare spending.[54] But this finding does not clearly illuminate the origins of the gender gap, raising instead a second pertinent question as to why women are more supportive of welfare spending. We can rule out any greater reliance among women on government policies because the gender gap is apparent across a broad spectrum of women who vary in household wealth, occupation, and work and family status.

The gap might be because of women's greater compassion and concern for the poor, consistent with evidence of sociotropic voting among women and pocketbook voting among men.[55] But this political compassion hypothesis raises a number of additional questions. Are women, in fact, more concerned about the plight of the poor than men? Do they rate themselves as more socially compassionate? Are they more forgiving and understanding when it comes to the origins and solutions to poverty? Does the impact of compassion have limits so that it is more focused on the protection of the young and elderly than on poverty more generally? And do women translate this compassion into support for specific candidates and policies? Schlesinger and Heldman provide partial supportive evidence, observing gender differences in emotional response to social problems, awareness of them among one's own family, and the perceived fairness of social institutions.[56] The compassion hypothesis would gain stronger support from evidence that the gender gap is fueled by women who score highly on empathy scales, rate themselves as compassionate, or who express sympathy with the plight of disadvantaged people.

Other factors also sporadically figure into the gender gap. Women's greater opposition to the use of force has fueled the gender gap in some years.[57] But these effects are variable over time and are unlikely to consistently drive the gender gap across elections. Others argue for the existence of a feminist gap, in which the gender gap is driven largely by women who identify as feminists.[58] It is important to remember, however, that traditional women's issues do not drive the gender gap, raising questions about whether the feminist gap conveys the impact of broader nongender political beliefs such as egalitarianism.

One clear political consequence of a robust gender gap is its likely future persistence, regardless of specific election year, salient issues, or particular candidates. Our analyses suggest that the gender gap in partisanship has solidified since 1988, and may now be firmly ensconced in American politics. It remains to be seen whether politicians can successfully manipulate the gap to further alter the current partisan balance. Men have clearly veered away from the Democratic Party while women remain loyalists, helping to explain the greater success of Republicans in recent decades. If the gender gap revolves centrally around social compassion, the Republican Party must determine how to pursue a conservative economic agenda while not appearing overly hard-hearted in order to attract additional women voters. George W. Bush's simple adoption of the term "compassionate conservative" obviously did little to undermine the gender gap. Democrats face the equally difficult challenge of appealing to men who are less supportive of social welfare spending without losing their image as concerned about the disadvantaged, a feat mastered successfully by Bill Clinton with the passage of welfare reform in 1996.

In sum, women are more divided than united politically, but they also display some limited political commonality. And although their political differences are large and suggest substantial caveats on the notion of the "women's vote," their commonalities are sufficient to determine electoral outcomes. More probing research is thus needed on the gender gap to better understand its origins and responsiveness to specific electoral forces. Perhaps the gap will persist regardless of the actions of the Republican and Democratic parties and their standard-bearers. But if the gender gap widens or narrows in the future, it could have a long-lasting impact on the American political landscape.

## Notes

1. Brooks and Manza, "Social Cleavages and Political Alignments"; Carroll, "Voting Choices," in Carroll and Fox, *Gender and Elections*.

2. Box-Steffensmeier, Bouf, and Lin, "Dynamics of the Partisan Gender Gap"; Chaney, Alvarez, and Nagler, "Explaining the Gender Gap"; Adell Cook and Wilcox, "Women Voters in the Year of the Woman," in Weisberg, *Democracy's Feast*.

3. Carroll, "Voting Choices," in Carroll and Fox, *Gender and Elections*.

4. Tate, *From Protest to Politics*.

5. Carroll, "Voting Choices."

6. Tate, *From Protest to Politics*.

7. Huddy, "Group Identity and Political Cohesion," in Sears, Huddy, and Jervis, *Oxford Handbook of Political Psychology*.

8. Chaney, Alvarez, and Nagler, "Explaining the Gender Gap"; Klein, *Gender Politics*; Shapiro and Mahajan, "Gender Differences in Policy Preferences"; Mansbridge, "Myth and Reality."

9. Klein, *Gender Politics*.

10. Mansbridge, "Myth and Reality."

11. Frankovic, "Sex and Politics."

12. Klein, *Gender Politics*; Mueller, "Empowerment of Women," in Mueller, *Politics of the Gender Gap*.

13. Chaney, Alvarez, and Nagler, "Explaining the Gender Gap"; Adell Cook and Wilcox, "Feminism and the Gender Gap"; Manza and Brooks, "Gender Gap in U.S. Presidential Elections."

14. Chaney, Alvarez, and Nagler, "Explaining the Gender Gap"; Adell Cook and Wilcox, "Feminism and the Gender Gap"; Mansbridge, "Myth and Reality."

15. Sapiro, "Theorizing Gender in Political Psychology Research," in Sears, Huddy, and Jervis, *Oxford Handbook of Political Psychology*.

16. Sears and Huddy, "On the Origins of the Political Disunity," in Tilly and Gurin, *Women, Politics, and Change*.

17. Chaney, Alvarez, and Nagler, "Explaining the Gender Gap."

18. Gilens, "Gender and Support for Reagan"; Kaufmann and Petrocik, "Changing Politics of American Men"; Manza and Brooks, "Gender Gap in U.S. Presidential Elections."

19. Piven, "Women and the State," in Rossi, *Gender and the Life Course*.

20. Box-Steffensmeier, Bouf, and Lin, "Dynamics of the Partisan Gender Gap."

21. Carroll, "Women's Autonomy and the Gender Gap," in Mueller, *Politics of the Gender Gap*; Carroll, "Voting Choices."

22. Erie and Rein, "Women and the Welfare State," in Mueller, *Politics of the Gender Gap*; Rosenbluth, Salmond, and Thies, "Welfare Works"; Manza and Brooks, "Gender Gap in U.S. Presidential Elections."

23. Berelson, Lazarsfeld, and McPhee, *Voting*; Campbell et al., *American Voter*.

24. Huddy, "Group Identity and Political Cohesion," in Sears, Huddy, and Jervis, *Oxford Handbook of Political Psychology*.

25. Jackman, *Velvet Glove*; Kinder and Sanders, *Divided by Color*; Kinder and Winter, "Exploring the Racial Divide"; Schuman et al., *Racial Attitudes in America*; Sigelman and Welch, *Black Americans' Views of Racial Inequality*; Tate, *From Protest to Politics*; Tuch, Sigelman, and Martin, "Fifty Years After Myrdal," in Tuch and Martin, *Racial Attitudes in the 1990s*; Welch et al., *Race and Place*.

26. Tate, *From Protest to Politics*.

27. Fiorina, Abrams, and Pope, *Culture War?*

28. Huddy, Feldman, and Dutton, "Role of Religion."

29. Stanley and Niemi, "Demise of the New Deal Coalition," in Weisberg, *Democracy's Feast*.

30. Berelson, Lazarsfeld, and McPhee, *Voting*; Campbell et al., *American Voter*; Stanley and Niemi, "Demise of the New Deal Coalition," in Weisberg, *Democracy's Feast*.

31. Hunter, *Culture Wars*.

32. Berelson, Lazarsfeld, and McPhee, *Voting*; Campbell et al., *American Voter*; Stanley and Niemi, "Demise of the New Deal Coalition," in Weisberg, *Democracy's Feast*.

33. Huddy, Feldman, and Dutton, "Role of Religion."

34. Stanley and Niemi, "Demise of the New Deal Coalition," in Weisberg, *Democracy's Feast*.

35. Sperry, *Are Republican Sprawlers*.

36. All analyses are unweighted because the ANES data set only contains weights for data collected from 1992 onward. There were only minor differences in our findings when the data are reanalyzed using weights, and these are noted in the relevant section of text.

37. Voters who supported independent candidates were removed from the vote tally in all years in order to compare across elections.

38. For the presidential voting models, there is insufficient racial diversity in the years from 1980 to 2004 to distinguish between multiple racial categories. For these models, a dummy variable is included to indicate the effect of white identification relative to identification as nonwhite. The enhanced sample size for partisanship models allows for greater racial differentiation. In these analyses, other race/ethnicity is treated as the missing category.

39. Because of reduced sample size, Jews were only distinguished in the analyses of partisanship, not vote choice. Other religion was the missing category in multivariate analyses.

40. High school or less was the omitted category in multivariate analyses.

41. Income categories are based on respondent reports of household income. Reported income was transformed from dollars to income percentiles. The income

ranges corresponding to each percentile varied by year (see the National Election Studies Cumulative Data File Appendix for more details). Here, low income corresponds to family incomes in the 0–33 percentile. Medium income reflects family incomes in the 34–67 percentile. In this analysis, medium income is the baseline category for the income variables. High income corresponds to household incomes in the 68–100 percentile range. In addition, we included a dummy variable for missing income to avoid list-wise deletion of these observations.

42. The question wording for the item about the number of children living in the respondent's household varied from the standard item in 1994 and 2000. Observations for these years are not included in the National Election Studies Cumulative Data File. Instead, this information was taken from the individual data sets for 1994 and 2000.

43. The post-baby boom cohort was treated as the missing category in analyses.

44. It was not possible to evaluate the influence of holding a postgraduate degree in 2004 because there were no respondents in this category. In addition, the effects of urban and rural residence could not be assessed in 2000 because it was not asked of respondents who were interviewed by phone or in 2004 because the question was not asked of any respondent.

45. Pomper, "Presidential Election," in Pomper, *Election of 2000.*

46. The slightly larger gender gap in 2004 holds up when the data are weighted.

47. For a similar finding, see Norrander, "Independence Gap and the Gender Gap," and Norrander, "The History of Gender Gaps," in Lois Duke Whitaker, *Voting the Gender Gap.*

48. Conway, Steurnagel, and Ahern, *Women and Political Participation.*

49. Single professional women were more supportive of Bill Clinton in 1992 than single professional men but that was the only year in which the coefficient was significant.

50. These effects are slightly weaker when the data are weighed. With weights, the coefficient for Catholic is no longer significant for vote choice in 1996, and coefficients for Protestant in 2000 and Jewish in 1996 and 2004 are no longer significant for partisanship.

51. The impact of fundamentalism is not significant in 1996 once the data are weighted.

52. The number of significant coefficients for some college or college education diminishes slightly with the addition of weights to eight.

53. Brooks and Manza, "Social Cleavages and Political Alignments"; Mattei and Mattei, "If Men Stayed Home"; Sapiro and Conover, "Variable Gender Basis of Electoral Politics."

54. Gilens, "Gender and Support for Reagan"; Kaufmann, "Culture Wars, Secular Realignment, and the Gender Gap"; Kaufmann and Petrocik, "Changing Politics of American Men"; Mattei, "Gender Gap in Presidential Evaluations."

55. Chaney, Alvarez, and Nagler, "Explaining the Gender Gap"; Welch and Hibbing, "Financial Conditions, Gender, and Voting."

56. Schlesinger and Heldman, "Gender Gap or Gender Gaps?"

57. Chaney, Alvarez, and Nagler, "Explaining the Gender Gap"; Frankovic, "Sex and Politics"; Gilens, "Gender and Support for Reagan."

58. Conover, "Feminists and the Gender Gap."

# 12

# THE GENDER GAP

## A Comparison across Racial and Ethnic Groups

M. MARGARET CONWAY

From *Voting the Gender Gap*,
edited by Lois Duke Whitaker (2008)

The term "gender gap" has been used to describe differences between
men and women in vote choice, voter turnout, other types of political
participation, policy preferences, and public opinion differences. Regardless of the topic studied, almost all research focusing on the United
States has examined the gender gap either exclusively among whites or
just within the white and African American groups. In part this paucity
of research can be attributed to the small numbers of minority group
members included in most national surveys. Only a few studies have
expanded analysis of the political gender gap to include Hispanics, Asian
Americans, and Native Americans. The extent to which a political gender
gap occurs within different racial and ethnic groups merits further study.

This article focuses on the gender gap among several racial and ethnic groups in the United States, comparing patterns found within those
groups. It first reviews prior research on the political gender gap; then
the gender gap patterns within white, African American, Hispanic, Asian
American, and American Indian racial or ethnic groups are examined,
using data from several surveys conducted between 1990 and 2004.

## Prior Research

Survey data collected since 1952 in the American National Election
Studies (ANES) provide evidence for the existence of the political gender

gap among whites and of change over time in its patterns. For example, prior to 1964, women more frequently voted for Republican Party presidential candidates than did men.[1] After 1964, women were more likely than men to vote for the Democratic Party presidential candidates.[2] Examining the gender gap in the 1992 presidential election, Franco Mattei suggests the most powerful contributor to the gender gap in voting behavior is beliefs about the proper role of federal government.[3] Other research based on survey data collected during the 1984, 1988, and 1992 elections points out that different levels of salience on economic issues contributed to the gender gap in voting behavior.[4] Since 1980, a gender gap has existed in voting for members of the House of Representatives, with women being more supportive of Democratic Party candidates.[5]

Previous research suggests that a gender gap also exists in other forms of political participation. In their study of political activity, Burns, Schlozman, and Verba found whites to be more politically active than African Americans, who were more politically active than Latinos. Within each racial or ethnic group, men were more politically active than women.[6] However, the disparities between groups in factors affecting political activity were structured more by race or ethnicity than by gender.[7]

Differences have also existed in patterns of party identification. Since 1964, a greater proportion of women than men have identified with the Democratic Party, and, since 1988, a greater proportion of men than women have reported a Republican Party identification.[8] Other studies have examined political ideology and party support among racial and ethnic groups. A study of Hispanic Americans using data from exit polls conducted in 1980, 1984, and 1988 concluded that Hispanic women were more liberal and more supportive of the Democratic Party than were Hispanic men.[9] Another study of the gender gap suggests that the shift in male-female differences in both partisanship and presidential voting may be explained by differences in policy attitudes. An alternative explanation points to the shifts occurring because of different weights that men and women apply to selected attitudes when making decisions about partisan identification and presidential vote choice. Research using survey data from the 1992 and 1996 election studies provides evidence that both explanations contribute to understanding citizens' choices.[10] Other factors besides the gender gap, including educational attainment, level of income, religious affiliation and religiosity, and organizational memberships, appear to influence party identification.[11]

Differences in men's and women's evaluations of presidents also exist. What might explain a gender gap in presidential evaluations? An examination of variations in support for Ronald Reagan, using data from the 1982 ANES study, concludes that the most important component of the gender gap in presidential approval was generated by differences in opinions on social and military issues.[12]

These differences in political attitudes may arise from a variety of sources. Possible sources include gender-based social roles, socioeconomic status, and value differences. Gender differences in political attitudes may arise because of compositional effects, which exist when women and men differ on an explanatory variable. A gender gap could also occur as a result of conditional effects that occur when a variable has differential effects on the political orientations of men and women.[13] Lending support to the compositional explanation is research that emphasizes women's autonomy, with increased autonomy resulting from women's increased participation in the labor force.[14]

How might a gender gap in support for government programs be explained? Women might be expected to be more supportive of government programs because they tend to be more compassionate in their reactions to social problems or because they are more aware of such problems among family and friends. Women may perceive gender differences in economic opportunities, with a greater perceived need for effective social programs. Women's personal experiences may also lead them to perceive more unfairness in the operation of social institutions, or they may be more likely to perceive government-sponsored social programs as ineffective.[15]

Another explanation for political gender gaps emphasizes differences in political interest, information, and efficacy. Prior research suggests that women tend to be less politically interested, informed, and efficacious than men. That could contribute to differences in both levels and patterns of political participation.[16]

### Prior Research on the Political Gender Gap within Ethnic and Racial Groups

The research discussed above focused primarily on white Americans. Do political gender gaps exist within racial and ethnic minorities? As noted above, research on the existence of a political gender gap among racial and ethnic minorities has been limited because few data sets contain large enough samples of minorities to permit valid generalizations. Exceptions are studies that use the U.S. Bureau of the Census Current Population Surveys conducted after the November general elections in even-numbered years. Research by Pei-te Lien compared patterns of voter registration and turnout across racial and ethnic groups using data from the 1992 post-election Current Population Survey. Her analysis of voter turnout rates found small but significant gender differences in voter registration rates among whites and blacks, but not among Latinos and Asians.[17] Subsequent research by Lien used data from the postelection studies conducted by the Bureau of the Census after both the 1992 and 1996 presidential elections. The samples were large enough to permit comparisons among non-Hispanic whites, blacks, Latinos, Asian and Pacific Islanders, and American Indians as well as between men and women within each racial group. Differences in levels of registration and turnout were far less distinct between men and women within each racial and ethnic group than they were between racial and ethnic groups. For example, Asian American men and women had acquired citizenship, registered, and voted at approximately the same rates. Comparing patterns of registration and voting between men and women among blacks, whites, American Indians, and Hispanics, black women were significantly more likely to register and vote than black men, and in 1992, American Indian women had significantly higher registration rates than American Indian men. When controls are applied for socioeconomic conditions and social connections, only among both blacks and whites were women more likely than men to register and vote.[18] To summarize, Lien's research suggests that differences in electoral participation between ethnic and racial groups in registration and voting may be greater than differences in electoral participation between men and women within a racial or ethnic group.

## Data

To examine gender differences in political behavior, attitudes, and policy preferences within ethnic and racial groups, the research reported here uses data from several surveys. One data set used is an ANES data file that combines the 1990, 1992, 1994, 1996, 1998, and 2000 data files. This data set permits research on the gender gap within the white, African American, Hispanic, Asian American, and American Indian racial and ethnic groups. Also used in the analysis are the 2004 ANES and the Pew Hispanic Center (PHC) 2004 political survey. The 2004 ANES data set enables additional analysis of the gender gap within white, black, and

Latino populations. The PHC data set permits analysis of the gender gap within white, black, and Latino racial and ethnic groups. In addition, inferences about the gender gap contained in the Joint Center for Political and Economic Studies' (JCPES) 2000 *National Opinion Poll* report and the center's *The Black Vote in 2004* are discussed. Gender differences in Asian Americans' political participation and political attitudes based on analyses of data collected in late 2000 and early 2001 by the Preliminary National Asian American Study (PNAAPS) are also presented.[19]

Four topics are considered in this article: (1) the extent to which gender gaps exist in voter registration and turnout; (2) other forms of political participation; (3) orientations toward government and public affairs; (4) and policy preferences on several issues. The discussion focuses on gender gaps within an ethnic or racial group that are statistically significant.

## Voting Turnout

Does a gender gap exist in voter turnout within each racial and ethnic group? Based on the ANES data sets used here, the answer would be no. Although a gender gap in turnout existed among whites during 1990 to 2000, it did not occur among the other groups studied. In contrast, analysis of the PHC 2004 data indicates that Hispanic women were significantly more likely than Hispanic men to vote in 2004. The report on the black vote in 2004 by JCPES, using data from the postelection U.S. Bureau of the Census Current Population Survey, suggests that a gender gap in turnout existed between black men and black women, with black women being more likely to vote. In other words, the evidence about a gender gap in voter turnout is mixed, varying both across time and among racial and ethnic groups (see Tables 12.1 and 12.2).

Table 12.1: Political Participation by Gender by Racial or Ethnic Group, 1990–2000

| | White | | African American | | Asian American | | Native American | | Latino | |
|---|---|---|---|---|---|---|---|---|---|---|
| | Men | Women | Men | Women | Men | Women | Men | Women | Men | Women |
| Voted | 69.2 | 66.3[a] | 60.2 | 57.0 | 57.6 | 57.3 | 50.7 | 49.4 | 50.4 | 47.7 |
| Engaged in at least one campaign activity | 36.5 | 27.2[c] | 30.5 | 19.8[c] | 26.3 | 18.2 | 29.0 | 27.6[a] | 32.8 | 18.7[c] |

Chi-square test of significance is indicated by the following (absence of indicator = not significant).
a = $p < .05$
b = $p < .01$
c = $p < .001$
*Source:* American National Election Study Combined File, 1990–2000.

Table 12.2: Political Participation by Gender by Racial or Ethnic Group, 2004

| | White | | African American | | Other | | Latino | |
|---|---|---|---|---|---|---|---|---|
| | Men | Women | Men | Women | Men | Women | Men | Women |
| Voted | 79.3 | 80.1 | 61.8 | 59.3 | 71.3 | 70.9 | 65.0 | 75.0 |
| Engaged in at least one non-voting political activity | 35.9 | 26.4[b] | 27.8 | 32.6 | 29.6 | 31.8 | 31.5 | 29.5 |

Chi square test of significance is reported.
Chi square: a = $p < .05$; b = $p < .01$; c = $p < .001$.
*Data source:* Pew Hispanic Center Survey 2004.

## Other Types of Political Participation

Other forms of political participation are also possible. One is to engage in campaign activities, such as volunteering in a campaign, donating money, and attending political meetings. Based on the ANES 1990 to 2000 data set, it appears that men more frequently than women in the white, African American, Native American, and Latino racial and ethnic groups participate in at least one campaign activity (see Table 12.1). Examining different types of campaign activity, white, black, and Latino men attend political meetings more frequently than did women, and white men more frequently reported giving money to political candidates or parties. In contrast, the Pew 2004 data suggest that gender differences in political activity occur only among whites.

## Party Identification

Does a gender gap exist in party identification? During 1990 to 2000, a gender gap in party identification existed among both Hispanics and American Indians as well as among whites. However, no gender gap in party identification existed within either the African American or Asian American groups. The PHC 2004 survey also provides evidence of a gender gap in party identification among American Indians, with women significantly more likely to identify as Democrats than men and less likely to identify as Republicans. However, in that survey, women and men in the white, black, and Hispanic racial and ethnic groups did not differ significantly in party identification.

## Attentiveness to Government and Public Affairs

Are gender differences evident within racial and ethnic groups in their attentiveness to government and public affairs, their concern with election outcomes, and their political attitudes? Analysis of the combined 1990 to 2000 ANES data set suggests that a gender gap in attentiveness to politics exists among not only whites and African Americans but also among Hispanics and American Indians. In all four groups, women are less likely than men to pay attention to what is going on in government and public affairs.

A gender gap in attention paid to politics occurred among African Americans and whites in 2004, but not among Hispanics. When the question is interest in the current election, in the 1990s, gender differences exist within African American, Asian American, and Hispanic groups, with women being less interested than men.

Turning to identifying as a liberal or a conservative, in all groups but Hispanics, men were significantly more likely than women to indicate that they were politically conservative (see Table 12.3). Why are Latino women more frequently identifying as conservative than Latino men? Several explanations are possible. Religiosity may be greater among Latino women, and that may influence their self-identification as politically conservative. It may reflect significant differences on policy issues, such as legalization of abortion. Also noteworthy is the significant difference in the proportion of Native American men and women who identify as conservative; the gender gap in ideological identification is larger among Native Americans than for any other group. That may reflect greater dissatisfaction among Native American men with government policies that affect Native Americans or more frequent unsatisfactory contact with federal government officials who significantly affect life on Indian reservations. Or it might reflect stronger support for more traditional Native American values. Further exploration of these gender gap differences among ethnic groups in ideological identification is warranted.

Are there gender differences in political trust within any of the racial and ethnic groups? Not during the 1990s. However, there are differences between groups in levels of political trust. Although a majority of all groups are distrustful of government, the proportion in the lower two levels of trust range from 54 percent among Latinos to 70 percent among Native Americans.

Are there gender differences related to election outcomes? Analyses of the ANES 1990–2000 data found no significant gender differences in caring who won the presidential and congressional elections. In 2004, only among whites did a gender gap exist in caring who won the presidential election, with men caring more than women.

Table 12.3: Political Attitudes by Gender and Racial or Ethnic Group, 1990–2000

| | White | | African American | | Asian American | | Native American | | Latino | |
|---|---|---|---|---|---|---|---|---|---|---|
| | Men | Women | Men | Women | Men | Women | Men | Women | Men | Women |
| Follow public affairs some or most of the time | 72.8 | 58.3$^c$ | 71.2 | 55.8$^c$ | 66.5 | 51.2 | 66.5 | 55.8$^b$ | 60.4 | 44.1$^c$ |
| Care who wins election a good deal | 77.6 | 77.1 | 76.6 | 76.9 | 71.7 | 70.9 | 76.5 | 81.8 | 73.3 | 69.4 |
| Election interest very much | 31.8 | 27.2$^c$ | 37.9 | 23.9$^c$ | 30.6 | 14.7$^a$ | 32.3 | 26.2 | 21.9 | 17.9$^a$ |
| Trust in government low | 69.4 | 70.2 | 70.7 | 67.5 | 55.7 | 64.8 | 72.3 | 69.0 | 55.5 | 54.7 |
| *Ideology* | | | | | | | | | | |
| Percent liberal | 22.3 | 26.0 | 30.0 | 33.8 | 27.2 | 30.0 | 18.4 | 31.4 | 27.1 | 15.6 |
| Percent conservative | 49.6 | 38.4$^c$ | 29.3 | 24.9 | 45.7 | 31.7 | 51.5 | 33.3$^a$ | 33.7 | 40.9$^a$ |

Chi square test of significance is indicated by the following (absence of indicator = not significant): a = $p < .05$; b = $p < .01$; c = $p < .001$.

*Source:* American National Election Studies Combined File, 1990–2000.

Does a gender gap exist in identifying oneself as a liberal or a conservative? During the 1990s, a gender gap existed among whites and Latinos, with men in both groups more frequently labeling themselves as conservatives.

## Policy Preferences

One issue that stirs controversy and policy debate is abortion policy. Are there gender differences on abortion policy within each racial and ethnic group? When provided with four choices on the issue of abortion policy, with the choices ranging from "by law, abortion should never be permitted" to "by law, a women should always be able to obtain an abortion as a matter of personal choice," a gender gap in abortion policy preferences was evident in 1990 to 2000 among both Hispanics and whites, but not among Asian Americans, African Americans, and American Indians. Hispanic men were more supportive than Hispanic women of abortion as a matter of personal choice. White women were slightly more supportive than white men of the two extremes of the abortion policy options. In contrast, in 2004, no significant differences existed between men and women within any of the racial and ethnic groups on the abortion policy question.

Another controversial policy issue is the provision of health insurance. Asked to indicate whether they preferred a government insurance plan or a private insurance plan, in the 1990–2000 ANES combined data file, white women were more likely to prefer a government insurance plan than were white men. No significant differences between men and women occurred in any of the other racial and ethnic groups. In 2004, a similar pattern prevailed, with white women preferring governmental provision of health insurance and white men preferring private provision of health insurance. No significant gender differences occurred on that policy issue within the Hispanic and African American groups in 2004.

Are there gender differences within these groups on the issue of the appropriate roles for women in contemporary society? When asked to place themselves on a seven-point scale, with "women and men should have an equal role" at one end of the continuum and "women's place is in the home" at the other, gender differences existed between men and women among both blacks and whites in the 1990–2000 ANES data set. In both groups, women were significantly more supportive of an equal role for women. In contrast, in the 2004 ANES survey, 55 percent of black men and 65 percent of black women supported the view that women and men should have an equal role, compared to approximately 60 percent of both white men and women supporting an equal role for women.

Controversy swirls around the role of government in American society. Does a gender gap exist in opinion on that issue? Should the government cut spending and reduce services or increase spending and services? Both black women and men and white women and men differed on that issue during the 1990s. Women were more supportive of the role of government, preferring higher levels of spending and more provision of government services. A gender gap did not exist on that issue among Asian Americans, Native Americans, and Latinos. In the 2004 PHC survey, the question focusing on that issue was worded differently and a gender gap on that issue was not present among Hispanic, black, and white survey respondents, but it was among respondents in the "other" ethnic group.

In the 2004 PHC study, survey respondents were queried as to their policy preferences on the issue of gay marriage. The survey item asked if they favored or opposed a constitutional amendment that would define marriage as a union between one man and one woman, thereby prohibiting legally sanctioned marriages for same-sex couples. A gender gap did not exist on that issue in any of the racial and ethnic groups.

Is there a gender gap in political participation, party identification, and policy preferences among Asian Americans? Another study, focusing only on Asian Americans, provides additional evidence that some differences do exist. The gender gap patterns reported here focus on Asian Americans as a group.[20] The survey that provided the data for the analysis by Lien, Conway, and Wong sampled six Asian American ethnic groups—Chinese, Japanese, Vietnamese, Filipinos, Indians, and Korean Americans.

Asian American men have higher levels of political knowledge and political interest than Asian American women. The men are also more likely to report identifying with the Republican Party than are the women, but both men and women are more likely to identify as Democrats than as Republicans. Men are more likely to report being contacted in political mobilization efforts, but men and women do not differ in political organization memberships. Men have higher levels of trust in state and local governments and are more likely than women to perceive local governments as responsive to citizens' complaints.

To some extent, gender gap differences among Asian Americans are a function of nativity. For example, foreign-born men express greater interest in politics than do foreign-born women. In contrast, native-born Asian American men and women do not differ in their levels of political interest. When foreign-born Asian Americans are queried about the extent to which they trust the U.S. government compared to the government in their home country, men are more likely than women to report they trust the U.S. government more. Men are also more likely than women to believe they have more influence over the U.S. government than they had over the home country government. Among native-born Asian Americans, men are more likely than women to perceive government as responsive to their concerns.

Despite these differences in beliefs about American government, the Asian American men and women surveyed in the PNAAPS study in 2000 and 2001 do not differ in their levels of voter turnout. Men and women also do not differ in their levels of participation in other forms of political activity.[21]

Among the differences that prior research suggest as relevant in influencing patterns of political behavior and political orientations are levels of political interest, information and efficacy, awareness of social problems, and compassion for those who face such problems. Individuals also differ in economic opportunities, personal values, social status, and social roles.

The next step in the analysis of the political gender gap among racial and ethnic groups is to test models incorporating relevant variables. That would permit comparison of their effects on men and women within racial and ethnic groups, across racial and ethnic groups, and across time.[22]

## A Preliminary Test of a Model of Voting Turnout

Do attitudes, policy preferences, and sociological characteristics have similar effects in stimulating participation of both men and women in different racial/ethnic groups? A preliminary examination of that issue, using regression analysis, is presented in Tables 12.4 and 12.5. The tables report the results of an analysis of the effects of a variety of frequently discussed influences on patterns of voter registration and turnout of both men and women within each racial/ethnic group. The analysis uses data from the American National Election Studies from 1990 through 2000. The dependent variable, a measure of voter registration and turnout, is scored 0 if the individual is not registered and did not vote in the previous election, 1 if registered but did not vote, and 2 if he or she voted in the election. Several attitude measures are included as explanatory variables; these are trust in government, assessment of personal economic well-being during the prior year, party identification (Democratic, independent, or Republican), strength of party identification, and indicators of the strength of self-identification as a liberal or a conservative. Policy orientation measures include an abortion policy preference measure, support for government spending less, support for the government providing more services, and an assessment of past national economic conditions. Sociological variables include marital status, employment status, being in a professional or clerical occupation, having a union member in one's family, educational attainment, length of residence in the community, length of residence in the home, family income level, frequency of church attendance, and two measures of religious denomination affiliation (Protestant and Catholic). Also included are frequency of following what happens in government and politics and an assessment of personal financial well-being during the previous year.

Variables significant in accounting for both white men's and white women's voting participation include preferences on abortion policy,

Table 12.4: Did a Gender Gap Exist in Policy Preferences? 1990–2000

|  | White | African American | Asian American | Native American | Latino |
|---|---|---|---|---|---|
| Equal role for women | yes | no | no | no | no |
| Government role in health insurance | yes | no | no | no | no |
| Abortion legal by law | yes | no | no | no | yes |
| Government spending and services level | yes | yes | no | no | no |

*Yes* indicated chi square significant at $p < .05$.
*Source:* American National Election Study File 1990–2000.

Table 12.5: Gender Gap in Policy Preferences by Racial/Ethnic Group, 2004

|  | White | African American | Hispanic | Other |
|---|---|---|---|---|
| Abortion | ns | ns | ns | $p < .05$ |
| Gay Marriage | ns | ns | ns | ns |
| Health Insurance | $p < .05$ | ns | ns | ns |
| Tax Cuts v. More Services | ns | ns | ns | $p < .01$ |

Chi Square Test of Significance: ns = not significant.
*Data source:* Pew Hispanic Center Survey 2004.

assessment of the previous year's performance of the economy, strength of a conservative political identity, and strength of party identification. A number of personal characteristics are also significant; those include having a family member in a union, being married, level of educational attainment, length of residence in the home, income level, frequency of church attendance, and Protestant religious affiliation. A Catholic religious affiliation and being a liberal were also significant in explaining voting turnout among white men but not among white women. Among white women, employment in a clerical occupation also contributes to explaining voting participation.

In contrast, fewer of the variables predicted electoral participation among African American men and women. Among African American men, preferences on abortion policy laws, strength of party identification, and following what occurs in government and politics are significant predictors of participation, as were membership in a union household, frequency of church attendance, and length of residence in the household. Still fewer variables included in the analysis were significant predictors of voter turnout among African American women; those variables include level of trust in government, length of residence in the home, level of educational attainment, frequency of church attendance in the home, and strength of party identification.

Variables in the participation model are least effective in accounting for electoral participation patterns among Native Americans. Only one of the included variables (level of educational attainment) is statistically significant in explaining voting registration and turnout among men. Only three are significant in explaining electoral participation among Native American women (following government and politics, being married, and level of income). Among both Latino Americans and Asian Americans, more variables in the analysis were significant in accounting for participation by women than by men.

Several general conclusions can be drawn from the analysis of the impact of these variables on the patterns of men's and women's electoral participation within and between racial/ethnic groups. The variables included in this analysis are more useful in explaining voter registration and turnout among white Americans than among members of other groups. Prior research on electoral participation has for the most part used data sets that primarily include white Americans. Thus, it is not surprising that the variables included in the model used here are better at explaining election participation among both white women and men.

Fourteen of the twenty-three explanatory variables are significant in accounting for electoral participation among both white men and women. Only five of the twenty-three are significant for both men and women among Latinos, four for African Americans, two for Asian Americans, and none for both men and women among Native Americans. Gender differences in the impact of these variables varies within racial/ethnic groups; for example, among Asian American women, ten are significant, but only five among Asian American men, and, as noted above, only two are the same variables. One inference that might be drawn is that whatever gender gaps exist within each of the racial/ethnic group examined here, explanatory models more focused on the experiences, relevant attitudes, and policy concerns within each group need to be specified and examined.

Statistical analyses using the same variables to account for participation in campaign activities were even less successful. Campaign participation is undoubtedly stimulated by both the context of the campaign and by citizens' involvement in organizations that make them more likely to be recruited by campaign organizers. A much wider variety of issue concerns also provides a stimulus to campaign participation.

## Discussion and Conclusions

The research presented here suggests that the political gender gap varies across ethnic and racial groups, across time, and across political objects (vote choice, voter turnout, other forms of political participation, political attitudes, and policy preferences) as the conditions stimulating a gender gap change. The political, social, and economic contexts of citizens' lives change over time, and the salience of the components of those contexts also change over time. Conditional effects exist; variables can have differential effects on women and men. Compositional differences also exist; women and men may differ on the explanatory variables. Obviously, relevance is also a function of personal characteristics such as gender and race or ethnicity and how those identified are internalized and integrated.

Future research examining differences in racial and ethnic patterns of political participation needs to draw more specifically on the experiences and social circumstances of racial and ethnic minorities. Additional data sets that include a broader and more appropriate set of variables, reflecting the life experiences of racial and ethnic minorities, need to be collected.

### Notes

1. Clark and Clark, "Gender Gap in 1996," in Whitaker, *Women in Politics*, Table 2.22.

2. Clark and Clark, "Gender Gap in 1996," in Whitaker, *Women in Politics*, Table 2.22; Seltzer, Newman, and Leighton, *Sex as a Political Variable*, Table 3.1.

3. Mattei, "Gender Gap in Presidential Evaluations."

4. Chaney, Alvarez, and Nagler, "Explaining the Gender Gap."

5. Selzer, Newman, and Leighton, *Sex as a Political Variable*, Tables 3.3 and 3.4.

6. Burns, Schlozman, and Verba, *Private Roots of Public Action*, Figure 11.1, 278.

7. See ibid., Chapter 11.

8. Selzer, Newman, and Leighton, *Sex as a Political Variable*, Table 3.5.

9. Welch and Sigelman, "Gender Gap among Hispanics?"

10. Kaufmann and Petrocik, "Changing Politics of American Men."

11. Mattei and Mattei, "If the Men Stayed Home," Table 3, 425, and Table 4.

12. Gilens, "Gender and Support for Reagan."

13. Howell and Day, "Complexities of the Gender Gap."

14. Manza and Brooks, "Gender Gap in U.S. Presidential Elections."

15. Schlesinger and Heldman, "Gender Gap or Gender Gaps?"

16. Verba, Burns, and Schlozman, "Knowing and Caring about Politics"; Conway, Steuernagel, and Ahern, *Women and Political Participation*, 52, Table 3–6.

17. Lien, "Does the Gender Gap in Political Attitudes and Behavior Vary?"

18. Lien, "Who Votes in Multiracial America?" in Alex-Assensoh and Hanks, *Black and Multiracial Politics*.

19. Combining the ANES data files provides enough cases to permit analysis of the gender gap within white, African American, Asian American, American Indian, and Hispanic groups. The 2004 Pew Hispanic Survey (PHS) permits analysis of the gender gap among Hispanics, whites, and African Americans. The PNAAPS and JCPES surveys are studies of just one racial group and do not permit comparisons across ethnic and racial groups within the context of those surveys.

20. The U.S. Bureau of the Census identifies twenty-eight different Asian Pacific Islander ethnic groups in the United States. The groups vary in the timing of group patterns of immigration to the United States, religion, historical experiences in the home country and in the United States, and socioeconomic characteristics.

21. Lien and Conway, "Are There Gender Gaps in Political Attitudes and Behavior Patterns?"; Lien, Conway, and Wong, *Politics of Asian Americans*, Chapter 5.

22. For examples of the testing for the effects of different variables on the gender gap at one point in time, see Burns, Schlozman, and Verba, *Private Roots of Political Action*, Tables 11.11 and 11.14; Lien, Conway, and Wong, *Politics of Asian Americans*, Tables 6.4 and 6.5b.

# ORIGINAL PUBLICATIONS

Behling, Laura L. *The Masculine Women in America, 1890–1935*. University of Illinois Press, 2001.

Boisseau, TJ, and Abigail M. Markwyn, eds. *Gendering the Fair: Histories of Women and Gender at World's Fairs*. University of Illinois Press, 2010.

Gallagher, Julie A. *Black Women and Politics in New York City*. University of Illinois Press, 2012.

Hewitt, Nancy A. *Southern Discomfort: Women's Activism in Tampa, Florida 1880s-1920s*. University of Illinois Press, 2001.

Holsaert, Faith S., Martha Prescod Norman Noonan, Judy Richardson, Betty Garman Robinson, Jean Smith Young, and Dorothy M. Zellner, eds. *Hands on the Freedom Plow: Personal Accounts by Women in SNCC*. University of Illinois Press, 2010.

Jensen, Kimberly. *Mobilizing Minerva: American Women in the First World War*. University of Illinois Press, 2008.

Moses, Claire Goldberg, and Heidi Hartmann, eds. *U.S. Women in Struggle: A Feminist Studies Anthology*. University of Illinois Press, 1995.

Scott, Bonnie Kime, ed. *Gender in Modernism: New Geographies, Complex Intersections*. University of Illinois Press, 2007.

Whitaker, Lois Duke, ed. *Voting the Gender Gap*. University of Illinois Press, 2008.

# CONTRIBUTORS

**LAURA L. BEHLING** is professor of English at Knox College, Illinois. Her scholarly works include *The Masculine Woman in America, 1890–1935* (University of Illinois Press, 2001) and *Gross Anatomies: Fictions of the Physical in American Literature and Culture* (Susquehanna University Press, 2008). She has also edited a Civil War–era composite memoir, *Hospital Transports: A Memoir of the Embarkation of the Sick and Wounded from the Peninsula of Virginia in 1863* (SUNY Press, 2005).

**ERIN CASSESE** is an associate professor in the Department of Political Science and International Relations at the University of Delaware. Her research on women's political attitudes and behavior has appeared in outlets including *Political Behavior*, *Political Psychology*, *Sex Roles*, and *Politics & Gender*.

**MARY CHAPMAN** is professor of English at the University of British Columbia in Vancouver, B.C., Canada. She is the author of the award-winning *Making Noise, Making News: US Suffrage Print Culture in Modernism* (Oxford University Press, 2014), and the coeditor of *Treacherous Texts: An Anthology of US Suffrage Literature, 1846–1946* (Rutgers University Press, 2011) and *Sentimental Men: Masculinity and the Politics of Affect* (University of California Press, 1999).

**M. MARGARET CONWAY** is distinguished professor emeritus of political science at the University of Florida. She is the author of *Political Participation in the United States*, 3rd edition (CQ Press, 2000) and coauthor of *Diversity and Community: The Political Behavior of Asian Americans*, 3rd edition (Routledge, 2004), *Women and Public Policy*, 2nd edition (CQ Press, 1999), *Women and Political Participation* (CQ Press, 1997), and other books.

**CAROLYN DANIELS** remained in Terrell County for several years after her home was bombed. Then she moved to Albany, Georgia, where she opened a grocery store and was an insurance agent for black-owned Atlanta Life Insurance Company. When she later became a resident of Atlanta, she continued to write insurance for Atlanta Life and sold Avon cosmetics for more than nineteen years. For many years she was a geriatric nurse and volunteered with the Red Cross. She was active in the choir Daughters of Bethel, the stewardess board, and the Sunday school at her church, Big Bethel A.M.E. Upon her retirement, she lived with her son and his family in Atlanta.

**ELLEN CAROL DUBOIS** is professor emeritus of history at UCLA. She is the author of *Woman Suffrage and Women's Rights: Essays* (New York University Press, 1997), *Harriot Stanton Blatch and the Winning of Woman Suffrage* (Yale University Press, 1997), and *Feminism and Suffrage: The Emergence of an Independent Women's Movement in America, 1848–1869* (Cornell University Press, 1978). She is the coauthor or coeditor of numerous other books, including most recently *Through Women's Eyes: An American History with Documents*, 5th edition (Bedford/St. Martin's, 2018).

**JULIE A. GALLAGHER** is an associate professor of history at Pennsylvania State University, Brandywine. She is the author of *Black Women and Politics in New York City* (University of Illinois Press, 2012) and coeditor with Barbara Winslow of *Reshaping Women's History: Voices on Nontraditional Women Historians* (University of Illinois Press, 2018).

**BARBARA GREEN** is associate professor of English and concurrent professor in gender studies at the University of Notre Dame. She is the author of *Feminist Periodicals and Daily Life: Women and Modernity in British Culture* (Palgrave Macmillan, 2017), *Spectacular Confessions: Autobiography, Performative Activism, and the Sites of Suffrage, 1905–1938* (St. Martin's Press, 1997), and coeditor of *Women's Periodicals and Print Culture in Britain, 1918–1939* (Edinburgh University Press, 2017).

**NANCY A. HEWITT** is distinguished professor emerita at Rutgers University and the author most recently of *Radical Friend: Amy Kirby Post and Her Activist Worlds* (University of North Carolina Press, 2018) and coauthor of *Exploring American Histories*, 3rd edition (Bedford/St. Martin's, 2019).

**LEONIE HUDDY** is a professor of political science at Stony Brook University. She is the coeditor of the *Oxford Handbook of Political Psychology* (Oxford University Press, 2013) and former editor of the journal *Political Psychology*. Her work has appeared in numerous journals, including the *American Political Science Review*, the *American Journal of Political Science, Journal of Politics, Public Opinion Quarterly*, and *Political Psychology*.

**KIMBERLY JENSEN** is professor of history and gender studies at Western Oregon University. She is the author of *Mobilizing Minerva: American Women and the First World War* (University of Illinois Press, 2008), *Oregon's Doctor to the World: Esther Pohl Lovejoy and a Life in Activism* (University of Washington Press, 2012), and coeditor of *Women and Transnational Activism in Historical Perspective* (Republic of Letters, 2010).

**MARY-KATE LIZOTTE** is an associate professor of political science at Augusta University in the Department of Social Sciences. She earned her Ph.D. in political science from Stony Brook University. Her research focuses on American political behavior with a particular interest in gender. Much of her work is concerned with the origins and implications of gender differences in public opinion. In addition to her work on public opinion, she has also published research on the gender gap in voting, political knowledge, and party identification.

**LADY CONSTANCE LYTTON** (1869–1923) was a British suffragette activist, writer, speaker, and campaigner. She was a member of the Women's Social and Political Union, known as the most militant group of suffragettes who campaigned for the vote for women, and she was imprisoned four times for her work with this group. She wrote pamphlets and articles on the topic of women's rights, and her book, *Prisons and Prisoners*, was published in 1914.

**ANDREA G. RADKE-MOSS** is a faculty member in the Department of History, Geography, and Political Science at Brigham Young University–Idaho. Her research interests include western women at the 1893 Chicago World's Columbian Exposition, women and higher education, suffrage, school teachers, and Mormon women's experiences in the Mormon-Missouri War of 1838. She has published award-winning articles in *Great Plains Quarterly* and *Mormon Historical Studies*, and is the author of *Bright Epoch: Women and Coeducation in the American West* (University of Nebraska Press, 2008).

**BONNIE THORNTON DILL** is dean of the University of Maryland's College of Arts and Humanities. A pioneering scholar on the intersections of race, class, and gender in the U.S. with an emphasis on African-American women, work, and families, she is founding director of both the Center for Research on Women at the University of Memphis and the Consortium on Race, Gender, and Ethnicity at the University of Maryland. Her scholarship includes three books and numerous articles. She is former president of the National Women's Studies Association; former vice president of the American Sociological Association; and former chair of the Committee of Scholars for *Ms.* magazine.

# INDEX

The University of Illinois Press
is a founding member of the
Association of University Presses.

---

Composed in 10/13 Georgia
with Raleigh LT Std display
by Lisa Connery
at the University of Illinois Press
Cover designed by Jennifer S. Fisher
Cover photo: Three women installing a sign advertising
a suffrage event featuring Anna Howard Shaw, c. 1915
(Library of Congress Prints and Photographs Division).
Background images from Shutterstock.com.

University of Illinois Press
1325 South Oak Street
Champaign, IL 61820–6903
www.press.uillinois.edu